Urban Preparation

Young Black Men Moving from Chicago's South Side to Success in Higher Education

Chezare A. Warren

HARVARD EDUCATION PRESS
CAMBRIDGE, MASSACHUSETTS

SERIES | RACE AND EDUCATION

Paperback ISBN 978-1-68253-077-1
Library Edition ISBN 978-1-68253-078-8

Library of Congress Cataloging-in-Publication Data

Names: Warren, Chezare A., author. | Brooms, Derrick R., author.
Title: Urban preparation : young black men moving from Chicago's South Side to success in higher education / Chezare A. Warren.
Other titles: Race and education series.
Description: Cambridge, Massachusetts : Harvard Education Press, [2017] | Series: Race and education series | Includes bibliographical references and index.
Identifiers: LCCN 2017018170| ISBN 9781682530771 (pbk.) | ISBN 9781682530788 (library edition)
Subjects: LCSH: Urban Prep Academies. | Charter schools—Illinois—Chicago—Case studies. | High school environment—Illinois—Chicago—Case studies. | African American youth—Education (Secondary)—Illinois—Chicago—Case studies. | Single-sex schools—Illinois—Chicago—Case studies. | Education, Urban—Illinois—Chicago—Case studies. | Achievement motivation in adolescence—Illinois—Chicago—Case studies. | Prediction of scholastic success—Illinois—Chicago—Case studies.
Classification: LCC LC2779 .W37 2017 | DDC 371.0509773/11—dc23 LC record available at https://lccn.loc.gov/2017018170

Published by Harvard Education Press,
an imprint of the Harvard Education Publishing Group

Harvard Education Press
8 Story Street
Cambridge, MA 02138

Cover Design: Endpaper Studio
Cover Photo: Hill Street Studios/Getty Images

The typefaces used in this book are Adobe Garamond Pro and Helvetica Neue.

For the young Black men
and boys who've allowed me
to mentor them, educate them,
and tell their stories.

And to my nephew,
Piercen Michael Fitzgerald Wright,
and Black boys everywhere—
may the ugliness of this world
never dim your light.

Contents

Foreword

by H. Richard Milner IV
Race and Education Series Editor

The publication of Chezare A. Warren's *Urban Preparation: Young Black Men Moving from Chicago's South Side to Success in Higher Education* marks the advent of Harvard Education Press's Race and Education series. A central goal of the series is to advance a critical, forward-thinking body of research on race that contributes to policy, theory, practice, and action. Although the series will advance scholarship in race studies, a central objective is to assist educators—real teachers, school counselors, administrators, coaches, and outside-of-school providers—in their efforts to center the very humanity of students whose needs are far from being understood, responded to, and met in schools and in society.

Grounded in and substantiated by empirical research, the series aims to highlight action designed to help solve problems of race in education. In this sense, it will look to address both societal issues and educational practices. The books included in the series will be developed to highlight scholarship from leading researchers in the field as well as emerging scholars and will investigate mechanisms, systems, structures and practices that have a real bearing on students' opportunities to learn.

Racial justice is arguably the most important educational imperative of our time. Considering the inextricable links between society and education, educators have the potential to help equip students with knowledge, tools, attitudes, dispositions, mind-sets, beliefs, and practices to create a world that is truly equitable for its citizenry. Series titles will attend to issues both inside and outside of schools, shedding light on what matters and how we, in education, can improve practices that systemically improve the life chances of students.

The centrality of race to education reform and transformation can scarcely be overstated. If we avoid addressing race, or if we continue to address it only marginally, the big problems of education will likely persist. Too many of the most pressing challenges in education are a function of racial inequities, as manifested through bias, racism, and other forms of discrimination. To be clear, many of these manifestations of race are implicit, tacit to individuals who benefit from a caste system designed to meet and perpetuate the interests of those in power and to maintain an unjust status quo. Understanding the role and salience of race on the individual level, therefore, is as important as examining broader systems, structures, and institutions. Indeed, individuals create inequitable systems, and this series will address individual as well as broader structures and systems.

Several interrelated objectives guide the series:

- to study race and develop explicit recommendations for eliminating racism, discrimination, and other forms of oppression from educational efforts and institutions
- to address race by means of multidisciplinary expertise and approaches
- to examine various layers of inequity through micro-, meso-, and macro-level lenses that will expose individual and systemic barriers that prevent equitable opportunities for students of color
- to explore the many assets and strengths of students, communities, and families, thereby challenging inaccurate narratives, policies, and practices which suggest that students of color need "fixing" and instead reinforcing how students of color succeed when mechanisms are in place to support them
- to advance scholarly attention to aspects of racism and discrimination while also (and most importantly) offering real, action-driven assistance to educators and others who work with and on behalf of students of color inside and outside of schools as institutions

Above all, this series asks the important question, *Do we have the fortitude to center race in our work, or will we continue going about our business, our work, as usual?* I am always mindful of curriculum theorist Beverly Gordon's provocative observation that "critiquing your own assumptions about the world—especially if you believe the world works for you"—is an arduous endeavor.[1] At the very heart of this series is an explicit challenge to those in power to work for the good of humanity, to interrupt systems, policies, and practices that work only for some while others remain underserved. It asks: How do the effects of poverty and compromised opportunities in transportation, housing, and employment manifest themselves in how communities respond to social (in)justice? What role does and should education play in understanding and responding to these manifestations? What roles do teachers play in helping students develop insights about the salience of race in society? How do education policy makers respond to these realities when making decisions about what gets covered in the curriculum? The books in this series will address many of these questions about race, racism, and discrimination to advance what we know in education and to move us toward a more equitable education system.

The reasons for focusing on the intersection of race and education are many and varied, including:

- the overreferral of Black and Brown students to the office to punish them for "misbehavior"
- the disproportionate suspensions and expulsions of Black and Brown students
- the serious effects of poverty on student outcomes
- the underrepresentation and underenrollment of Black and Brown students in STEM areas
- the low numbers of Black and Brown teachers in the teaching force
- underprepared educators who are unable to respond to Black and Brown student needs
- myths about the achievement and socialization of Asian American students
- opportunity gaps across disciplines masked in the language of achievement gaps
- the unmet psychological and socioemotional needs of Black and Brown students

- the narrowing of the curriculum that push out the arts and physical education in many urban classrooms that serve Black and Brown students
- unconceptualized and unactualized health services that address the needs of the whole child
- poor collaborations and partnerships between schools and the families and communities they serve
- the cradle-/school-to-prison pipeline that ensnares too many Black and Brown students
- misunderstood identities of Black and Brown students, or their misincorporation into the fabric of education

I argue that as a society we risk continuing to reap the unfortunate consequences of an education system that is designed to *school* rather than *educate*.[2] The charge is for us to study and build knowledge about race in order to transform policies and practices to benefit our collective humanity. Think of the scores of students whose talents and dreams are underdeveloped and unactualized because we have failed them in our education system.

Indeed, a primary premise of the series is that we must learn from a diverse range of disciplines to build and sustain efforts on behalf of students who continue to be underserved in education. Thus, scholars from a variety of disciplines—sociology, psychology, health sciences, political science, legal studies, and social work—can assist us in reversing trends in education that continue to have devastating effects on student experiences and outcomes. What is clear from solid evidence is that these students succeed when appropriate mechanisms are in place. The Race and Education series will contribute to this tradition, centralizing those mechanisms that will help us reach our true ideal democracy. I am ready. I am hopeful that readers of the series are as well.

Welcome! #LetsDotheWork!

Urban Preparation

An Introduction

I wrote this text to subvert dominant narratives that insist on casting urban-dwelling young Black men and boys as "at-risk" or "disadvantaged."[1] *Urban Preparation: Young Black Men Moving from Chicago's South Side to Success in Higher Education* depicts the ecology of people, moments, lessons, incidents, and interactions that collectively help determine the journey to and through college for seventeen young Black men from Chicago's South Side. This book acknowledges the cultural strengths young Black men and boys bring with them to school and the important role of Black communities in their educational attainment. It refutes menacing plot lines that portray Black boys growing up in enclaves of concentrated poverty as hypervulnerable. These young men do not need another ill-conceived education reform to "fix" them. *They* are not broken; but they are too often exposed to broken education systems that conserve their academic vulnerability. *Urban Preparation* amplifies the voices of young Black men who grew up in densely populated, economically disenfranchised communities of color. Their points of view also counter pervasive stories of school failure that conveniently misplace critical analyses of the institutional structures that created, and presently sustain, the problem of Black male school underachievement.

Adversity does not discriminate based on race, gender, or class. These young men's exposure to risk in the urban environment at the intersection of these three identity markers underscores their development of various valuable cultural competencies. These are place-based intelligences they employ, and cultural resources they acquire, to adeptly negotiate and overcome some of life's most difficult circumstances. Hence, a central premise of *Urban Preparation* is that young Black men and boys are indeed resilient. They wield tremendous agency to effectively navigate the pathway from their home neighborhoods on Chicago's South Side to and through a four-year college or university despite numerous personal struggles and social and cultural barriers. My use of *agency* in this book centers on the supposition that young Black men and boys are actively involved in the experiences that shape their educational trajectories. They are not passive subjects being acted on. Instead, they take an active role, one way or another, in determining their education outcomes.

This book also aims to sharpen urban education reform efforts, and thus improve schooling outcomes for Black male youth by calling attention to the important implications of their perspectives on the matter—if we are listening closely to the details of their experiences inside and outside of school. Better understanding the factors that contribute to these young men's education trajectories help in the fight against structural and institutional impediments to education opportunity resulting from White supremacy and America's legacy of anti-Black racism.

The seventeen young Black men whose stories I tell here are members of the inaugural graduating class of Urban Prep Charter Academy for Young Men (UP), a single-sex high school for boys established in the Englewood neighborhood of Chicago's South Side (see figure 2.1). Today, with three campuses serving several hundred young Black men and boys throughout the city of Chicago, UP is widely celebrated for helping 100 percent of its graduates earn admittance to four-year colleges and universities. To date, however, little scholarly work has been published on the factors that undergird the school's success, broadly defined. The public, including those aiming to potentially replicate Urban Prep or its successes, know too little about the philosophies, practices, and circumstances behind the school's accomplishments. *Urban Preparation* aims to unveil the dimensions of UP's (in)effectiveness in both reversing trends in Black male school failure and preparing young Black men to be productive contributors to society.

Moreover, an urban school's partnership with families and communities is one component necessary to ensure that Black youth realize their greatest academic potential.[2] Beyond an impressive branding campaign centered on "changing the narrative" about young Black men and boys, it has been difficult to determine UP's long-term impact on urban education school improvement or education reform writ large, the material conditions of the Black communities where its campuses are located, and the life outcomes of its graduates.

Urban Preparation is one attempt to examine the relationship between urban living and urban schooling, as well as the important role of secondary education institutions for positioning young Black men to pursue a higher education, should they elect to do so.

The book has three chief aims:

- to describe the features of UP's organizational design and the influence of its institutional practices on its graduates' college preparation and persistence through the first-person perspectives of young Black men who were members of UP's inaugural graduating class
- to examine the intersections of place (growing up on Chicago's South Side) and space (attending Urban Prep) from a critical race perspective to better discern: the factors that contribute to developing the collegiate aspirations of young Black men who grow up in economically disenfranchised communities of color; strategies for cultivating antioppressive visions of Black manhood; and understanding about the young men's conceptions of becoming "successful Black men"
- to explore the types of schooling environments, experiences, and conditions most likely to narrow "opportunity gaps" for urban youth, and the implications of these factors for young Black men and boys' academic success and positive race and gender identity development

The Urban Prep College Persistence Study

In late June 2006, I left a position teaching eighth-grade math at Paderewski Elementary School in the North Lawndale community, a school in the Chicago Public Schools (CPS) system, to become the founding math teacher at Urban Prep. I had applied to the school and interviewed in the spring of 2006 but was not initially hired. After teaching summer school at Noble Street College Prep, where I had just been offered a job for the next academic year, I received a phone call from Dennis Lacewell, one of UP's founding principals, informing me that a math position had been created for me at Urban

Prep. With three professional opportunities looming, I had to decide whether to return to Paderewski, accept the position at Noble Street, or become the founding math teacher at Urban Prep. I chose Urban Prep.

Teaching at the nation's first all-boys public charter high school represented an opportunity to help build a school that would be(come) a national model for how to best educate young Black men and boys who attend urban schools. In my role, I was responsible for six sections of ninth-grade math, which meant I taught every student enrolled at Urban Prep in 2006–7 (except for a small group of students who were taught by a colleague). Beyond the classroom, I was involved in coauthoring the Urban Prep Creed, starting the school's musical ensemble, and interacting daily with 150 of some of the most brilliant Black boys I've ever met. Although my contract was not renewed for the following academic year, teaching at the school is still one of my proudest professional accomplishments.

After UP I went on to teach at a middle school on Chicago's South Side, completed my principal licensure, and worked as a mathematics instructional coach at two different CPS turnaround elementary schools. I enjoyed almost ten years of service as an urban educator and administrator before entering the professorate. I have not had any formal or informal affiliation with Urban Prep since 2007, but I have maintained cordial relationships with my former colleagues. And, thanks to social media, I have been able to reconnect with many former students, including several of the young men who are featured in this book. Working at UP helped to spark my passion to better understand the schooling conditions and teacher dispositions that enable young Black men and boys' high academic achievement. My sustained interest in expanding urban youths' access to high-quality public education opportunities inspired the research study behind this book.

Urban Preparation comes out of the Urban Prep College Persistence Study (UPCPS), which examined UP's role and function in the college persistence and retention of members of the school's first graduating class. I conducted this study with Dr. Derrick R. Brooms, another founding faculty member at Urban Prep; he worked at the school for four years before leaving in 2010. The participants in the UPCPS are our former students, and we collected data during the 2013–14 academic school year. At the time of data collection, each UPCPS participant was four years out of high school and on track to earning an undergraduate degree within six years of his initial college enrollment.[3] Derrick and I collaboratively conceived of the UPCPS, collected data together, and engaged in early analyses of the data. I am solely responsible for the final data analysis/interpretations, theoretical framing, and data reported in this book. The original ideas put forward in this text are mine alone, but *Urban Preparation* would not be possible without Derrick's contribution to developing and conducting the research project.

The seeds for the project were planted in 2007 during early conversations Derrick and I had with other founding faculty about the best organizational arrangements and pedagogical approaches for realizing the vision of an innovative urban high school for boys that would put each of its graduates on track to college. Derrick and I kept in touch over the years, and in 2012 we began imagining a research study that would allow us to learn from members of UP's inaugural graduating class. Since completing graduate school and securing positions in higher education, we have both maintained a steady commitment to doing empirical research that opposes widespread deficit discourses and perspectives about Black people, Black communities, and young Black men in particular. This commitment, in part, emerges from our experiences as urban educators. But, even more, it is our own cultural intuition as Black men—native South Siders, products of an urban environment and the Chicago Public Schools—that has motivated our continued intellectual engagement in this area of inquiry.

The primary data source for the UPCPS were the interviews we conducted with the young UP graduates. (A detailed account of the research methodology is presented in the appendix.) In gathering this data, Derrick and I were interested not only in the young men's journeys to college but also in the specific experiences they thought were important or valuable. We were concerned not just with the *what* of that journey but also with the *why*. From the beginning, Derrick and I openly communicated with the young men our reason for the research project: to understand their perspectives on how to improve schooling experiences for young Black men and boys growing up in high-poverty communities of color. The rapport we established with them—because of our role in their lives as teachers and, in Derrick's case, as a coach—was necessary to facilitate the integrity of this research and the trustworthiness of its findings.[4] Furthermore, research that represents this level of intimacy between the researcher and the researched requires a way of knowing that more fully aligns with the communities this text aims to represent.

In writing *Urban Preparation,* I relied on each of my multiple identities—man, educator, Black, race scholar, Chicagoan—to provide me with the epistemological and ontological perspectives necessary to gather "deep meaning" from these young men's personal narratives.[5] This allowed me to produce a text that is honest and authentic, deferential and critical, thoughtful and straightforward. I make no claims to neutrality or scientific objectivity. In fact, this research is fully subjective, so that I might be most responsible and accountable to the young men whose stories I tell, the communities from which they emerge, and the many young men just like them whose voices may never be heard in the mainstream.[6] The reader can argue with my interpretations, but the words and points of view revealed in conversation with these young Black men cannot be denied. Like Black lives, #BlackMensStoriesMatter.

Counterstorytelling and Experiential Knowledge

Critical race theorists argue that a function of racial oppression is the production of majoritarian stock stories that cast people of color negatively.[7] Solórzano and Yosso contend, for instance, that majoritarian stories include broad characterizations of "darker skin and poverty" as correlates to "bad neighborhoods and bad schools."[8] The word *urban* tends to conjure images of low-income, underresourced, high-poverty Black and Latinx communities—which are rarely acknowledged for the important cultural knowledge, skills, and resources they afford the youth raised there.[9] Stock stories about why young Black men and boys fail and the evidence of their alleged lack of school engagement, or care for their education, do little to disrupt widespread deficit perspectives about them in education discourse, theory, and practice. Dominant depictions and perceptions of them (and Black girls) as uncontrollable, deviant, and anti-intellectual tend to drive urban education reform efforts centered on discipline and control. This orientation underscores the logic used by school district officials to close or "turn around" neighborhood schools in order to "fix" poor Black communities or offer more "options" to

Black families (cue the proliferation of "no excuse" charter schools as an urban education reform strategy in almost every major US city).

The narratives in this book are written and framed using a critical race counterstorytelling methodology.[10] Counterstorytelling is the active pushing back against deficit perspectives about people of color through first-person narratives about a set of experiences, conditions, or circumstances. Counterstories are essential for presenting opposing pervasive deficit points of view, stories, and images like the ones I've just described. This methodological approach highlights important racial blind spots.[11] Parker and Lynn insist that storytelling "provides readers with a challenging account of preconceived notions of race."[12] In other words, the young men's personal narratives presented in this book are intended to complicate, unveil, and disrupt dominant discourses of race in urban education, and the intersections of race with class and gender. The counterstorytelling in chapters 2–5 reveal the logics of White supremacy and anti-Black racism that likely influence teaching and learning practices in urban schools and preK–12 youth development. These young men's words and perspectives humanize Black men and boys in ways not often accomplished in mainstream education research. Counterstories offer an empirical database from which to derive more justice-centered pedagogical orientations and shift dominant discourses of Black student school achievement.

Moreover, critical race scholarship intimately links theory and practice to the "activist social justice and change" needed to disrupt racist school practices that attempt to subordinate youth of color to positions of perpetual academic inferiority.[13] That being the case, I relied on the young men's experiential knowledge to construct their counterstory. *Experiential knowledge* represents the conventional sense making, understandings, and/or expertise afforded through personal experience useful for explaining or discerning racial subordination. Experiential knowledge is sound bites, if you will, that offer the alternative points of view necessary to better understand how race and racism restrict and/or pose threats to each young man's access to education opportunity as he moves along the education pipeline.

I constructed a counterstory based primarily on my reading and rereading of more than five hundred pages of interview transcripts. I analyzed these data to find patterns of experiential knowledge across the seventeen research participants (see the appendix). Together with knowledge gleaned from extant research literature and my own personal experience, as well as the logical juxtaposition of the young men's experiential knowledge, these data produced one compelling counterstory—a continuous narrative intended to oppose widely accepted assumptions, perceptions of, and narratives about urban Black male youth that function to maintain supremacy.

Experiential knowledge situates an individual's point of view as fundamental to interpreting the circumstances that lead to various racialized outcomes. The new knowledge generated by the young men, as a result of their lived experience as members of the very first graduating class of Urban Prep, as lifelong residents of the South Side of Chicago, and as graduates of a four-year college or university where many of them were in the racial minority, was essential for providing the most authentic account of the factors that support or impede urban-dwelling young Black men's college going and completion. Deep discussions of these factors appear in both the counterstory and my follow-up analyses.

It is my hope that this book casts doubt on any news report, research study, or media representation that fails to name race and, more specifically, anti-Blackness as a variable for determining Black male school failure. I also aim to compel educators and others to critically scrutinize the quality and intention of programs, (new) schools, or initiatives aimed at improving the school success of Black (male) youth.

Composite Characters and the Counterstory

The counterstory presented in chapters 2–5 is primarily based on the young men's experiences and other details specific to *real-life* places, people and scenarios, as well as interactions I had with them. Given my explicit aim to make this research accessible to a broader audience, I arranged actual research data (quotes from interviews with the UPCPS research participants) into one coherent, continuous narrative constructed around dominant themes that emerged from my data analysis. I created specific details, such as the setting, to construct a coherent story that reveals the racialized, classed, and gendered experiences of these young men.[14]

To be clear, the counterstory in *Urban Preparation* is not fictional. Everything about it is based on my field notes, the analytic memos I made during my interactions with the young men, the UPCPS interview data, my own professional experiences as an urban educator and founding math teacher at Urban Prep, and knowledge of the research literature.

The telling of this counterstory necessitated that I develop five composite characters. The composite characters are not imaginary; nor are they grounded in fictional details.[15] Researchers have long supported the use of composite characters in qualitative research scholarship.[16] I constructed the composite characters of Jeff, Winston, Quentin, Reggie, and Antwan by combining these young men's overlapping real-life experiences and their personal characteristics. In grouping the seventeen participants into five composites, I looked for similarities in disposition, family structure, college type attended (predominantly White institution versus historically black college or university), upbringing, and academic profile.

The setting of the counterstory is a real place in Chicago, and it depicts a similar dinner gathering that Derrick and I had with UPCPS participants about a year after we completed data collection. I included real aspects of the restaurant setting. The conversation in the counterstory centers around data Derrick and I collected during our one-on-one interviews with the young men. Even the coffee shop conversations in chapters 2–5 are amalgams of real-life discussions Derrick and I have had over the ten years since we worked together at Urban Prep. Moreover, all "dialogue" comes directly from a participant's comment during a research interview. Of course, when it was necessary to clarify, enhance readability, or further anonymize the seventeen young men, I did make minor revisions to this dialogue.

Urban Prep students, graduates, families, and (former) employees are a small-knit community, and the individuals from UP's first graduating class who are also college graduates is even smaller. And since certain experiences are deeply personal and specific, and therefore difficult to completely mask, I endeavored to protect their identities as best I could. Similarly, for this reason I used pseudonyms for any of the young men's mentions of individual's names, such as former teachers from UP.

Urban Prep Charter Academy for Young Men, the First All-Boys Public Charter High School in the United States

In conceiving of the Urban Prep Academies in 2002, fourth-generation Chicagoan Tim King set out to improve the educational outcomes of young Black men and boys in his hometown. After completing law school at Georgetown University, he returned to Chicago to run Hales Franciscan, a small private high school serving young Black men on the city's South Side. He would later pursue the idea of establishing a high school that would broaden access to college for urban-dwelling young Black men and boys.[17]

King recounts how the school's motto, "We Believe," was the sober reminder he needed to persevere after his application to establish the charter high school was twice rejected by Chicago's charter authorizing agency. On the third try, Urban Prep was granted a charter to become the nation's first all-boys public (charter) high school. The "We Believe" motto evidences a conviction held by King, UP's supporters, and multiple other stakeholders, and a staunch confidence in every Black boy's capacity to graduate from UP ready for college, no matter the external obstacles. This philosophy suggests that *believing* young Black men and boys can achieve academic success is necessary for *seeing* the substance of that success demonstrated. "Either you do or you don't [believe]"—there is no in between. The idea of believing shows up throughout *Urban Preparation* as a critical factor in these young men's preparation to finish high school, enroll in college, and attain success in higher education.

The first Urban Prep campus was established in 2006 as a single-sex, grades 9–12 college preparatory high school open to any male student living within the CPS district.[18] UP's founders used district data to identify three communities where the first campus might be opened. A needs assessment revealed that Englewood was lacking a high-quality secondary education option. The flagship campus began with a ninth-grade class of approximately 150 students. The school added a new group of students each year until it reached the maximum capacity of 600 students.[19] Today, there are three UP campuses, located in the Englewood, Bronzeville, and University Village/Little Italy communities. UP claims to use a blind lottery system to admit students, which means that factors such as a student's test scores, grades, or exceptional learning needs are not considered in the selection process. Students apply by completing a one-page application that includes a demographic section and a short questionnaire which invites them to identify their academic and educational interests. Transfer students have a special form they complete for admission that is different from young men applying for a seat in the freshman class. Once the maximum number of students has been met, the remaining students are waitlisted. At capacity, UP may enroll approximately 2,000 students across its three campuses. To date, the school has served primarily young Black men and boys, with about 80 percent of them receiving free or reduced-price lunches.

Urban Prep's mission is "to provide a comprehensive, high-quality college preparatory education to young men that results in [their] graduates succeeding in college."[20] "Succeeding in college" is understood to mean that UP graduates are prepared to earn a baccalaureate degree from a four-year college or university. The young men whose stories are featured in this text are 2010 graduates of UP's Englewood campus. Data from the 2015–16 Illinois Report Card show that there was a 94 percent high school graduation rate for students from this campus.[21] In 2016, ten years after UP opened its doors, the school celebrated its seventh year in a row of helping 100 percent of its graduates gain admission to a four-year college or university.[22] That same year, however, only 16 percent of those graduates were considered college ready leaving high school.[23]

A 2011 data report from the school, published a year after the graduation of UP's inaugural class, maintained that about 30 percent of Black boys who start high school at Urban Prep leave the school before completing their senior year. This data point is referenced as one of UP's successes, since it can be compared with attrition rates for young Black men from other Chicago high schools that hover at 56–61 percent. In the same 2011 report, UP announced that 94 percent of its 2010 graduates were enrolled in college, with 80 percent of them having completed the first year. I have not been able to locate a report that reveals the percentage of students from the inaugural graduating class who persisted through the second year and beyond. There is also no easily accessible, publicly available data about college persistence or completion rates for graduates of Urban Prep.[24]

Urban Prep's mission is underscored by four guiding aims:

- Prepare young men from urban settings to gain admission to and succeed in college.
- Provide a comprehensive learning experience through a college preparatory curriculum, extracurricular participation, and community service.
- Maintain high expectations for all students.
- Promote a positive environment that facilitates and nurtures respect for students, staff, and the community.

Key Design Elements

All incoming freshmen participate in a multiweek summer orientation, the Transition Program, prior to the start of their first year at the school. Additionally, students are required to adhere to a strict school dress code (khaki pants; a white, collared, buttoned shirt; black shoes; a school-issued red tie; and a black blazer). Each day begins with a schoolwide meeting referred to as Community. This is the time of day when students recite the Urban Prep Creed, which articulates aspects of Urban Prep's school culture emphasizing respect, responsibility, ritual, and relationships. Each student also meets daily with his small advisory group, referred to as a Pride. Finally, through its Arcs—four foundational dimensions or principles guiding the school's operations and organizational design—UP aims to provide its students a rigorous college-prep program, deepen their sense of responsibility, bolster their confidence and leadership capacity, and increase their understanding of the world around them.[25] (See figure I.1.)

Community. Community is convened, usually in the school gymnasium, at the beginning of each school day. It is the one time each day when every teacher, student, staff member, and administrator gathers together. Students greet one another by shaking hands and checking one another's uniform. School leaders acknowledge students for their superlative attendance, character, effort, and academic performance. One such celebration is recognizing when a young man has earned his first college acceptance, which is a moment marked by trading in his solid-red tie for a red-and-gold-striped tie. It is also the time and place when announcements are made about programming efforts,

FIGURE I.1 Distinctive elements of Urban Prep's organizational structure

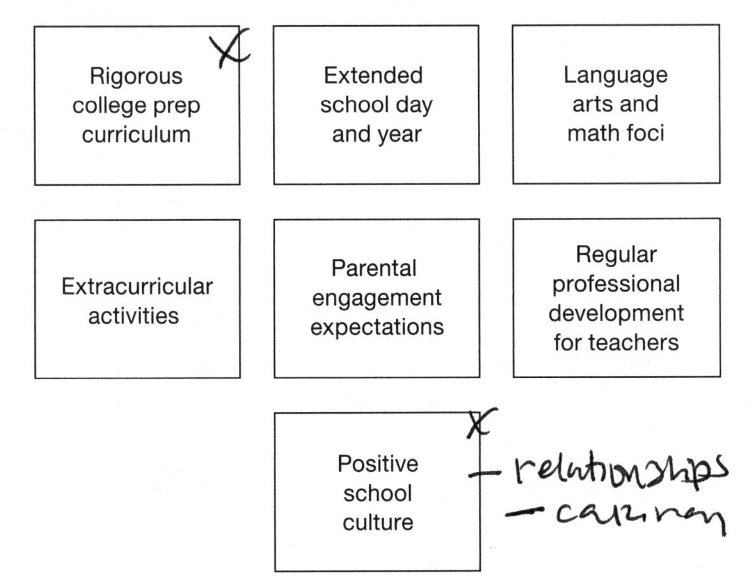

upcoming events, and other school-related activities. Community concludes with recitation of the Urban Prep Creed, "We Believe."

Creed. The Creed is a litany of self-affirmations that members of the UP community memorize and recite together each school day.

> We Believe. We are the young men of Urban Prep. We are college bound. We are exceptional—not because we say it, but because we work hard at it. We will not falter in the face of any obstacle placed before us. We are dedicated, committed and focused. We never succumb to mediocrity, uncertainty or fear. We never fail because we never give up. We make no excuses. We choose to live honestly, nonviolently and honorably. We respect ourselves and, in doing so, respect all people. We have a future for which we are accountable. We have a responsibility to our families, community and world. We are our brothers' keepers. We believe in ourselves. We believe in each other. We believe in Urban Prep. WE BELIEVE.

The Creed represents UP's cultural ethos. Most importantly, each line is a declaration intended to embolden the young men's academic self-efficacy so that they are prepared to seamlessly transition into college, overcome any challenging academic tasks and personal obstacle, and persist through college to complete their degree program.[26]

School culture and climate. UP's school culture and climate is a defining feature of the school's overall organizational design. In describing UP's educational philosophy, Tim King said, "At Urban Prep, we provide our young men with swords and shields. The sword is a high-quality education based on a rigorous and culturally relevant curriculum . . . The shield is the self-confidence, self-possession, and self-awareness necessary for protection in an often unfriendly and unforgiving world. Our students develop these shields, thanks to a school culture grounded in four elements that Urban Prep calls the '4 Rs': respect, responsibility, ritual, and relationships."[27] The 4 Rs are reinforced in myriad ways through UP's academic curriculum, extracurricular activities, athletic programs, and service learning initiatives. One way the school aims to encourage and model respect for the young men, for example, is by referring to each student by his surname (as opposed to his first name). Every man in the building, student or adult, is referred to as Mister. Also, during the time I worked at the school, male teachers were required to wear a buttoned shirt and a tie each day. Daily recitation of the Creed during Community is an important ritual the school observes. Students practice responsibility by keeping their uniforms clean and pressed. School administrators place a premium on building substantive interpersonal relationships with the young men, so much so that, during my time at the school, "relationships" was a category on the UP official teacher evaluation.

Prides. Urban Prep's mascot is a lion. Playing on this, the small, teacher-led advisory groups are called Prides, reinforcing the idea of family and collective responsibility for each other's well-being. Prides meet every day, and their focus on peer interaction is designed to counter students' tendency to think only about themselves and their individual achievements. They are like an in-school family. Students stay in the same Pride—with the same teacher leader and the same set of peers—throughout their time at Urban Prep. This space allows for peer and adult mentoring and the development of life skills, in addition to providing time to develop group service projects. Moreover, through participation in the Pride, the young men garner positive peer associations, build a sense of community and school spirit, and share and disseminate schoolwide communications. Students line up in their Pride groups during Community.

College preparation. Messages about college going are a central feature of UP's overall organizational design. The school's culture and climate establish the conditions necessary to put every young man on track to enroll in, and eventually complete, an undergraduate degree from a traditional four-year college or university. The academic program includes double periods of English all four years and core courses in math, history, and science, as well as two years of a foreign language. By the time students reach grade 12, they should have established a competitive college admissions portfolio that includes their participation in several extracurricular activities and community service projects, the equivalent of eight years of English/language arts coursework, and six years of math. Furthermore, students participate in college visits beginning their freshman year, and the college counseling department works to identify and match students with summer academic enrichment programs. Students tend to be selected for these programs based on grades, academic performance in specific subjects, and interest.

Reading *Urban Preparation*

In writing *Urban Preparation,* I did not intend in any way to exceptionalize these young men, their home lives, or their families' decisions to send them to UP for high school. Nor did I write this to provide a rosy or unrealistic picture of growing up on the South Side of Chicago, in the "hood." I characterize UPCPS as a fundamentally descriptive qualitative study, and *Urban Preparation* paints a vivid picture of these young men's journeys from their home communities to and through college with respect to the factors they perceive have contributed the most to their education trajectories. The counterstory in this book demonstrates how attempting to provide a high-quality education to young Black men and boys *without* paying critical attention to the legacy of anti-Blackness, patriarchy, heterosexism, and White supremacy only works to reproduce racialized inequity, oppression, and marginalization within Black communities, rather than eliminate them. While discussion in *Urban Preparation* tends to center around one school, the themes revealed reflect broader social phenomena. And though these young men do not see themselves as better than their peers who have not completed college, their successes (and trials) in pursuit of a higher education are instructive for advancing justice in the education of young Black men and boys (and Black urban youth) everywhere.

Chapter 1 reviews relevant research literature focusing on opportunity gaps and the impact of anti-Black racism on the education of Black youth in the United States. This chapter helps frame the issues contributing to young Black men's persistent school failure, and it also reveals the historical and sociopolitical contextual knowledge necessary to understand the contemporary significance of Urban Prep's founding.

Chapter 2 begins the counterstory and introduces life on Chicago's South Side through the eyes of the young men. UPCPS's participants describe what they most and least enjoyed about growing up on the South Side, their initial motivations for leaving home, their aspirations toward future success, and gaining access to opportunities that enable them to one day improve their own and their family's quality of life. In chapter 3, these young men reflect on the reasons they (or their families) decided they would attend Urban Prep and their transition into the school during their first and second years of high school. This chapter is an in-depth examination of the young men's acculturation to UP's schooling environment. It looks at their descriptions of "brotherhood" and be(com)ing a "successful Black man." Analyses unveil UP's role in shaping these young men's conceptions of manhood and masculinity. Chapter 4 continues the counterstory by exploring how these young men experienced their junior and senior years of high school. More specifically, the chapter foregrounds specific aspects of the young men's college planning, the messages they received (and/or internalized) about college going, and Urban Prep's effectiveness in preparing them to be college ready. Chapter 5 concludes the counterstory and provides an overview of these young men's descriptions of their transition into college and their persistence through to completion. The young men reflect thoughtfully on college life, including the roadblocks they faced during their matriculation as well as the factors that helped them circumnavigate threats to completing their undergraduate degrees. This chapter features important reflections from the young men about what they perceive to be the difference(s) between them and their classmates who did not complete college.

In broad strokes, chapters 6 and 7 provide important considerations necessary to deepen the reader's understanding of the forces that mediate the effectiveness of urban schools to provide high-quality educational experiences to young Black men and boys. In chapter 6, I put forward some ideas about an appropriate starting point for reimagining the education pipeline for young Black men and boys as something altogether different. I theorize the effects of anti-Blackness on the (im)possibilities of structural-level urban education improvement. I then reflect on ways to rethink notions of "success" necessary to foster a learning environment that ignites young Black men and boys' school engagement. I build on these considerations in chapter 7, where I present some final recommendations for strengthening urban education reform efforts. I contemplate the concept of "urban education reform" as well as the utility of coeducational versus single-sex schooling arrangements, charter versus traditional public schools, and the importance of listening to urban youth to bolster school improvement efforts.

Critical race scholars create counterstories based on real-life details to expose the oppression and racialized disparities associated with the intersections of race with class, gender, and other social identity markers.[28] The counterstorytelling I employ includes the counterstory *as well as* the scholarly interpretation of this narrative around larger issues of anti-Black racism and White supremacy. I break up the counterstorytelling chapters into three parts. Chapters 2–5 begin with a brief vignette featuring Damani and Glen (characters meant to represent Derrick and me), the two former UP teachers who inaugurated the reunion of alums from the first graduating class of Urban Prep. Their conversations reflect on and foreground discussions that unfold in each chapter and also provide some contextual knowledge about Urban Prep based on their own experiences working at the school during its early years.

The Zoom In portions of each chapter follow. These are the narrative parts of the counterstorytelling. The setting is Giordano's, a famous Chicago pizzeria. There is a group of UP graduates and two of their former teachers who tell specific stories of their journeys to college. The Zoom Out portions of each chapter analyze the significance of these shared reflections and experiences to the broader issues of race, class, gender, and sexuality for determining these young men's education trajectories.

Think of a camera lens—zooming in gets you up close to the object of scrutiny so that you can examine the particularities of the object or case; and zooming out allows you to see the bigger picture, where all the smaller details cohere to tell a larger story of general significance to the observer. In my counterstorytelling, Zoom Ins are about being attentive to the individual experiences, interactions, lessons, and moments of each young man's journey. Zoom Outs are about making sense, from a more scholarly perspective, of how or why these details matter for determining the education success of young Black men and boys in an anti-Black racist society.

Conclusion

Improving education outcomes for young Black men and boys begins with a firm understanding of where they're growing up. Schools do not operate in isolation from the community space surrounding the building. Understanding the factors that collectively help determine these young men's education trajectories is limited without attending to the specific roles communities and families play in the process. Knowledge of the sociocultural and sociopolitical context of urban schooling adds depth and nuance to assessing the value of having attended Urban Prep. *Urban Preparation* is not about Urban Prep the school, per se. The title of the book is meant to represent the meaning associated with growing up in an urban environment. It is a statement of opposition to deficit discourses fixated on foregrounding the perils of poverty and disadvantage as predictors of future academic success. These narratives fail to adequately account for the resiliency and agency of urban youth. And because terms like *urban/inner city/ghetto* are used to socially construct Black and Latinx communities as places of destitution, desperation, and disinvestment, educators are left to establish schools around (or based on) perceived deficits rather than on the cultural strengths and expertise of urban youth.

More than anything, I hope this book adds substantively to conversations about how to expand access to education opportunity for young Black men and boys. Some would argue that the "promise of equal education opportunity" for Black people is a farce. Nonetheless, a commitment to at least reducing or minimizing barriers to education opportunity necessitates an orientation toward justice, not simply creating more diverse or inclusive schooling environments.

Attending to justice means having a reasonable command of the historical and political context shaping contemporary public schooling arrangements. This includes knowledge of neoliberalism, the persistent challenges of improving urban schools in Black communities, and the political forces that allow unsubstantiated narratives of academic success to endure without concrete evidence of an education institution's pedagogical effectiveness. Justice is questioning the public's pathological preoccupation with, and fetishistic consumption of, Black boys in tidy black blazers, shirts, and ties and the simultaneous exploitation of Black youth and families in the communities where these boys are being raised.

Justice is insisting on the creation of single-sex schools that make *explicit* commitments to embracing and honoring diverse forms of Black manhood and gender performance. Justice requires that we push back against the ways that certain charter schools in Black communities become exceptionalized and, by default, actively underwrite master narratives that characterize traditional public neighborhood high schools as "drop-out factories."[29] Such stock stories do nothing for reimagining these spaces so that they no longer exist as sites of Black pain and suffering while we keep "waiting for Superman" to save Black youth.[30] Justice involves being intentional about allowing young Black men and boys to conceive of a future for which they can be proud, instead of simply preparing them to talk, dress, and behave in ways palatable to a society that does not see them as fully human.

The counterstorytelling in *Urban Preparation* belongs to, and is written in honor of, these young men. They have graciously shared their lived experiences in the hope that educators and researchers learn to think, say, and write something different about them. Some of what is said may be surprising. At other times their stories will resonate with some readers' personal experiences, while other reflections may directly challenge one's cultural sensibilities. But all of what they say is insightful and educative. I ask readers to be open-minded, to embrace the parts of this book that are unsettling, and to come away with an idea of how they will inspire change and resist the status quo of present-day urban schooling. We all have a part to play.

1

Improving Urban Education for Young Black Men and Boys

with Derrick R. Brooms,
Associate Professor of Sociology,
University of Louisville

In her 2006 American Educational Research Association presidential address, Gloria Ladson-Billings challenged the research community to reconsider "achievement gap" language by focusing more deliberately on the governing systems, moral codes, political agendas, and history of institutional wrongdoing that created such a "gap" in the first place.[1] More recently, scholars have responded to this call by foregrounding other gaps, from wealth to quality childcare, to explain the failure of public schools to adequately educate diverse youth.[2] Others posit that the persistence of "opportunity gaps" points to why poor Black and Latino youth are consistently overrepresented for indicators of school failure across academic content areas and underrepresented for indicators of school success.[3] In fact, Prudence Carter and Kevin Welner assert that "achievement gaps arise from opportunity gaps."[4] These scholars acknowledge that before we can understand what a student does in school, we must interrogate how the structure of the school actually limits young people from maximizing their full academic potential. White supremacy and anti-Black racism are central for both explaining why opportunity gaps persist in urban education and how they work to sustain Black male academic vulnerability in the United States.

Consistent with perspectives in critical race theory, I agree that (anti-Black) racism is a permanent fixture of American society.[5] Studying these young men's education trajectories illuminated the many ways that the intersection of race with class mediates access to education opportunity for urban youth. For this reason, I begin this chapter with a discussion that clarifies the legacy of racism in public education. I do this to offer a context for discerning the significance of schools like Urban Prep, which was founded in part to disrupt pervasive deficit narratives about Black male youth growing up in urban America. When economic inequality intersects racial oppression, opportunity gaps emerge, which do nothing more than reinforce numerous structural limitations to high academic achievement for Black youth. Again, if contemporary Black youth growing up poor are to obtain an education that prepares them for multiple postsecondary options and participation in the global economy, then schools must consider how, and to what degree, they are organized to challenge white supremacist cishetero patriarchal capitalism.

Framing the problem in this way helps situate why there is a need for greater race consciousness in education praxis. Not considering race and its intersections with other social identity hierarchies poses more threats than it does opportunities for improving the educational experiences of young Black men and boys, which includes better preparing them for postsecondary success.[6] Thoughtful interrogation of young Black men's experiential knowledge is among the most useful tools available to education researchers for undoing the "commonsense" practices and policies that maintain Black males' school-induced psychological oppression, suffering, and/or cultural assimilation.

Black Education and the Legacy of Anti-Black Racism

An adage credited to Winston Churchill still rings eerily true today: "Those that fail to learn from history are doomed to repeat it." Another famous, unattributed, quote advises that "history repeats itself because no one was listening the first time." The history of Black people's education in the United States offers a valuable lens for distinguishing the factors that facilitate the failure of public schools to adequately educate young Black men and boys. This history acknowledges that Black people have always cared deeply about becoming literate and have fought for their access to education.[7] On the contrary, this history also unveils the numerous barriers to education attainment. White racial collusions to maintain White people's superior class status have made the struggle for educational equity one that endures even through to the present time. Volumes of research evidence across multiple academic disciplines confirm that race and racism have been, and will very likely remain, central to explaining disparities in academic achievement for Black youth, especially those languishing in poverty.[8]

Racism in contemporary American society is not best understood by overt acts of discrimination or prejudice committed against non-White people. If we consider racism as a system of privilege and power that advantages White people and disadvantages non-White people, then *being racist* stretches beyond the boundaries of a single, isolated incident of physical violence.[9] Anti-Black racism represents an accumulation of assaults—an *observable* trend of symbolic and enacted brute force inflicted on Black communities by those paid to serve, protect, and educate. This sort of assault is evident in the words and images used to describe Black people publicly and privately, such as when governmental agents pejoratively use the term *inner city* as code for poor Black and Latinx people. This assault is also enacted by individuals in positions of authority who automatically approach Black people with suspicion, fear, apprehension, and contempt.

The dehumanization of Black people, or the act of rendering them not fully human, originates in the mind of those who (unconsciously) center Whiteness and White cultural norms as "good" and "right" and "normal." Anti-Black racism, Islamophobia, settler colonialism, and anti-indigeneity, for example, are the by-products of White supremacy. All US social institutions are structured to center White logic, intellect, and emotionality.[10] Anti-Black racism, and anti-Blackness more specifically, is specific to the ways that Black bodies get socially constructed as inherently problematic, deviant, and inhuman.

In one of the earliest sociological studies in US history, W. E. B. Du Bois problematized the quandary of being both Black *and* American.[11] In *The Souls of Black Folk,* Du Bois argued that these dual identities live in parallel worlds—separate, but entrenched.[12] He went on to argue that the "color-line" would be the primary problem of the twentieth century, noting the precariousness of being Black and having to survive in a country that measures and affirms almost everything to the norms of Whiteness, or being/acting/performing as White (or "American").[13] His notion of *double consciousness*—the sense that Black people are always viewing themselves through the lens of White hopes and standards—helps explain why Black youth are socialized to cope with oppressive social conditions in neglected urban communities rather than find ways to subvert or change these conditions. This is especially true in institutions of education founded by and for Black people, such as Urban Prep.

Carter G. Woodson, in *Miseducation of the Negro,* extended Du Bois's contention, emphasizing how Black peoples' education by the oppressor, in the oppressor's schools, produces the sensibilities, ideology, and perspective that maintains their own oppression. "The Negro has never been educated. He has merely been informed about other things, which he has not been permitted to do."[14] This suggests that a Black person's "education" simply reminds them of the rights and privileges reserved for White people, such that everyone knows their "place" in society. For centuries, while Indigenous people have resisted White settlers aiming to expand the US nation-state, Black people have resisted colonization of the mind. In the case of Native Americans and Black people, "education" by White settlers has always had the explicit aim of erasing their home culture (cultural assimilation) by replacing our capacity to think, independent of the oppressor, with the sociocultural perspectives that only work to maintain the oppressor's superiority (white supremacy).[15]

Woodson further contended that "educated" Black people have not been taught to be creative and critical of the world so that they might improve social conditions for all Black people. Instead, their education has taught them to internalize and reproduce anti-Blackness.[16] That is, Black people have been socialized in school to exalt those ideas, philosophies, and ways of being that covertly operate to conserve their racial subordination. At the same time, they are learning to be disgusted with the cultural practices and performances most associated with Blackness. The result is a propensity to embrace holistically the norms of Whiteness.

Therefore, any contemporary education institution's orientation toward "success" (i.e., thinking, dressing, behaving, and talking in ways most palatable to White people or mainstream American society) will likely come into conflict with young Black men and boys' inherent desire to resist external boundaries to authentic self-expression. Du Bois's scholarship underscores the fallibility of hegemonic conceptions of success (like those I discuss in chapter 3). Historically, education as a means of upward mobility was never imagined to produce material benefits for a culturally and linguistically diverse citizenry. Subscribing to dominant notions of success renders people of color vulnerable, since attempts to *be successful* often force them to give up or compromise aspects of their personhood. Consider, for example, national debates about institutional policies requiring Black people to relax their natural hair or cut their dreadlocks.[17] Similarly, Derrick Bell emphasizes that no matter what Black people do to achieve parity with White people, their quality of life will remain inferior until White people decide to collectively dismantle the enduring system of inequity created by their ancestors.[18] Despite the bleakness of Bell's claim about the permanence of race and racial realism, history also reveals that Black people are resilient. They have always found a way when there was literally no way in sight—and education attainment is no exception.

Black Education, Resilience, and Resistance to Racism

Landmark court decisions such as *Brown v. Board of Education* did not effectively dismantle the consequences of racism on the schooling of Black youth. If nothing else, the *Brown* decision inaugurated many new challenges for the education of Black people in the United States. Multiple research volumes chronicling the fight for racial equity in education remind us of the ugly history of schooling for Black families prior to and after the 1954 Supreme Court decision.[19] Scholars emphasize the persistence, engagement, and cultural orientations of Black educators in segregated schools as well as the numerous challenges that integration has posed for Black communities. Bell argues through his theory of interest convergence that the *Brown* decision had more to do with advancing White interests than it did with closing gaps in education access for Black youth.[20] Even forty years after *Brown,* Black people in the United States struggle to understand the benefit of the (in)famous court case. William Tate, Gloria Ladson-Billings, and Carl Grant contend that the *Brown* decision heralded a restrictive form of equality, which suggests that the case significantly limited Black families' ability to benefit equally from the schooling arrangements mandated by the nation's highest court.[21]

Research confirms that the school was an extension of Black communities. One factor that made segregated schools effective despite having unequal access to high-quality instructional materials, for instance, was the fact that children were regularly culturally affirmed and taught cultural pride in tandem with traditional school subjects.[22] No degree of racism could limit the potential of segregated Black educators to produce intellectually astute young people. Most prominently, committed teachers and school leaders regularly included and collaborated with Black families in the education of their youth. Similarly, multiple case studies demonstrate that partnering with urban communities is vital for urban educators.[23] Holding to the notion that #BlackCommunitiesMatter, understanding effective approaches to educating today's Black youth and young Black men without considering the community's role is ill-informed. It is this philosophical assumption that sparked my desire to chronicle these young men's stories beginning with life on the South Side of Chicago.

The legally sanctioned, egregious acts of terror endured by people of African descent in the United States during slavery could not strip away the commitment Black men and women had about being educated. Reading and writing was such a priority to Black families in the South that many started their own independent schools and colleges (through the freedmen's educational movement) immediately following their emancipation from slavery.[24] The industrializing of agriculture in the late nineteenth century required a working class to shoulder the intense labor associated with the agriculture-driven economy. Without the institution of slavery, the laws that governed its operations, and legal protections for the White elite, landowners were left to invent other approaches to maintain agronomic productivity. One such approach was to restrain the desire of Black freedmen to educate their own children.

The "White architects of Black education" insisted that if Black youth were to be educated, it would only be so that they could be trained to meet market demands for labor—"White industrialists and landowners were to be the chief beneficiaries of Black industrial training."[25] This is a much earlier example of Bell's interest convergence principle, which maintains that White people will only make political and legal concessions when there is some direct benefit for them.[26] In other words, interest convergence is the point where Black people's needs intersect or converge with opportunities for White people to preserve hegemony. That said, urban industrialists and northerners funded White missionaries, many of whom were women, to travel to the South to dismantle all-Black community schools and "civilize" Black children. Today, White women still dominate the teaching profession, continuing to enter the field at high numbers, primarily through traditional teacher preparation programs.[27] These missionaries facilitated a form of schooling that emphasized Black youth's physical capabilities rather than their intellectual capacities. This was schooling with an end in mind: to relegate Black people to a permanent working class. Black people were never imagined to be more than White people's property, even after the end of slavery in the United States.

Improving Urban Education for Young Black Men and the Permanence of Racism

Sadly, considering the permanence of racism and the US's abominable history of genocide and settler colonialism, it is hard to imagine how the institution of public education can ever be restructured to better respond to the needs of Black (male) youth. One result of this history has been the persistence of dominant narratives about Black neighborhoods in large, economically diverse, densely populated cities as being culturally deprived pits of despair. The Englewood community on Chicago's South Side is one of those "high crime, low-income," predominantly Black communities that has received widespread negative attention from the national media. Movies like *Chiraq* mock Black residents and distract attention from the structural forces that have created the material conditions inspiring the movie's production.[28] Films like this fuel public discourse and minimize the significance of anti-Black racism, capitalism, toxic Black masculinity, and patriarchy. Each has created, and fosters, the very problem the filmmaker purports to want to solve.[29] Stock stories about Englewood, and other Chicago South Side and West Side neighborhoods like it, help position Urban Prep as a light in darkness—a beacon of hope to rescue Black children from the generational cycle of drugs, gangs, and poverty. These and other mainstream depictions of urban schools in movies like *Freedom Writers* and *Dangerous Minds* have been important for distinguishing UP as an education option "better" suited to young Black men and boys. Nevertheless, we still don't know what makes the school a better urban education option, and why.

Opportunity Gaps and "Inequalities of Opportunity" in Urban Education

Scholars have identified "opportunity gaps" as an important unit of analysis for naming factors that invisibly limit the capacity of urban schools to make the promise of "equal opportunity" for high academic achievement available to urban youth.[30] Opportunity gaps represent disparities in access to culturally appropriate and responsive school resources, practices, personnel, and learning experiences needed to optimize the learning environment. They also significantly reduce a school's capacity to provide ample opportunities for youth to experience being, or at least feeling, successful in school. Opportunity gaps are the confluence of education misfortune, long-standing economic inequality, and generational racial inequity.[31] The longer individuals from various racial groups are denied equal opportunity in various domains of life (housing, health care, employment, etc.), the greater the threat to their education attainment.

Economic inequality in the US makes it increasingly difficult to design learning spaces that effectively encourage the participation of urban-dwelling young Black men and boys. They help explain how the legacy of racism in the United States considerably reduces the capacity of educators to establish school environments that affirm and respond appropriately to young Black men's cultural differences. One such example can be traced back to how teachers are professionally prepared. Teacher preparation programs in the United States tend to favor the social and cultural norms of Whiteness.[32] This includes the failure of teacher educators to actively oppose deficit perspectives about teaching in poor communities of color.

Opportunity gaps have more to do with *inputs* than *outcomes*. Ideology, professional practice, the development of policy, a school's cultural ethos, and other professional priorities are inputs manipulated by education practitioners. These variables either strengthen or severely limit students' potential to achieve academic success. Considering what is known about the legacy of racism in the United States, and the failure of public education to actively oppose factors that exacerbate racial inequity, opportunity gaps undoubtedly obfuscate well-meaning urban school reform efforts. Thus, charter school organizations, established in the contemporary neoliberal context, fall incredibly short of appropriately responding to the ways racism covertly produces and maintains opportunity gaps in urban schooling.

I differentiate between two levels of opportunity gaps. *Classroom* opportunity gaps are beliefs and orientations toward cultural difference that fail to acknowledge the racialized experiences (and histories) of ethnically diverse students.[33] For example, a student who has fully adopted or internalized the prevailing social and cultural norms of a particular institution and is prepared to demonstrate the knowledge valued by that institution, will likely find great success in that institution. But a student who thinks, dresses, talks, or behaves outside the norms of an institution, one that is not designed to account for and respond to such diversity, is likely at an automatic disadvantage for ever achieving success there. In other words, success is tied to one's willingness to succumb to the dominant ways of being most valued by an institution.

Institutional opportunity gaps represent an entire student body's lack of access to the human or material resources in a school necessary to maximize their academic success. Such gaps represent the institution's inability to ensure full expression of students' greatest academic potential.[34] Dilapidated facilities, outdated curriculum materials, overcrowded classrooms, and minimal social support services and personnel pose significant barriers to all students' high academic achievement. An example of institutional opportunity gaps are the deplorable school conditions precipitating the Detroit Public Schools' 2016 teacher "sickouts."[35] Similarly, it was conditions like these that produced the complaints which led to the *Brown* case: the injury was not centrally located in Black people's lack of access to White schools but, rather, their lack of access to the same material conditions that White children enjoyed.[36] Whether classroom or institutional, opportunity gaps weaken any attempt a school makes at providing an already underserved group of students equal opportunity for achieving school success (table 1.1).

Classroom and institutional opportunity gaps are perpetuated by educators with good intentions who engender beliefs about students of color that lead them to act in ways that limit students' potential for high achievement. H. Richard Milner draws on a wide body of scholarship to develop an

TABLE 1.1 Research examples of opportunity gaps in urban schools serving predominantly youth of color

OPPORTUNITY GAPS	
Institutional	*Classroom*
• Less-qualified teachers[a] • Inequitable funding allocations/ Lack of material resources[b] • Lack of culturally responsive and affirming curriculum, learning experiences, and school practices[c]	• Deficit perspectives of culturally diverse youth and communities[d] • Racial illiteracy and racial stress[e] • Misguided beliefs about racial and cultural differences[f]

Sources:

a. C. Ascher and N. Fruchter, "Teacher Quality and Student Performance in New York City's Low-Performing Schools," *Journal of Education for Students Placed at Risk* 6, no. 3 (2001): 199–214; Linda Darling-Hammond, "Inequality and the Right to Learn: Access to Qualified Teachers in California's Public Schools," *Teachers College Record* 106, no. 10 (2004): 1936–66, doi:10.1111/j.1467-9620.2004.00422.x; Linda Darling-Hammond, "Securing the Right to Learn: Policy and Practice for Powerful Teaching and Learning," *Educational Researcher* 35, no. 7 (2006): 13–24, doi:10.3102/0013189x035007013.

b. Jonathan Kozol, *Savage Inequalities: Children in America's Schools* (New York: Crown, 1991); Jonathan Kozol, *The Shame of the Nation: The Restoration of Apartheid Schooling in America* (New York: Crown, 2005).

c. Gary R. Howard, *We Can't Teach What We Don't Know: White Teachers, Multiracial Schools* (New York: Teachers College Press, 1999); Tyrone C. Howard, *Why Race and Culture Matter in Schools: Closing the Achievement Gap in America's Classrooms* (New York: Teachers College Press, 2010).

d. Richard R. Valencia, *Dismantling Contemporary Deficit Thinking: Educational Thought and Practice* (New York: Routledge, 2010).

e. Howard C Stevenson, *Promoting Racial Literacy in Schools: Differences That Make a Difference* (New York: Teachers College Press, 2014).

f. H. Richard Milner, *Start Where You Are, but Don't Stay There: Understanding Diversity, Opportunity Gaps, and Teaching in Today's Classrooms* (Cambridge, MA: Harvard Education Press, 2010).

"opportunity gap explanatory framework" that outlines the greatest threats to equal opportunity for students of color and those from low-income families.[37] I have extrapolated what each of the five dimensions denotes about an educator's beliefs:

- *Color blindness.* The belief that race is of little consequence to students' schooling experiences and is insignificant for negotiating culturally affirming interactions with youth

- *Cultural conflicts.* The consequence of beliefs that position students' cultural frames of reference and lived experiences as subsidiary or peripheral to dominant perspectives guiding standard (Eurocentric) teaching and learning practices
- *Myth of meritocracy.* The belief that academic achievement is chiefly a function of effort and internal motivation rather than matters of social context, access, and other external variables; belief that merit, not wealth and economic advantage, predicts success
- *Low expectations and deficit mind-sets.* Beliefs about student ability based on perceptions of cultural deficiency, a perceived lack of experience, or the result of a youth's home life
- *Context-neutral mind-sets.* The belief that an understanding of place, or the physical, social, cultural, historical, and political contexts where teaching happens, do not matter for creating culturally responsive learning experiences for diverse youth

Teachers who recognize and abstain from such beliefs are much more likely to narrow classroom opportunity gaps in their professional decision making. Nonetheless, broader discussions of inequality of opportunity are necessary to further unravel the structural barriers to students' high academic success.

Prudence Carter and Sean Reardon distinguish "inequality of opportunity" from "inequality of outcomes" by lamenting that access to "power and life chances" significantly improves the likelihood of "attainment of desirable outcomes" for certain groups of people.[38] The limited access to wealth and/or other forms of power for Black youth from economically depressed communities underscores the important responsibility urban schools have to expose young people to a range of educational opportunities that level the future economic playing field. These efforts should not, however, come at the expense of students' own healthy racial and ethnic identity development. Additionally, this exposure should not disaffirm or diminish the multiple forms of culture youth of color bring to school.[39] Teachers act as levers for mitigating the damning effects of structural inequity (including the intersections of race and poverty) that are the result of opportunity gaps too often present in urban schools.[40] Christopher Jencks illustrates how the meaning of equal opportunity in educational practice is less discernible than the intention of teachers and schools to provide it to all youth.[41] Many schools want to do better by Black students and youth of color but fail to have a language or approach that adequately addresses disparities in access to opportunity. Opportunity gaps provide a lens by which to frame and engage the long-term work of sustainable urban school improvement.

Understanding opportunity gaps and their relationship to broader discourse around "equal opportunity" is at the core of *Urban Preparation*. Young Black men growing up in large cities likely come in close contact with numerous classroom and institutional opportunity gaps in their preK–12 education. There are different forces, however, in the urban environment that these young men contend with that can inform how a school organizes its academic and social supports. Pedro Noguera argues that urban school improvement for Black males requires acquiring knowledge of the sociocultural and environmental contexts from which these young men emerge.[42] Studying "grit" is not the answer, as this paradigm attributes Black males' failure or success as primarily a function of their own physical or intellectual effort. Instead, I include in *Urban Preparation* an examination of one single-sex school's efforts to disrupt opportunity gaps for young Black men, and the efficacy of those efforts as understood through these young men's first-person perspectives.

Single-Sex Schools and Young Men of Color

According to the US Department of Education, single-sex education is "education at the elementary, secondary, or postsecondary level in which males or females attend school exclusively with members of their own sex."[43] Reports indicate that in 2011–12, more than five hundred public schools across the United States offered single-sex options in some form, in single-sex classroom instruction or in entirely single-sex schools, where most or all of students' school activities are in an all-boys or all-girls setting.[44] Supporters of single-sex schooling assert that separating boys and girls, by classrooms or schools, increases students' academic achievement.[45] Advocates of all-male schools contend that centering boys' social and emotional development, combined with strong mentoring and an academic focus, can help males succeed in the classroom.[46] Over the last fifteen years, the creation of single-sex schools has been embraced primarily as an intervention strategy, to "ameliorat[e] the risks and hardships commonly associated with the academic performance and social development of Black and Latino young men" and thereby improve the educational and personal trajectories of this population that has been identified as "at risk" rather than "at promise."[47]

Abigail James and Herbert Richards found in their study that single-sex educational environments for boys helped them avoid gendered stereotypes of "appropriate" interests and aspirations.[48] Boys who were educated in a single-sex environment expressed strong academic attitudes and affiliation for their secondary school. Attending a single-sex school served as a significant predictor for students' increased interest in a variety of subjects such as English, reading, and history. Additionally, students' attitudes toward these and other verbal subjects were increased, and these interests and skills remained throughout students' college and careers. Furthermore, James and Richards's study suggests that students from single-sex schools displayed a significant attachment to their school, both during their time as students and after graduation. Other research suggests that it is critical for schools to create environments designed to protect young men of color from various risk factors, which includes acknowledging and building on their resilience to organize culturally responsive schooling experiences.[49]

Despite a dramatic increase in the number of public single-sex schools, there has been a shortage of research supporting the academic benefits of isolating young Black men and boys from girls. And while single-sex schools have been the subject of much research, the overwhelming majority of this tends to focus on how single-sex schools differ from coeducational institutions and classrooms. There is a dearth of studies that critically examine student experiences within these educational spaces. Thus, discerning the role and function of Urban Prep for supporting its graduates' college persistence is a worthwhile aim of this text.

Conclusion

Over the last decade, a significant number of single-sex charter schools for boys of color have been established in major US cities. Eddie Fergus, Pedro Noguera, and Margary Martin describe the contribution of such schools to reversing trends in the education of Black and Latino males in their book *Schooling for*

Resilience.[50] They insist that much more work needs to be done to clarify how the race and gender of males of color contribute to the academic and social problems they face in school. They found very little evidence that these schools are *better* academic options for young men of color and note that the "good intentions" of funders and education reformers are not enough to "generate real solutions" necessary to strengthen the young men's educational attainment. However, these schools have made institutionalized commitments to young men of color that positively impact their overall educational experiences in school. No work has been published that centers the nuanced voices of young Black men boys who attend these schools. This is research that makes tangible contributions to understanding the impact of urban public (charter) schools like Urban Prep.

History provides some contextual details for making sense of present-day schooling conditions for young Black men and boys.[51] Examining the intersections of race, class, and gender in the experiences of these young men's journeys from Chicago's South Side to and through college necessitated that I begin with a discussion of Black people's education in the United States and the history of anti-Black racism. Improving that education means becoming increasingly aware of the implications of White supremacy and anti-Blackness. It also means giving explicit attention to the intersections of race with other interlocking systems of oppression (religious and linguistic imperialism, heterosexism, patriarchy, ableism, capitalism, etc.).

Awareness is the first step toward disrupting institutional arrangements that build on, extend, and embolden White supremacist ideology. This is the fundamental American viewpoint by which wealthy, White, Christian, cisgender, heterosexual, able-bodied men set the standard for (and are elevated to) the apex of all social identity hierarchies. In other words, contemporary public schools must avoid organizing themselves in such a way that their practices and philosophies subtly imply that students should aspire to reach this apex. Instead, learning environments must be established that minimize threats to a young person's freedom to express the fullness of their humanity. These are the conditions that help to reduce opportunity gaps and enable young men like those featured in this book to "overcome" risk factors in their upbringing. Like a mirror, the counterstory that follows makes apparent that which easily goes unnoticed.

2

Living and Learning on the South Side of Chicago

Chicago had not yet transitioned into the fullness of its reputation as one of the most frigid places on Earth, but the low temperatures on that December night two weeks before Christmas foreshadowed what was sure to be a record-breaking cold winter. Armored in the necessary outerwear for the season, Glen and Damani waved goodbye to the young men and began walking briskly down Michigan Avenue toward their cars. They were on an emotional high. In excitedly recounting what they'd heard at the dinner reunion, the two couldn't help but feel proud about where life had taken five of their former Urban Prep students.

As they neared the intersection where they should have parted ways, they found themselves walking slower and slower, their conversation having become too involved for even a casual stroll. They stopped at the corner of 16th and State. Glen gestured toward the coffeeshop behind them, asking Damani, "You got some time?" Anxious for relief from the the icy windchill that native Chicagoans refer to as the "hawk," the two men scuttled inside. It had been over a decade since the opening of Urban Prep, and in the nine years since Glen left the school, he and Damani had been in and out of touch. Damani was a professor in a sociology department at a midsized public institution in the South, and Glen was a teacher educator at a large land-grant university in the Midwest. The men agreed that this dinner was long overdue. They also agree that while it was great to reconnect with their former students and hear about their experiences at Urban Prep and life during and after college, these young men's journeys really began well before they entered Urban Prep. Glen and Damani realized that when they started teaching at Urban Prep, they did not have a good understanding of what life outside of school was like for their students. They acknowledged that every adult came into Urban Prep with his or her own view of what it was like growing up on the South Side. These realizations launched a two-plus-hour conversation in which Glen and Damani recounted the details of the dinner conversation. Their discussion was punctuated by moments of deep contemplation as they reflected on, and marveled at, their former students' perseverance, resilience, and agency.

> My least favorite part—that it's the hood. It is! That's all I've known. I've learned to adapt to it. I know more, but that's all I've been accustomed to growing up. I'm comfortable with this. I learned to adapt.
>
> **REGGIE**

This chapter is a portrait of living and learning on Chicago's South Side as seen through the eyes of seventeen of its sons. It's a glimpse of the events, experiences, and incidences that inspired these young men's dreams for the future. Their stories of life in Englewood, West Englewood, Auburn Gresham, Chatham, South Shore, and other South Side neighborhoods both counter and complicate dominant mainstream depictions of Black men and women in these communities. Not ashamed of growing up on the South Side, these young men described their birthplace as the incubator where they learned how to effectively mitigate threats to their physical, emotional, and material well-being, and they owed much of their present success to the messages, skills, and "street" knowledge they acquired from home, on the South Side.

Through their comments and reflections, the young men revealed a good deal about the difficulties they faced growing up, with much of that "struggle" being connected to poverty and their susceptibility to neighborhood violence. Their childhood conceptions of success centered on "doing something" with their lives that would make their families proud. These young men developed agency at an early age, when they had to learn how to effectively navigate urban environmental risk exposure.[1] I use *risk* to refer to anything the young men were exposed to that threatened their physical, emotional, or psychological well-being. Gang violence, the lure of crime and the victimization, as well as their own and their families' struggles with joblessness, access to quality health care, and the criminalization of Black bodies (e.g., stop-and-frisk practices) can each be considered a risk factor. These young men were not passive subjects being acted on by neighborhood and school influences. Instead, they were (and still are) active decision makers whose input and visions of the future became central to determining their educational trajectories. The young men's descriptions of life in the "hood" help clarify aspects of their motivation to finish high school and persist through college.

This chapter represents a Sankofa moment in these young men's lives.[2] They looked back to remember and contemplate the significance of the beginning of their journeys to and through college, journeys that began on the South Side of Chicago.

Watching Mama's Struggle

ZOOM IN

The seven men greeted one another with handshakes and hugs. After all the text messages and e-mail exchanges, they were finally meeting for a long overdue dinner reunion. Quentin, Antwan, Reggie, Jeff, and Winston attended colleges or universities outside the city, with all but Reggie having returned to Chicago after college. And their former teachers, Glen and Damani, also native Chicagoans, no longer lived or worked in the city. So it took some work to get them all together, and, as the bright green, blue, and red lights adorning the restaurant's entrance signaled, Christmas was the one time they were all "home."

The aromas were intoxicating, and as they settled in around a high-top table with a classic red-and-white plaid tablecloth, Glen remarked, "Living in another city really makes you appreciate the small things about home—like good pizza!" Everyone agreed, nodding enthusiastically as they picked up menus and turned their attention to which golden-buttery-crusted cheesy pie of goodness they wanted to order. A silence set in.

Glen, breaking the ice, said, "Facebook is cool, but we can't wait to hear more about what's been going on since we last saw you guys almost seven years ago. Tell us about college! Y'all left the South Side—What ultimately made you go away

FIGURE 2.1 Map of Chicago's South Side and median household incomes

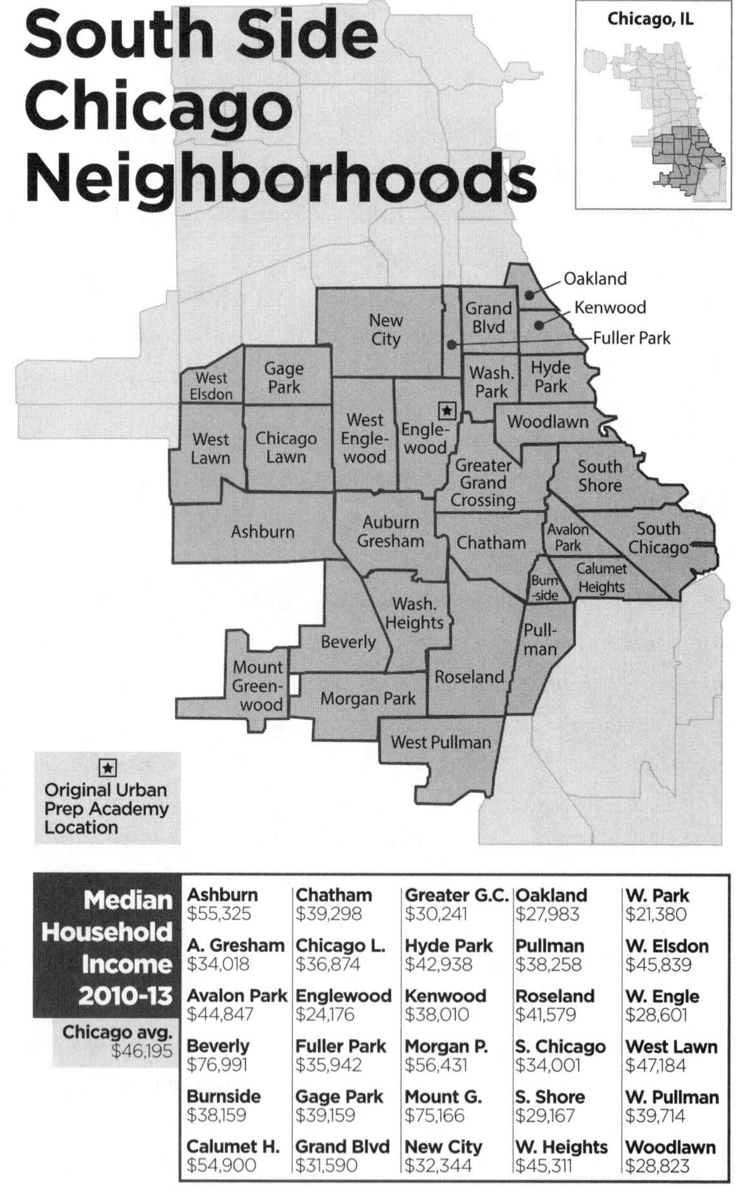

Ashburn $55,325	**Chatham** $39,298	**Greater G.C.** $30,241	**Oakland** $27,983	**W. Park** $21,380
A. Gresham $34,018	**Chicago L.** $36,874	**Hyde Park** $42,938	**Pullman** $38,258	**W. Elsdon** $45,839
Avalon Park $44,847	**Englewood** $24,176	**Kenwood** $38,010	**Roseland** $41,579	**W. Engle** $28,601
Beverly $76,991	**Fuller Park** $35,942	**Morgan P.** $56,431	**S. Chicago** $34,001	**West Lawn** $47,184
Burnside $38,159	**Gage Park** $39,159	**Mount G.** $75,166	**S. Shore** $29,167	**W. Pullman** $39,714
Calumet H. $54,900	**Grand Blvd** $31,590	**New City** $32,344	**W. Heights** $45,311	**Woodlawn** $28,823

Source: US Census data, 2010–13. Map designed by Cody Harrell.

to school? Catch us up!" Quentin, not usually the first to speak up, jump-started the conversation.

QUENTIN: A lot of times in my childhood I saw my mom struggle. I'm the first to go to a four-year university in the family. Seeing my mama struggle, that's one reason. The struggle, at least that I've seen, influenced me to just want to do better for myself, because I didn't want to go through that when I grew up. It was just tough on everybody in the family. My mother really struggled. That really encouraged me to go to college, because I learned from some friends, you know, and seeing what was going on in the neighborhood, that I really couldn't do that much to help her if I didn't get through college.

The other young men nodded in agreement, Quentin's words clearly resonating with them. At that moment, Damani and Glen realized how hard it was for the young men to imagine going to college without considering how it could potentially improve their families' lives. His mama's "struggle" was the motivation Quentin needed to want to do better. Reggie, inspired by Quentin's remarks, was eager to offer his perspective of why he went away to college.

REGGIE: I believe it was the whole idea of making my great aunt proud. The idea that she never pushed me to be a doctor or lawyer or anything. "Just make something of your life." That's all she would say. I could be a janitor or anything, "just make something out of your life."

WINSTON: Yeah, I think my mom was the most influential person because, I mean, even just seeing what she did and how she had an associate's and she went on to get a bachelor's and transitioned to a master's. She got her bachelor's shortly before I graduated high school.

JEFF: My parents were all for it. They were very supportive whether I wanted to go or I didn't want to go. They left the decision up to me. We never had conflicting decisions of my mother or father making me want to go to college because neither one of them went to college. They've always told me that college isn't for everyone, even though in my eyes they seemed successful without going to college. They have pretty decent jobs. I know that those opportunities that they were given are not the same as now. I felt like going to school was best for me. Also, getting out of my comfort zone and going into a new area where I can grow more and learn more about how to be independent and a man.

REGGIE: Well, I wanted better for myself. I grew up seeing people on the corner selling drugs. I really didn't know the meaning of a successful Black man before I went to college, or before I came to Urban Prep. I always believed that college was a fairy tale. It didn't really exist. I thought it was a place that was only for white people. I didn't think there was anything after high school. But at home, I didn't really get any messages about college.

The waiter, who'd been standing by waiting patiently for Reggie to finish, asked for drink orders. Conversation stopped as everyone studied the menu. After ordering, Antwan recalled his family's initial response to his desire to one day attend college.

ANTWAN: Debt! That was one of the big things they said to me. They was like, "If you go to college you'll find yourself in debt. You won't find a job after college, or it'll be hard." They told me that, before I even went, that you're going to have some financial challenges. "We won't be able to support you in the ways that you want us to." They was like, "If you go to college you still ain't gon' do nothing. You gon' have a lot of debt and financial problems." I was basically raised in an environment with competition, and they didn't want me to think that I was better than them.

Antwan's comments struck a cord with Damani. He recalled how frightening it was for him to attend an elite, private, historically White university not far from home, something no one else in his family had ever done. The young men agreed that, for them, the risk of going to college far outweighed the risk of staying in the neighborhood. They recognized that it took a lot of courage and confidence to follow through with this decision and that the struggles they observed as children were enough to convince them that they had to give college a try.

The waiter returned with the drinks and stood ready to take orders. "That'll be, what, two sausage-and-cheese-stuffed pizzas, one cheese-and-spinach-stuffed pizza, and one pepperoni-and-onion-cheese-stuffed pizza to start, please." Glen ordered. "These young men are hungry!"

ZOOM OUT

For *these* young men, there was very little pressure from home to go to college. Their parents/guardians cared about their education, but they did not insist that they get a college degree. The decision to attend college ultimately belonged to the young men. That does not mean they made that decision without some external influences. Data from the Urban Prep College Persistence Study suggest that most important to these young men's families was that they learned to make decisions that would produce a comfortable quality of life free from the ongoing difficulties of generational poverty and overexposure to street violence. For instance, Reggie's making "something" of himself anchored his great-aunt's hope that he would live a future life that countered the negativity of the community where she was raising him.

Even though these young men did not articulate a specific recipe for (college) success, the young men's mamas still cared deeply that their sons achieve it. (Here, *mama* refers to anyone who acted as the guardian or caregiver; for many of these young men, these were aunts, grandmothers, or other women relatives.) And these young men envisioned doing something to alleviate their mamas' "struggle," although it wasn't always clear exactly what that was.

Taking cues from their mamas and from life on the South Side, the young men learned to begin making decisions centered on their will to survive, which, in essence, placed numerous limitations on their autonomy. Being poor and Black and male living on the South Side put immediate demands on the types of decisions these young men could make, such as the places they could go and the people with whom they could interact, to not compromise their own or their family's physical safety. The weight of poverty, having to negotiate (and avoid) gang territory/interactions, and the persistent susceptibility to neighborhood violence created numerous social boundaries for these young men, and significantly narrowed their visions of the future. As adolescents, they had a difficult time conceptualizing "going to college" as a means of achieving "success." Reggie indicated that college was a "fairy tale."

Though there were a few exceptions in their stories, "mama's struggle" was something each young man internalized, something they could not escape. But it was also something that would inspire them over the next eight or nine years of schooling. Their mamas' inimitable resolve to survive at all costs served as the inspiration these young men drew from to endure their own struggle to achieve future goals, which includes completing high school, enrolling in college, and completing an undergraduate degree program.

In the context of the reunion dinner conversation, the idea of struggle is not in and of itself necessarily violent or unsettling, though it could be in other contexts. Instead, it is a space for wrestling with various difficulties or obstacles to achieve a reasonable resolution. Hence, the young men's use of *struggle* is both negative and positive. There is the negative experience associated with the need to carefully and strategically navigate unfamiliar neighborhoods to get to school safely. But the positive aspect emerges from the intellectual act of weighing and contemplating multiple alternatives to solve a complex, real-life problem. Taking active steps to bravely and intelligently reduce one's vulnerability to a set of distressing circumstances is the substance of struggle. Struggle encourages problem solving.[3] This is not to say that being poor is necessarily a good thing; but learning to effectively negotiate the cirumstances that poverty generates does develop character, tenacity, and resilience.[4] As the stories of these UP alums' journeys to college make clear, each of these traits contributed to their persistence to and through college.

It is in and through struggle that Black people across generations have learned to demonstrate *resilience*, the capacity to adeptly bounce back from adversity.[5] Young Black men from urban environments are, indeed, resilient.[6] One significant factor contributing to the development of this resilience is "college going familial capital," the "rich knowledge, information, and inspiration" men of color receive from their families that motivate their postsecondary aspirations.[7] It is out of mama's struggle and the family's hope that they do "something" with their lives that these young UP graduates began to establish an ideological frame and a commitment aimed at finding and achieving future success. At this point in their journey, prior to entering Urban Prep, going to college was a distant variable in their definition of future success. College-going would later emerge as an opportunity to disrupt the cycle of struggle.

Similar to Frederick Douglass's assertion that "without struggle, there is no progress," struggle represents perseverance despite, or in the face of, formidable obstacles.[8] For these young men, the toughness, ingenuity, creativity, and flexibility they demonstrate in persisting through college was first cultivated at home on the South Side. The roots of their desire to be successful also, in one way or another, emerged out of mama's struggle and the struggle of navigating the space between home and school. The substance of their remarkable capacity to never give up once they set their minds toward accomplishing a goal centers on their basic human instinct to survive, which includes observing how the adults in their lives practice survival.

This is not about grit. Grit assumes we live in a meritocracy and presupposes that the young men's successes rise and fall based on what they do or do not do. These young men succeed, first, *because of* where they're from, not in spite of it. The political and economic circumstances that created the structural disadvantage they faced navigating the South Side are an aside to this particular discussion, but this knowledge is important to understanding the factors that restricted these young men's access to education opportunity.

This is where Urban Prep comes in. UP emerges as central for inspiring the young men's beliefs in future possibilities that extended far outside the South Side—which includes college going—and the difficulties of "hood" life.

Living in the Hood

ZOOM IN

Damani ordered a few appetizers—to tide them over until the pizzas arrived—as the group began to discuss how the word hood *sometimes gets construed pejoratively, like* ghetto, *and how that misconception plays into their own and their mamas' struggles.*

ANTWAN: When I was in high school I stayed in West Englewood. In relation to Urban Prep, it was no more than about five to ten minutes away from our school. It's a particularly, definitely a rough neighborhood. The way I describe it to people who ask me where I'm from, because they don't know the Chicago area too well, I say, "It's the place that ABC7 is always featuring. Or, whenever you see something about police lights or violence or something, it's that place that the ABC7 guy was talking about."

JEFF: I wish I didn't have to experience some of the violence, but I'm glad I did. That showed me I was "street smart" [*using air quotes*]. A lot of people aren't street smart. They are vulnerable to a lot of stuff that may go on, especially in the city of Chicago and Englewood. Some people just aren't street smart! I was working to be street smart as well as smart in the school. I knew that there was the time to do work, and outside of school I knew how to avoid a lot of situations. If everybody was walking one way, I walked the opposite way just to not set myself up, or something like that, in a potential danger or anything. I learned that earlier on, too. But, I mean, it was like the usual stuff you see on TV, stuff like shooting, drugs, and all that stuff. But it was like a community of people. Amidst all that stuff that was going on, we were still friends, and close.

Damani interjected, telling them how, when he was an undergraduate, Black students used the word ghetto *to differentiate themselves from other, poorer Black people. Jeff reacted with surprise. This prompted a few of the men to comment on how they thought the South Side had changed over the course of their childhood and young adulthood.*

WINSTON: I do remember that the neighborhood was in transition, so you had a lot of, like—I don't know. We had some new apartments that was built across the street from us, and there was a lot of violence. It was on the increase. A lot of that was happening, but a lot of times I wasn't even there because I was either at school or doing something else. [The people that moved into the neighborhood] brought the violence with them.

QUENTIN: When I was young, before high school, when I was in grammar school, it wasn't that bad, but, like, once I started high school, the projects started to get torn down, so like more people started to move from the projects to my neighborhood. What made it a lot harder for a lot of people that lived there, it just became more violent. My family didn't let me go outside that much anymore because they got a lot of violence over there. It was just a sad neighborhood for my family and especially my brothers and my sisters because we couldn't go outside if we wanted to.

The men talked at length about how outsiders tend to think of the hood—a characteristically rough neighborhood, like the place Quentin had just described—as a place to be escaped, yet these places are just called home for the people who live in those neighborhoods. Despite differences in upbringing and family structure, Winston, Reggie, Antwan, Jeff, and Quentin shared the common experience of being from the South Side, and they believed that the community helped make them sharper, more intuitive, and more aware of the many traps that too easily ensnare those who are less street smart.[9] *Glen then asked them what they thought was the worst part of living on the South Side.*

WINSTON: I think—I don't know. I think it's the violence. I know for a fact it was the violence. Just knowing that you have to be careful, of course, when you go, what happens. Just all the shootings and the negative vibes that you get from people and all those things. People get shot at two o'clock in the morning, and you wondering what's going on. This never happened before. And you used to be able to go outside, and it's not like that no more. It's not that comfortable feeling where you can just go outside just anytime or just chill outside. You've got to be aware of your surroundings. That was something that I definitely didn't like, because I wasn't used to that growing up.

In early 2000s, when these young men were entering Urban Prep, parts of Chicago were gentrifying. Housing projects like Cabrini Green were being destroyed, many schools were closing to make way for new charter school "options," and Black youth were being shuffled around in the mix of it all. Glen found it interesting how the men sometimes talked about where they grew up as a place where they currently live, in the present tense. This was because their families are still there, though they were away at school. It was still home.

REGGIE: I just felt like—I'm not saying I was scared of death or anything, but I was just afraid of my life just being taken. I know what I want to do in life. I know what I want to be in life, and I don't want my life to be taken by living in this type of environment. Anything could happen. I was blessed to make it out alive. There were a lot of people getting killed for no reason. There were days when I'd go outside and I'd see blood on the sidewalk. Sometimes I'd think it could be me. There kids about twelve years old standing on the corner selling drugs. Just a shame. Definitely was my least favorite part about my neighborhood growing up.

ANTWAN: Sometimes, being here, you got depressed. Sometimes we would have discussions about having low self-esteem or sometimes we would go on outings to places like downtown. You don't see those things too often, and you feel out of place. You wondered, "Why don't we have this type of stuff where we stay? Why don't we have these types of things?"

WINSTON: Englewood was pretty convenient, but the neighborhood was really, really bad. There was a lot of trouble in that neighborhood, but I never came across any trouble. I would just hear about it from the other Urban Prep students.

QUENTIN: You couldn't even go outside without having to worry about a drive-by shooting or anything. Last summer, somebody I went to high school with, and grammar school, he got shot, almost got killed. Like a block away from the house. I grew up with this dude. He's like my little brother. That's what I call him. That's, like, the worst part. There's another person that I grew up with that got killed. I found out about that last year. There's a lot of people that I knew got killed, and that's the worst part of that neighborhood.

ANTWAN: It's crazy. I lived right across the street from St. Sabina, so it wasn't that bad. But as soon as you cross the street, you're right in the middle of all the crime, gang violence, and drug violence and all that stuff. I feel like I always had to watch my back everywhere I went. We once had a break-in, and it was just stuff like that where I just feared for my family's safety and stuff like that.

The appetizers arrived, and as they passed around the plates, they compared notes on what it was like growing up on the South Side. They clearly shared a pride in where they were from, but that didn't mean they weren't critical of the unfortunate circumstance of normalized neighborhood violence.

ANTWAN: "I'm from Chicago." We say that with pride—"I'm from Chicago. Murder capital of the USA. You don't want to mess with me because I'm from Chicago." You say that type of stuff, but at the end of the day, it's still sad that you take pride in the fact that your city's *that.* It's not something that you want. Even though your cousins might bang, that might be the lifestyle you grow up in, I don't think anybody's that dumb to actually want that type of life. If you give them any other outlet, they're going to want to get it. It's harder for others just because of circumstances. Nobody wants that life, and college was that, was one of those options, possibilities to get away from it. I didn't want to come back. I [went] to college to get away.

The men were moved by Antwan's passion, and several of them echoed his comment about going away to college to escape the violence. Damani didn't think that Antwan had a clear understanding of the structural circumstances that lead to violent behavior, but he could see how he was confident in his belief that Black people were not born violent.

QUENTIN: I used to come back to this every break. Having to experience the stuff every time you want to come back home—you got to deal with so-and-so, or something happening on the block or shootings happening around the corner. Things like that. Other than that, this would be a real decent neighborhood, if it wasn't so bad.

Nodding in agreement, Winston described the tension he felt hanging out with some of his old friends in the neighborhood when he visited Chicago during his college years.

WINSTON: I was always the type of guy where if I wanted to do something, I don't see any reason why we shouldn't do it or I can't do it. And then if you tell me I can't do it because these guys are over here or you can't go to this area, I understood it but then I didn't understand it, because I felt like I was always trapped by my association to other people.

Shaking his head in regret, and pausing several times as he spoke, Jeff shared his experience navigating the space to and from school.

JEFF: Going to and from school, what we had to deal with going to school—what I had to deal with going to school, and from school, was a lot. A lot of times when my little brother first started going to the school, he would ask me, "Why are we going this different way today or why are we . . . ?" He would ask questions. I didn't really want to tell him because I didn't want him to be scared. Instead of going down the street where I knew that a lot of people were going to be, I went around a different way to just miss all of that. I'd have to reach out and be very candid about that with my teachers, that "if I stay late and work with you on this assignment" that I couldn't necessarily walk home. I'd have to call a ride. I wouldn't be able to just stay and put my education forward because of where my neighborhood is.

Glen and Damani noticed how the young men sat up a little taller in their chairs when describing how they had avoided the negative consequences of risk exposures in their neighborhoods. Glen, Reggie, and Damani listened as Quentin, Jeff, Winston, and Antwan spoke about having to navigate threats to their physical well-being. Quentin turned the conversation back to Urban Prep and refuted the characterization of all young Black men from neighborhoods like theirs as "thugs" and "gang members."

QUENTIN: We had dudes that was in gangs. Dudes that wasn't in gangs but they hung around the gangs. We had the cool dudes, or whatever. We had the generals of certain gangs and things like that. Everybody. It was a diverse group of black males at Urban Prep, for sure. The guys that I hung around just happened to fit a lot of stereotypes or whatever that you might see on the news or that you might not see on the news. Okay, well, yeah. Some were more focused on academics, some weren't. Everybody had their different paths in life, you know. Everybody had different support systems at home.

ZOOM OUT

Colloquial use of the term *hood,* much like *urban,* often conjures up apparitions of violence, images of Black and Latinx people living in abject poverty, and visions of run-down buildings, vacant lots, and liquor stores with people loitering out front. The schema produced by the use of words like *hood* and *urban* are rooted in the reality that, too often, one is likely to find such conditions in places like Englewood. In my own experience, growing up on the North Side of Chicago, in Rogers Park, calling someone "hood" was an insault. It marked that person's behavior or values as lower class or subordinate to more widely accepted norms for social interaction, dress, or speech.

The larger issue is the accompanying belief about, and perception of, young people who are growing up in economically disenfranchised, densely populated communities of color and what deficit beliefs about being from the hood mean for the types of (education) opportunities available to them. There is no skirting the fact that these places are as "rough" and "violent" as the young men described. But these circumstances cannot be allowed to essentialize urban-dwelling young Black men and boys into one monolithic group. Some students at Urban Prep were closer to danger than others in terms of their affiliations and habits outside of school. Urban Prep was a Black male melting pot of sorts. The range of difference within the student body added substantively to the relationships the young men cultivated with one another over their four years at the school.

Scholars suggest that young people who are born in neighborhoods like the South Side communities described in this counterstory are likely to have far fewer opportunities for upward mobility than do their peers from more affluent neighborhoods.[10] These young men defied these odds. They made it clear that they had an aversion to the violence they experienced in their neighborhoods. They understood that these conditions limited their ability to move freely through the physical place they called home, and they resented such restrictions on their autonomy. Still, the counterstory raises questions about what role their high school played in reshaping their thinking. Winston recalled resenting limits on his autonomous decision making because he had to think first about acting in ways that protected his physical well-being. He still had agency, but there were strict boundaries for how it could be expended. Such boundaries were most usually connected to various risk factors operating outside of the young men's control.

Essential to these young men's survival was developing the expert knowledge needed to navigate the South Side—*street smarts,* as Jeff called it. Exposure to risk, which may include gang recruitment, gang involvement, or a susceptibility to random street violence, was among the early obstacles these young men learned to overcome as they persisted toward achieving their education goals. Nonetheless, there was consensus in the data that these aspects of life on the South Side did not make it an innately bad place to grow up. As Antwan noted, the most common depictions of communities like Englewood do not represent the conditions that anyone would choose to live in. These are conditions they have inherited from decades of neglect that, in one way or another, can be traced back to the insidious racism in US local, regional, and federal laws and policies.[11] The young men regretted having seen, and sometimes experienced, so much street violence, but they recognized that this adversity was important for making them smarter and more aware. They did not have the chance (or privilege) to feel vulnerable, as this could pose a threat to their physical well-being. They invested that energy in figuring out how to survive and make their circumstances work to their advantage.

The young men alluded to how increases in violence robbed them of some of the freedom and safety they once enjoyed in their home communities as they moved out of boyhood into their teenage years. Pauline Lipman's connection between a rise in violence, sweeping neoliberal market reforms, and gentrification have left the "rights to the city" hanging in the balance.[12] Increased violence in neighborhoods is one unintended consequence of groups of youth having to travel through unfamiliar neighborhoods to get to a new school after their own neighborhood schools have been closed. (One instance of such violence was the 2012 death of Derrion Albert, who was hit with a wood plank while we was on his way home from Fenger High School in 2012.[13])

As Antwan observed, the conditions that create violence deserve much more attention from public officials, not just educators who daily have to respond to the fallout of such violence. This is not a problem of the schools alone; it is an issue of significance at the municipal level. Disproportionate coverage of violent acts in urban spaces is a distraction from the root causes, which include racist policies enacted by city governments that lead to segregated, densely populated, high-poverty communities of color in wealthy US cities like Chicago.

The Urban Prep grads also spoke about how they learned to adapt to various negative neighborhood influences by acknowledging that it wasn't always a comfortable process, but necessary. Their ability to bounce back and learn strategies to buffer risk exposure was the substance of these young men's resilience. Jeff's comments about getting himself and his younger brother to and from school safely reveal such strategies. The young men's resilience was evident in their application of expert cultural knowledge, skills, and resources—or cultural capital. This form of knowledge is rarely appreciated by a school, and educators often expect urban youth, and young Black men in particular, to give up this sort of place-based, neighborhood-specific cultural intelligence in exchange for more dominant (Eurocentric) forms of cultural knowledge.[14]

Critical race theory scholar Tara Yosso puts forward community cultural wealth as a strengths-based theoretical perspective useful for deciphering the valuable skills, knowledge, and abilities youth of color bring to school.[15] Her framework assumes the critical race perspective, that nothing is wrong with communities of color; the problems they face are rooted in institutional racism and other forms of discrimination that fail to value and account for their experiential knowledge of the policies, cultural norms, and practices of that institution. Within this community cultural wealth frame, the young men's dreams of alleviating mama's struggle by one day being able to make them proud could be considered what Yosso terms "aspirational capital." The young men held very tightly to their aspirations to return home from college with a degree. Their trajectories through the neighborhood, and through Urban Prep, helped them acquire social capital, or valuable "networks of people and community resources," which served them well in college and at various times throughout and after their matriculation.[16]

In maneuvering through their neighborhoods and college campuses, these young men also demonstrated an ability to problem solve. They made well-reasoned decisions when posed with perplexing alternatives. These young men learned to connect broader structures of racial inequity to experiences navigating familiar social barriers in the neighborhoods where they grew up. The idea of "street smarts over school smarts" is one advantage that growing up on the South Side afforded these young men, that educators and researchers do not easily recognize, understand, and/or appreciate.

As Yosso points out, young people of color draw on numerous "social and psychological 'critical navigational skills' to maneuver through structures of inequality permeated by racism."[17] For these young men, effectively navigating a segregated Black neighborhood suffering from a lack of investment by the political elite is not much different than navigating a predominantly White institution of higher education. Organizations, offices, and agencies historically established to support Black people's financial, physical, social, and emotional well-being are consistently underresourced. At the same time, Black people continue to struggle to gain access to the positions of power that directly influence large-scale institutional and structural transformations. These structural barriers pose a unique risk to young Black men's progress and their opportunity to advance with minimal disruptions to their educational attainment.

Balanced Views of Life on the South Side

ZOOM IN

The pizzas finally arrived, and everyone made room for the four hot pans in the center of the table. The waiter carefully cuts up and plates thick, steaming slices, and the men pass them around the table until everyone is served. This did not slow down the conversation, though. In between their first bites, the table discussion turned reflective, with the young men recalling what they liked about growing up on the South Side.

ANTWAN: Still, the hood has a better sense of community. Sure, there's violence, and gang this and blah blah this. But at the end of the day, it's still a community, and people still care for each other. That's one of the biggest things that I really do appreciate about West Englewood. There's always something there. Everything may not be up to par, or up to our expectations as a people, as a race, but there's still something there. There's still resources there. It's accessible. There's accessibility in West Englewood, because you know where your resources lie and go out there and get them . . .

DAMANI: What else did you all really like about growing up on the South Side?

QUENTIN: Uh, family. Because, you know, that's where I felt most safe, because I had a lot of family. I really enjoyed living over there.

ANTWAN: I liked going to summer camps [offered through the park districts], but sometimes I got into trouble along with the neighborhood kids.

WINSTON: Growing up I enjoyed going outside. We'd go outside for hours, and my mom would be like, "Okay, now it's time to come in." We'd just go outside. All the kids played with each other. We got into it, but at the end of the day we were still neighbors. We'd get into it, and the next day they'd say, "Can they come outside?" It was definitely cool, but, like I said earlier, that had definitely stopped once people started moving into the neighborhood, once the old people started moving out.

REGGIE: One thing I did like about the neighborhood was, even though people were gang members and stuff like that, there was a community. People did look after each other. Food trucks used to come around, and people gathered . . .

Reggie was interrupted by the loud singing of "Happy Birthday" at a nearby table. While he searched for his thoughts, Quentin picked up the conversational thread.

QUENTIN: Some of the people that I met, they're not doing as well as I'm doing every day. That kind of sucks, but I can still talk to those people any time I want to. Some people, they'd be like, "Quentin think he is better than me," and stuff like that, but they haven't disowned me or anything. I guess we have to talk to them and continue to talk to them. That's one of the best parts of that neighborhood.

WINSTON: [The neighborhood] was like a sense of family. Not that we were really close. We just identified with each other. It was a joy to be around the people, and we had fun with each other. I don't know. It was just a realness to it, I guess. This was important to me because we moved a lot. I think my favorite thing about it was my own different types of perspective that each community gave, because they gave off a different type of energy. And then when you're in the area, you're influenced by the energy of a community, that tends to affect your outlook. Every time I would move, I would literally have a different outlook on life and how things are in general. It was fun to go somewhere else new, even if it wasn't in a good area, because I'd always meet the right people, and that would always affect me in a certain way. Well, there are good people in bad neighborhoods.

ANTWAN: And I most liked my friends, growing up with my friends. We used to always talk about what we was gon' do and how we was gon' make a difference. Just coming up with plans about making it out of the situation that we was in even though we didn't really have the vision. Not having the vision but still having a visual.

WINSTON: Just the people. People and convenience. Not too far from everything—not too far from downtown, not too far from farther south, not too far from my family. Everybody lived on the low end.

The conversation quieted as the men began taking their pizza seriously. Someone at a nearby table commented, "Y'all just got so quiet. Must be good!" The men chuckled. It didn't take long, though, for conversation about their South Side days to resume.

ANTWAN: Participating in programs and organizations and things like that. Going to school, that was another one. There would be times and days where we didn't eat at home. I would look forward to going to school—for the "edumacation," but knowing that we could get a lunch. Most of us looked at school as an outlet for getting away from what was going on outside.

JEFF: My favorite part is it's right by the expressway. It's not really into the city. A lot of people don't come down our street, so it's pretty quiet. It's more just secluded but still "in the hood." It's pretty much where we stay.

QUENTIN: As I think more about it, living there—I mean, that's where I grew up, so I guess that's, in a sense, my favorite part about growing up on the South Side. It's convenient. The 87th Street bus is right there. The rail line's around the way. I can get to Oak Lawn real quick, if I need to. I guess, for the most part, what I do like about living out there is the buses that I take are close by, so it's kind of convenient. It helps me to transition from my side of the city to downtown pretty quickly. That's definitely something that I enjoy about living in my neighborhood. It's closer to some stores. There's many pros about living in a neighborhood.

ANTWAN: My other favorite part of living there was the convenience—just like a couple of blocks to school and back. I could just walk there, and I didn't have to take, like, five buses. My mom didn't have a lot of money, and it just really helped to be able to walk to school and back. So that would be my favorite part of living in the neighborhood.

WINSTON: I'd also say my favorite thing is that there was always something going on. Living in [a wealthy, predominantly White Chicago suburb], you see a different sense of community. Nobody's around, everybody's all cooped up in their big fancy houses, everybody's just worried about their own sort of lives. West Englewood—I can't say the same for that. It's a better sense of community.

ANTWAN: I was involved through the church. We met every Friday around seven or eight o'clock at night. We had a round discussion about our week and what we can do to better ourself. We hosted events like marches against violence, events like feeding the homeless, a bunch of fund-raisers, and stuff like that. [Pause to reflect further.]

I'd say I gained a lot from it. I can't really remember how I got involved in it. I want to say word of mouth; maybe I was at home not doing nothing. I went into it with an open mind. It helped me better myself as a person. It brought me closer to God. I met new people.

The conversation volleyed back and forth among the young men. Glen and Damani listened attentively, trying not to interrupt the young men's reminiscences with too many questions. Antwan was particularly engaged, giving the men quite a bit to think about. He tended to talked with his hands, as if he were directing a chorus of words.

ANTWAN: It was just that all odds were against us as young Black males. All odds were against us. But, it was like once you stepped inside the [UP] campus, it was like a safe zone. You were safe there, and they believed in you there. Once you stepped outside the safe zone, it was like everybody was against you. The neighborhood with all the violence, making it safely back home—it was just crazy. Going to school, coming home—it was just crazy. Every day you wake up it was, like, "I just gotta make it to the safe zone. I gotta make it to the safe zone. If I make it then I'm okay." Then it got to the point where once you got to be a junior and senior you just started counting down the days.

JEFF: I know there are a lot of students that didn't have fathers at home or grew up in neighborhoods worse than mine that were actively in gangs. Urban Prep gave them a place, a safe haven to go. Whether they decided to stay for the short period of time they did or whether they didn't, for however long they were at Urban Prep, it was that safe haven where they could be, where they knew somebody cared and made their life better.

ZOOM OUT

Concentrations of poverty, food deserts, and few institutional assets, such as parks, well-resourced community centers, universities, or places of worship, characterize the difficulties of urban life experienced by these young men.[18] They resented the conditions of the South Side without regretting having lived there. This was home; the place where they had family, friends, church, and the convenience of proximity, programs, and activities. Everyone was trying to survive, which sometimes meant feeling like "everybody was against you."

The discussion of the difficulties of South Side living allowed them to reflect on what they appreciated about growing up in the hood. They'd not often been asked what they liked about being from Chicago's South Side. Their interactions with educators tended to send the implicit message that escaping the South Side was their best hope for a better future. But that is not the stance these young men took in discussions with them.

Elsewhere I reflect critically on the assumptions I developed about Black youth given my own privilege as an educated Black man.[19] Part of the reason I became a teacher was because I wanted to "save" young Black men by setting them on a path toward the American Dream—prosperity and the pursuit of happiness. Hearing about these young men's experiences reminded me of just how much what I (thought I) knew about the young people I taught in North Lawndale, Englewood, Austin, and Auburn-Gresham was un(der)informed. This severely limited my capacity to see more clearly what my Black students needed from me as their teacher and to recognize the skills and knowledge they brought to school that I could use to minimize opportunity gaps in the classroom learning environment.[20] While I had a similar upbringing to some of the young men who participated in the UPCPS, I grew up in a different era. Also, I have completely different interests and cultural influences. And, in the classroom, nobody ever challenged me about what I knew relative to the sociocultural context where I was teaching. From my experience, colleagues believed being a Black man teaching Black kids was enough. But that couldn't be further from the truth. If I'd had a deeper sense of what the young people I taught valued in their communities, I would have been more effective early in my teaching career.

The network of people and the conveniences the young men spoke of are key components of any vital community. These aspects of South Side living are characteristic of the historic significance of Black communities' contributions to the education of Black youth.[21] These young men's experiences growing up on the South Side evidence the importance of family, loyalty, and cultivating strong community links. They described their villages, descriptions akin to Afrocultural values of communalism.[22] Historically, before *Brown v. Board of Education,* Black teachers were members of the communities where their jobs were situated. There were very few school-neighborhood distinctions; teachers were residents of the neighborhood and members of, not visitors to, the community.

This is significant, since the young men's lives *outside* of school informed their orientation toward school and their proclivities to (dis)engage in certain schooling environments.[23] For example, the young men recognized the threats to safety that gang banging posed, but their discussion humanized these individuals. These "gang bangers" were their neighbors' children, and the drug dealers were some of the same people who granted the young men safe passage to school or looked out for them when they were younger. Each was a member of a larger community, a part of what they appreciated about living on the South Side. This is not to suggest that gang banging adds value to urban spaces. But it is to say that these are *still* people, human beings, whose need to survive, though unfavorable to many, leads them to participate in underground economies.[24]

Antwan's description of Urban Prep as a safe zone and Jeff's description of the school as a safe haven indicate that UP provided an oasis from the violence, both physical and symbolic, that its students experienced outside of school. *Symbolic violence* refers to the invisible microassaults experienced during simple interactions with various social institutions. An example is developing a fear of police because of patterns of abuse experienced by community members when interacting with law enforcement officers.[25] Scholars acknowledge that high school–age young Black men need to attend schools with protective factors built into the design in order to counteract the psychological, emotional, and physical consequences of risk exposure.[26] One such protective factor is the interpersonal relationships these young men form with their Black male teachers and school administrators, many of whom come from the very same neighborhoods where they now teach, much like Glen and Damani. Relationships across stakeholder groups in a school matter for ensuring Black male school success.[27] The young college graduates who participated in the UPCPS found value in these student-teacher relationships. They perceived that these teachers could directly identify with what they enjoyed and disliked about growing up on the South Side. These relationships were pivotal for boosting the young men's academic efficacy and engagement in school.

As Antwan pointed out, people tend to see only the violence on the ten o'clock news. Communities like these receive little credit for all of what is happening that is positive. The gloom and doom of growing up in an urban environment perpetuates the kinds of schematic references of Black neighborhoods, like Englewood, that reformers use to rationalize dismantling neighborhood schools. Reformers and those with a vested interest in the remaking, or gentrifying, of predominantly Black and Latinx communities for the purposes of wealth accumulation, for instance, rely on such stock stories. Without them, it is difficult to justify dismantling entire neighborhoods, displacing their residents, and possessing land that had been occupied for generations by people of color. This neoliberal approach is a hallmark of contemporary urban school reform, and Urban Prep was established within this political climate.[28]

A problem with this type of reform is the penchant of a school's design team to not consider the rich cultural strengths of the Black communities the school will inhabit. Weak school-community partnerships emerge as reformers project dominant, ill-informed perceptions of parent involvement and engagement onto Black parents and families.[29] Compounding this problem is the failure of school leaders to consider "opportunities in geography" as sites of collaboration and capacity building.[30] This is significant for preparing Black youth to pursue multiple postsecondary pathways.

Neoliberal school reform corporatizes public education, which breeds competition and further dehumanizes and deprofessionalizes the teaching and learning enterprise in communities that have the greatest material needs. Urban schools in communities of color seem expendable when (unelected) Chicago school board members choose to close fifty schools in one school year. Such actions precede major shifts in mainstream discourse and understandings of education as a *public good*—a civil right and service provided by the government to level the playing field for youth who have been historically underserved.[31] In places where everyone is just trying to survive day to day, parents are fighting for the best "product" (schooling option). Thus, privately run charter school networks like Urban Prep Academies, enter public debates about improving urban education with an agenda, all the while clamoring for their share of the market (Black and Latinx children). This is not to dismiss the good work that some charter schools are doing, even though the differences in academic performance between charters and traditional public schools vary quite a bit by state.[32] Charter schools should not and cannot be positioned as a panacea to problems that extend far outside of the school walls.

Of great concern is what happens to traditional public neighborhood schools that are left to languish, while charter schools get heralded as *the* answer to urban school reform. For example, even on the issue of preparing urban youth for college—an explicit aim of Urban Prep—stubborn racialized disparities in college readiness for all youth of color persist.[33] This threatens any school's goal of getting its graduates both accepted into and prepared to succeed in college. Still, the institutional imperative of "college for all" implies that schools like Urban Prep are only populated with students who are serious about education, which sends a covert message that students at other traditional neighborhood schools, and the guardians who send them there, are not serious about obtaining a high-quality education.[34] These kids are no different from the young men in this study. But because Urban Prep monopolizes the public's attention by reporting that every one of its graduates has been accepted to college, too few people consider what happens to the many other Black youth enrolled at neighborhood high schools right down the street or to the students with whom UP shares a building.

Conclusion

The influence of life in the hood on these young Black men cannot begin and end with narrow discussions of gang affiliations, street violence, and the ravages of poverty. Such a picture is incomplete and imbalanced. Considering today's neoliberal school reform climate, this view of urban life accentuates the Whiteness of good intentions by reformers and others who seek to establish "college for all" schools in communities of color.[35] After all, predominantly White (and/or wealthy) communities do not receive this same attention by school reformers or charter school operators looking to expand their operations.

For this reason, these young men's reflections are indispensable for better understanding and responding to impediments to young Black men's and boys' high academic achievement. They provide important alternate perspectives necessary to rethink prevailing assumptions about what urban youth need from their schools. They offer critical lenses for assessing the feasibility and capacity of urban educators to appropriately meet those needs. After all, pursuing an education should not require forcing young people to disassociate themselves or detach from their neighborhoods. This type of "education" only works to sanitize aspects of their racial identity, or diminishing features of their cultural expression and heritage. Instead, educators teaching in urban schools must understand the value and strength young people have acquired as a result of growing up in those neighborhoods and respond accordingly.[36]

3

UP Years 1 and 2

Schooling Environment

The coffee shop was quiet. Laptop keyboard clicks and smooth jazz playing faintly through a couple of wall speakers made for good background noise. Glen and Damani could feel themselves getting carried away in discussion. Their playful, thoughtful exchange had transported them back to moments in the past that defined their professional career trajectories. "Keep it down," they reminded one another jovially, careful to avoid disrupting the other customers who appeared to be hard at work. But they couldn't contain their excitement. In revisiting the conversation from dinner, the two college professors were reminded of the many important role models, encouraging words, interactions, and exposures that shaped their own journeys from Chicago's South Side to and through college.

Glen joked in between sips of his soy caramel macchiato, "When all of us first gathered that summer to think about how this school might prepare these young men to become successful, I'm not sure we fully understood the gravity of what we were doing." Damani agreed. "I don't remember us ever debating or explicitly agreeing as a faculty that college was the most viable pathway to success." Glen nodded, adding, "I think it just made sense though, that we wanted these boys to reach for the stars, and college seemed like the best way to do that at the time. Most importantly, though, every single adult in the building had a deep love for those boys. No doubt about it." This launched the men into discussions of the implicit messaging about manhood and (hegemonic) masculinity that were transmitted in the schooling environment and of how well UP acknowledged each young man's cultural difference, versus essentializing them and treating them as if their family upbringings, for example, were all the same.[1]

"Being a student at UP was something special for these young men. They had no regrets, and neither do I having taught there. UP has had a significant impact on these young men's educational trajectories," Damani noted. "We probably could've been more expansive in our thinking about education opportunity and the concept of becoming 'successful Black men,' though." Glen agreed, "I can see that. But we did what we thought was best for the young men at the time."

> I guess the first two years [it was about] adjustments, making adjustments. The last two years I was aiming, I was achieving goals.
>
> **REGGIE**

Deciding where to attend high school marked an important turning point in these young men's visions of and aspirations for the future. Attending Urban Prep was the first step on the path to a four-year college or university. This chapter features an examination of the young men's early transition into Urban Prep, focusing in particular on their first two years of high school. During that time, their interactions with the school's adult stakeholders, culture, and climate underscored their aspiration to attend college, gave them confidence in their ability, emboldened them to enroll in and complete college, and established conceptions of manhood and masculinity that they carried with them into and through college.

This transition is better understood by exploring the messages the young men received and the lessons they learned about becoming a "successful Black man." First, I explore the mechanisms Urban Prep employed to attract students and families to the school, and what these suggest about the school's philosophy around notions of "success." I then describe the young men's adjustment to a single-sex high school and the ways they make sense of this newfound "brotherhood." This includes examining the utility of the school's other design elements, such as Prides, Community, the rewards system, and the daily recitation of the Urban Prep Creed. Finally, I consider the young men's descriptions of the adult Black men internal school stakeholders—most of whom were teachers their first and second years at UP—and what these and other interactions in the schooling environment meant for their early gender identity development specific to notions of manhood and masculinity.

Making the Decision to Attend Urban Prep

ZOOM IN

"I see you gettin' kinda light up top, Glen," joked Antwan, noticing his former teacher's subtle balding pattern. Glen rubbed the top of his head, quipping, "That's what age will do to you, young man. Just you wait!" Everyone laughed. Jeff then asked the group, "So, what made y'all want to go to Urban Prep?" This moved the conversation from life on the South Side to a more focused discussion of the young men's transition into Urban Prep, starting with what initially prompted the young men to enroll in the college prep high school.

ANTWAN: One of my elementary school counselors recommended that I go there. I guess she seen something in me. She didn't want me to be like all the other boys—those falling victim to temptations. It was crazy. She suggested that I go there even though I had all these other applications. She was like, "Nah, you gon' go here." After the orientation I was just sold once they said, "We're going to send you to college," and I was just like, "I'ma go here." Once [the school counselor and Antwan's family] made that decision, it was like, "You're going to Urban Prep." I didn't even apply to other places.

REGGIE: I think [UP] wanted Black men to do better in life and not be the typical Black man or stereotype of African American men. I didn't want to fall up under that category. That's just something I didn't want to do, so I felt going to UP was my calling.

WINSTON: People didn't really care about education [at neighborhood high schools]. It was just—We knew people who went there, and they didn't really do anything. And my mom wanted me to go to college, and they felt like Urban Prep was the right move. Believe it or not, I'll just say the fact that nobody else in my neighborhood was doing what I was doing. I was going to college, and I knew many people in my neighborhood wasn't. Just the different *opportunities* I had.

ANTWAN: I wanted to go to Lindblom initially. I made the right decisions though. But I feel like for everybody, just because of the situation in the neighborhoods we grew up in, I feel like definitely the way Urban Prep is structured, you know, people are there to support you, that believe in you, that you're not doing it by yourself. I feel like that helps a lot of students out. I made that right decision.

As educators, and knowing what they did about traditional public high schools, Glen and Damani were troubled to hear Winston describe those schools as places where "people didn't really care about education." Following up on Antwan's comment, Glen asked, "I know some of y'all applied to other schools outside of the neighborhood, so what sealed the deal for attending UP?"

JEFF: I was into computers earlier on. The computers caught my attention. That's why I went. I didn't even think about the fact that there wasn't going to be any girls, because I wasn't—I was young. My focus wasn't really on girls at the time because I was young. I was still young. I was more into the computers.
QUENTIN: Yeah, what really got my attention was the laptops. They brought up the word *laptops,* or whatever. I think that kind of sold everybody, like the whole laptop thing. So, that's what drove me to go home and tell my mother about it. I really ignored the all-male thing. I tried to go to, like, the Whitney Young, the Lincoln Park, all the top schools, and stuff like that, but at the time my scores were low. One day my friend came to school with the folder for Urban Prep, and he said, "You get a free laptop if you come." I'm like, "Word, you get a free laptop. I've been needing to get my own computer." Yeah, after everything, because I couldn't go nowhere else after that. My mom went to orientation. They hooked her too, so she made me go.
JEFF: I had taken the selective enrollment test for Whitney Young and Lane Tech and Walter Payton, and didn't pass that. I'm like, "Man, I'm definitely not going to X High School."[2] Anybody who knows anything about South Side Chicago knows that X High School is not the place you really want to send your child, especially if you know they can achieve academic excellence and you want that to be heightened. UP sent out these fliers saying, "Hey, there's an orientation for this new school." They had these four guys on the flier dressed up in these red ties, white shirts, black blazers, all of that. I was just like, "I'm going there."

ZOOM OUT

I remember how the cheers of excitement about finally receiving the laptops turned to lament when the new freshmen learned that they would have a double-period English class every day. UP appealed to an idealized notion of success by distinguishing itself as "college preparatory." Also, its guarantee of access to technology and more time spent on instruction made the school a very attractive choice to families and elementary school educators on the South Side. At the same time, Urban Prep benefited from the dominant perception that local schools failed to provide an adequate education to young people on the South Side. Through its recruitment campaign, Urban Prep distinguished itself as a *better* schooling option. In a community of Black families who wanted the best for their sons, and for young men who wanted to find success—to alleviate mama's struggle and make something of their lives—UP was a superlative option. With its laptops and brochures featuring "four guys . . . dressed up," Urban Prep stood out.

The public is inundated with images and messages of success that feature a fairly standard model: shirts and ties, college preparatory schools, "standard" American vernacular English, low haircuts, and so on. Yet, too few young Black boys can turn on the television and see diverse depictions of Black men with whom they can personally identify. Unfortunately, many young Black men and boys growing up in urban environments don't regularly encounter positive representations of adult Black men who at least appreciate, let alone mirror, how these young men dress and speak. Ordinary, everyday Black men who may hail from similar neighborhoods, who have faced similar challenges, and who embody the same cultural sensibilities as urban-dwelling young Black men and boys are too often pathologized and judged unfairly because of how they look.

Men whose cultural repertoires parallel those of the Reggie, Antwan, Jeff, Winston, and Quentin tend to be widely depicted as animalistic, hypersexual, deviant, anti-intellectual, and a "menace to society."[3] These types of images perpetuate public fear of Black men, just as public policy such as "stop and frisk," a result of "broken windows" policing, has done little for public safety beyond further penalizing Black people for being Black, for fighting to "breathe" on New York City streets.[4] The War on Drugs ushered the United

States into an era of mass incarceration, which Michelle Alexander has named the New Jim Crow.[5] In this climate, urban-dwelling Black boys continue to be imagined as thugs, while Black girls are imagined as loud and ratchet and ghetto.[6] These perceptions tend not to align with popular notions of "success." So, naturally, for families who want to avoid putting their sons in a high school where violence is normalized, and where they fear that their children's education will be subpar, Urban Prep is a strong high school option.

To that end, Urban Prep has remained intentional and strategic about building and maintaining its brand and squeaky clean public image. This way the school is attractive to funders and the families of young Black men growing up in some of Chicago's most neglected Black communities. Pamphlets, websites, and advertisements feature young men who are always "properly" dressed—pants belted above the waist, white shirt tucked in, tie, blazer, black shoes—and sporting low haircuts and clean-shaven faces. These demonstrations of conservative gender performance project images of cisgender young Black men and boys. These school materials depict a schema of what a safe, respectable Black male citizen looks like.

These images reassure the public that these Black boys are exceptional, nonthreatening—"different" from other (mischievous) Black boys and men who wear hoodies and sag their pants. These images also tell the public that supporting Urban Prep is an investment in the well-being and safety of the public, because these Black boys are not like other Black youth who attend the bad neighborhood high schools, where students don't care about receiving an education. *These* Black boys, the ones who attend Urban Prep, are on track to become "successful Black men"—middle-to-upper-class, Christian, heterosexual, well-spoken, college-educated Black men. And it is these images, featuring young Black men wearing the caps of the colleges they plan to attend, that drive the impressive press campaign celebrating Urban Prep's "success" in getting 100 percent of its seniors accepted to a four-year college or university. Nevermind if they actually attend college. This imaging tells its own story to parents and families: Urban Prep will set their sons on a trajectory toward high educational achievement.

At the same time, such imaging works to reify dominant standards for success that fail to appreciate the unique voices, experiences, aesthetic preferences, interests, desires, and talents of young Black men from the "hood." There is a very real tension between providing young Black men and boys with a quality school option without acculturating them toward a more anti-Black standard of success and Black manhood.

Extending the work of Black feminism and critical race feminism, Frank Rudy Cooper argues that normative social identity hierarchies cause Black men to operate within the binary of good Black man or bad Black man.[7] Being a bad Black man means acquiescing to pervasive stereotypes that construct them as animalistic and hypersexual, for example. This social construction then compels them to want to actively assume the good Black man image to avoid the negative consequences associated with the bad Black man image. Alternatively, the good Black man image centers on emulating heterosexual, Christian, middle-class White men. So many educated Black men, and those committed to improving the lives of younger Black men through mentorship or teaching or other formal and informal interactions, are stuck in the middle trying not to reinforce the bad Black man image. They do this while at the same time attempting to resist assimilation into the image of White(male)ness.

Respectability is mired in this contradiction, and the intensity of this identity negotiation ends up too often leading well-intentioned Black men to prop up oppressive hierarchies that continue to marginalize Black women, transgender Black people, and others who have been minoritized because of their sexual orientation. This is evident in Black men's inconsistency in standing up to injustices against those who are multiply subordinated, such as Black trans people. I have come to recognize my own complicity in maintaining and perpetuating cisgender heteropatriarchal relations during my time working at Urban Prep and beyond. The first step is awareness.

The young men's comments suggest that Urban Prep's efforts to shift deficit narratives of young Black men by preparing them to go to college were driven by an active desire to subvert the bad Black man image most associated with "brothas" from the Englewood community, where the school was founded. At the same time, teachers' interactions with the young men inadvertently privileged the good Black man image (e.g., employed, married, college educated, God fearing) to the degree that the schooling environment was likely marginalizing for women and for young men who may have identified as same-gender-loving. These findings parallel Eddie Fergus and colleagues' conclusions that single-sex schools for boys of color tend to "propagate masculine images" that school actors believe will help the boys find success in school and life.[8] These images privilege heterosexual men in the school who project a normative masculinity that socially constructs them as nonthreatening, but still manly. Certainly, Urban Prep was engaged in redefining masculinity for its students in an effort to counter "street" images of Black men.[9] This implicitly made manhood a normalizing function of the school. Less clear is how the school took these opportunities to help its young Black men recognize the role they played in interrupting assaults committed against women, sexual minorities, and others who are marginalized because they do not fit inside static gender binaries and roles.

The bipolarity of the "good" versus "bad" Black man image leaves little room for development of a complex, nuanced perspective of Black manhood, heterosexual or otherwise. Just as these young men were proud to be South Siders, they were also proud to be Black. But the stress of working to not associate with the bad Black man image can take its toll on Black men as they navigate the road to "success."[10] This is because their labor, modeled and advocated by adult Black men in high school, is ultimately an assimilationist incentive to dissociate from Black people, Black communities, Blackness, and other forms of Black cultural expression and knowledge. Put simply, without some attention to how schools disrupt binaries within Black masculinities, schools like Urban Prep unknowingly collude with systems of domination which also undermine efforts to establish culturally responsive social relations.

For Urban Prep, the college-going Black male image is exalted as the epitome of success, and it is an image around which the schooling environment is organized. This mission, however, was created *for* the young men, not *with* them. Because *all* Black lives matter, and because "injustice anywhere is a threat to justice everywhere," teaching Black boys to be successful Black men means also teaching them to be antisexist and antihomophobic.[11] It means teaching them to identify the multiple ways they are privileged, and to see how their various identities can work to marginalize others in various contexts.

Another aspect of Urban Prep's draw was the sense among educators who recommended the school, and the young men's families, that attending the college prep high school would transform these young men into respectable citizens. The desire to prove young Black men's decency and worthiness to the mainstream, and thereby underscore the importance of a school like UP that is "changing the narrative," can be dangerous. This is especially true when there is not equal attention given to the structural forces that lead to deficit narratives of Black people, and the deterioration of Black communities.[12] Respectability politics reinforces social class distinctions within the Black community and, at the same time, insists that individuals act in ways that project their worthiness to be treated with the same dignity and fairness owed any citizen. Michelle Smith says, "Respectability politics evince a distinct worldview: marginalized classes will receive their share of political influence and social standing not because democratic values and law require it but because they demonstrate their compatibility with the 'mainstream' or non-marginalized class."[13] Hence, engaging in respectability politics does not adequately account for, or respond to, the material conditions that maintain and perpetuate the United States's legacy of White supremacy and institutional racism. Those embodying this politic tend to be more concerned with an individual's personal behavior in public spaces, or other cultural aesthetics, than they are with equipping Black people to disrupt the social, political, and economic order.[14]

Respectability politics are most prominently imposed on poor, working-class citizens by Black elites as their contribution to "uplifting the race." This makes sense when one considers UP founder Tim King's family background. Getting young Black men positioned to successfully enroll in and complete college is a significant and important aim. While the push for respectability has, historically, worked to improve the lives of Black people who were willing to acquiesce to norms of Whiteness, respectability does little to prepare young people to critique and resist aspects of racial socialization that only work to distance them from loved ones and communities that helped rear them. As in the case of men like Philando Castile and Terence Crutcher, men with families who were pursuing higher education, respectability will not, and has not, saved us from the brutalities of state violence.[15]

At the core of this analysis is the question of how much of Urban Prep's work is centered on simply transforming young Black men into an image of Black manhood that more neatly fits them into an anti-Black, cishetero, capitalist, patriarchal society, and how much of the school's work is helping young people be critical of such a society. Respectability politics is an important lens for examining the root causes of resistance by students, especially those who did not stay all four years at Urban Prep. This lens might also better contextualize the rationale these young men provided to explain why they persisted in college when other classmates did not (more on this in chapter 5). The decision to attend Urban Prep seems to be part of a larger project of acculturation by the school that is rooted in genuinely good intentions.

But as Edmund Gordon says, "How do we prepare young people not just to fit in and survive in a dysfunctional system, but how to change the system to be more appropriate to their own needs? . . . My prescription for education for Black men is to take that resistance and to enable it. Help young men become competent resisters. A part of their education ought to teach them what you do about a system that is not working for you: You change it."[16]

"We Are the Young Men of Urban Prep"

ZOOM IN

"Is everything okay?" the waiter asked as he filled each man's water glass. The men nodded, their mouths full of pizza. Damani thanked the waiter and then asked the group, "So, be honest. What was that first year of high school like for you, the very first 'young men of Urban Prep'? How would you describe your freshman year?"

QUENTIN: Hell! [*The men laugh and pound the table.*] I didn't want to go, so it was like I was being forced to go. So it was, you know, initially it was really hell, because I didn't want to be there, even though sometimes I enjoyed it. So, the first year—my first year of school was, you know, pretty tough.

ANTWAN: Yeah, I hated it our freshman year, but I ended up liking Urban Prep a whole lot after my freshman year. On the other hand, when I got to high school I was like, "Man, this is living it up! I can surf the Web and I could look stuff up." I still struggled the same as any eighth grader transitioning. I still hadn't grasped time management, putting forth your best effort, learning how to be in high school—like, communicating with teachers, getting to class on time.

JEFF: I first learned how to tie a tie my freshman year, or whatever. So I still tie a tie to this very day, and that's one lesson. But something I guess more tangible, just learning how to carry yourself like a man. That was something that Urban Prep of course preached on a regular day-in-and-day-out basis, but seeing it be done on a regular basis by teachers and things like that, wearing the same suits and ties that we're wearing. It kind of gave me a more broader view of, you know, what it is to be a man and what I need to do, or whatever. That's definitely one skill. Just carrying myself like a man and walking like a man, talking like a man. Making sure you speak with good conviction, whatever, in everything that you do.

WINSTON: At first it started off weak, I didn't like it. I wanted to transfer. I just thought it was a bunch of boys, a whole bunch of guys. It was different because all the guys or all the teachers would preach to you all the time.

QUENTIN: When I was getting ready to go there, I thought you got to look like the Fresh Prince of Bel-Air and all that stuff like that, so I'm not about to do it. I ended up going anyway. So it was like from 8:30 to 4:30 I was stuck in the soup, in this building where we were restricted to do *this,* and *this*, and *that.* We couldn't do *this, this,* and *that.* It was kind of tough, just the transition from grammar school to high school. I didn't know what to expect. It was tough on me. But Urban Prep, they helped me out a lot, and they offered all those study sessions and staying after school and all that stuff.

JEFF: The long hours, 8:30 to 4:30, was a long time to me too. Coming to Urban Prep, within my first year of having to, you know, wear a suit and tie type things, it kind of gave me a different mind state when it came to education or academic values. I wanted to try and do as good as possible because I wanted to go to college eventually.

ANTWAN: Wearing a uniform every day—I feel like that was something a little bit hard. We had to learn how to tie a tie. We learned the importance of our appearance. We got used to being able to wear a suit, so it's not something foreign to us. So if we did go to an interview or something like that, we knew how to do it. Most challenging aspect, yeah, I guess, was wearing a uniform. I loathed wearing a uniform. I hate wearing uniforms. Part of the reason I took up my major in college was so I don't have to wear a uniform in the future.

QUENTIN: It was just the environment that we were in, and outside, you know, it was too dangerous to go back and forth to school. And then we had to dress up. It was just a whole lot of things, a lot of things that just made me dislike it more and more and more. Then we had this random guy telling me what to do. It was just something that I wasn't used to. I feel like they demanded too much.

WINSTON: See, the tucking in of your shirt—you would just be surprised how people would fight that so hard. In my mind, I said, "Look, we're in here for, like what? Six or eight hours. That's six to eight hours of a day. You got your blazer on. No one's going to see your shirt tucked in anyway. It's class. It was easy to follow the rules for me. The rules to me weren't hard. I would get mad when they would break them and then they went and forced more rules.

REGGIE: But if you didn't follow the rules, there were consequences. One teacher made us learn and say "Invictus," yes, with no paper, no nothing, and that was punishment. I enjoyed it because I didn't want it, and that pushed me. If you don't want to do push-ups, you don't want to lift weights, you don't want to do squats for thirty minutes, do what you've got to do. That's something I appreciated.

Damani broke in. "You know you never liked to follow the rules," he said, grinning, as he looked in Reggie's direction. Reggie, feigning surprise, looked behind him and responded, "Yeah, whatever, sir. You got jokes!" Quentin and Jeff started poking fun at Reggie, but he redirected the conversation to talk about another aspect of his freshmen year.

REGGIE: Freshman year of high school—it was scary. I thought people were gay.

Hearing the word gay, *the men stopped chewing and leaned in to listen closely to hear where Reggie was going with this revelation.*

REGGIE: It was an all-boys school, and I didn't know what the heck would happen. It was an all-boys school and I was paranoid. I told myself that I had to chill out. After that I adapted, and I took it from there. I was very nervous. I thought people would hit on me and I was worried. I was childish. When you're young you have a childish mind. I just had to get it out of my head. At other schools, I was always trying to impress girls—trying to get the freshest shoes, trying to wear the flyest shirts. I didn't have to worry about that [at UP]. I didn't have to worry about bickering.

JEFF: Yeah, I didn't really try to fit into too many crowds, but I got along with everybody in a sense. Except for all the dudes that wanted to be tough 24/7. I couldn't fit into that because I'm not tough 24/7. You got to take a break. You got to chill. I kind of got along with everybody. I was just a genuine little dude, cool dude. So that's how I kind of sum my freshman year. Just like moving through all the cracks to figure out what I wanted to be eventually.

QUENTIN: The football team was the big thing at Urban Prep. When I realized I wasn't like everyone else, I stopped trying to fit in and just decided to be me and not really worry what everyone has to say about me. That helped me throughout my entire time at Urban Prep. Freshman year was definitely a challenge just trying to fit in.

Glen and Damani picked up on the subtle mentions of sexuality in Reggie's remarks, his fear of being hit on by other guys, and also in Quentin's comment that he "wasn't like everyone else."

JEFF: After my freshman year, I got over the fact that I was at an all-boys school. Maybe a little bit into my sophomore year, I just forget it's an all-boys school. But it was like kicking it with the guys everyday. It's like seeing your guys everyday. You act up. We was silly. We made chants, or whatever. That really made the high school experience for me. That's what made the high school experience at Urban Prep real. The all boys—it was a brotherhood. A legit brotherhood, or whatever, within Urban Prep. We didn't realize at the time, until we graduated, that it was a brotherhood, but it was a brotherhood at Urban Prep. The brotherhood aspect, you know. That made Urban Prep the best for me.

Talking with his hands—as usual—Jeff knocked over his glass of water, spilling it on Quentin's cell phone. "My bad, man," he offered contritely, passing him napkins to dry up the mess he'd made. Quentin nodded in response and excused himself to go to the restroom, where maybe the hand dryers would minimize any damage. As he left, Winston weighed in on how interactions with peers made his transition into the school difficult.

WINSTON: Just dealing with peers. School was easy. That's the only thing I hated about Urban Prep. If one person did it, everybody suffered. Everybody would still suffer from it because the people who did bad things were known for doing bad things, so they would get expelled, come back, and still do the bad things. The people who did the good things either didn't really care about the punishment system or their grades were too bad to voice their opinion about the punishment system because, literally, the way Urban Prep worked, if your grades were bad, you had no voice. If you had a bad grade, there was nothing you could do. There was nothing you could say. There was nothing you could add, even if it was valuable. You would have to go to the people who had good grades. Even if you were doing something legit, you got in trouble. All of my punishments at Urban Prep was because somebody thought I was doing something I wasn't.

ANTWAN: Honestly, the whole all-boys thing, I think that helped though. The whole all-male setup kept us focused, more focused than we probably would have been if we were likely with girls. Not saying I'm pro unisex school, but there's good things about being in a school of the same sex.

JEFF: Going to school with all boys helped me figure out that there are a lot more stories than my story, I guess. That was challenging for me because at Urban Prep you had everybody from all over the city of Chicago, mostly the South Side, that came from, like, these troubling homes or whatever. With me, you know, my story of my life wasn't like that. I felt like it wasn't as—I was a lot more fortunate than some of my peers. I was a lot more fortunate, and that was a wake-up call for me in a certain sense. It was challenging in a way that it just made me realize that there's a lot more going on than what I see, you know, in my community. I knew that, but seeing it was completely different. That was kind of like my challenging wake-up call.

Quentin returned, giving a "thumbs-up," and settled right back into the conversational flow.

QUENTIN: It was interesting. I can't remember everything about my freshman year, but I do remember just learning the ropes, being around all males. I wasn't used to being around all guys. Most of my friends in the past would be all girls. Something different. You see all types of personalities and attitudes. It was like a public school, but it wasn't. Just being around all males helped me understand myself as a growing young man as well. It also helped me not fear seeing a bunch of dudes on the corner, because I see those type of dudes all the time. Being around all dudes wasn't necessarily distracting, like I thought it would be. It didn't really bother me. After adjusting to the entire Urban Prep community, it was not so bad at all, being around all dudes all the time for eight hours a day. I was able to be academically successful. I think my freshman year was pretty successful.

JEFF: The lack of girls at Urban Prep definitely caused me to be more focused. In eighth grade, it was eight, seven girls, like, "All right, we cool," you know. Do a little work, try to get some numbers from time to time while I'm in class. But without the distractions of females being around, it was easier to be focused on what's going on, what the teacher was teaching.

The waiter interrupted. "How are you all doing over here? Can I get anyone anything?" Jeff ordered a pitcher of beer—but, reflexively, he first glanced over at his former teacher, Glen, as if he expected him to frown on his consumption of alcohol. "It's fine, Jeff," Glen chuckled. "Y'all are grown men now." The others laughed, recognizing, and appreciating, Jeff's deference toward his former teachers.

ZOOM OUT

There is a fine line between assimilation and acculturation, particularly when creating a learning environment that is safe, culturally responsive, and personally affirming. Yet, the evidence suggests that during the transition into high school, Urban Prep may have failed to recognize, appreciate, and expand on the cultural knowledge these young men had acquired over time, or to acknowledge the values that governed how they performed their racial, gender, and sexual identities. I remember how many of the young men would remove their shirts, ties, blazers, and dress shoes in front of their locker before leaving the school building each day. There was a neighborhood high school a couple blocks away from UP, and the young men often had physical altercations with students from that school. I did not know it at the time, but their uniform identified them as UP students, which sometimes made them a target during their treks to and from school. Taking off the uniform each day also symbolized how the young men stepped back into their real lives away from the Urban Prep gaze.

Accounting for the complex intersections of race, gender, sexuality, and class is a necessary and worthwhile investment in designing antioppressive schooling environments for Black boys.[17] There are numerous examples in the literature of diverse youth who resist school policies and practices that they feel violate aspects of their lived realities.[18] For the sake of my analysis, I use Eric Toshalis's definition of *student resistance,* which includes any behavior, verbal or nonverbal communication, or situation that demonstrates a student's unwillingness to comply or acquiesce to the requests, norms, knowledge, or perspectives put forward by the school or one of its agents.[19] Evident through their reflections, in their early days at Urban Prep, the young men demonstrated resistance not only in their reluctance to assimilate to demands on their dress and behavior but throughout the process of unlearning behaviors and knowledge they felt were natural, normal, and necessary for safely navigating their South Side neighborhoods. Resistance is not necessarily about an individual teacher or an authority figure; young people resist to survive in what they perceive to be an assaultive school environment.[20]

"No excuse" charter schools, for instance, which work to create learning environments centered on going to college, have the potential to be quite oppressive to Black youth. They can do real damage to students' self-worth and cultural pride.[21] This is because the methods they employ include indoctrinating students with philosophies that they then use to control and manipulate student behavior. Students become what Joanne Golann calls "worker-learners" who act in ways just to appease authority instead of becoming more critical thinkers.[22]

My first teaching job was at a KIPP school in Chicago. I was horrified to watch the students at the predominantly Black middle school have to earn their desks and uniform shirts by behaving in the ways set forth by the school: being silent in the hallways, walking in straight lines, and S.L.A.N.T.ing (sitting up straight, leaning toward the speaker, activating your thinking, nodding in agreement, and tracking the speaker). Charter schools like KIPP that intend to help kids of color "climb the mountain to college" really reflect "undemocratic and militaristic values."[23] Brian Lack finds that underneath the values that KIPP espouses is an implicit message to students that if they fail, it is because they have not worked hard enough.[24] This perpetuates notions of meritocracy that fail to account for the many ways that institutional racism and White supremacist ideologies stymie or restrict access to educational opportunity.[25]

Some might consider KIPP's philosophies and practices as laying the groundwork for academic rigor and high expectations. Yet, suburban schools with predominantly White student populations would never require students to earn their desks, or expect students to sit, talk, dress, and even celebrate a classmate's success in the exact same way.[26] Researchers suggest that charter schools overall are not doing a better job of educating youth of color or closing stubborn achievement gaps.[27] These schools' pedagogical approaches can, however, do real damage to a Black child's creativity, imagination, sense of self-worth, and cultural pride.

I'm not necessarily equating Urban Prep's schooling environment to this type of charter. What I am saying is that "college for all" charters established in predominantly Black neighborhoods with the intent of "fixing" urban youth do little to undo White logics of power and domination that center on controlling Black bodies. This includes modeling what success is and is not. In describing their transition into Urban Prep and their demonstrations of resistance, the young men indicated that there was an element of control that felt constraining to them. Up for debate is whether or not UP's approach to establishing the school's cultural ethos and expectations was good or bad for the majority of young men attending the college prep high school. Evidence of resistance does suggest that the young men contended with potentially oppressive elements in the schooling environment that are worth further investigation.

A study of urban single-sex schools serving predominantly young men of color found that educators' conceptions of the problems and challenges facing boys of color were central to the design and deployment of various programs, professional practices, and strategies.[28] This was the case for Urban Prep, where every action and initiative was rooted in the aim to get *these* Black boys from Englewood admitted and enrolled in four-year colleges and universities. A key design element was making Urban Prep single-sex. Tim King's dream was to create a public schooling alternative that would expand young South Side Black men and boys' access to education opportunity. He thought that a single-sex schooling environment would help the young men be more focused.

While the UPCPS participants noted their initial prejudices about attending an "all-boys" school ("I thought everyone would be gay"), they admitted that over time they came to see the benefits of attending such a school ("Without girls, I felt less distracted"). Many of them referenced the "brotherhood" they developed with one another. T. Elon Dancy maintains that brotherhood binds Black men one to another based on shared experiences of oppression, and it is established through a number of "brother codes" that are enacted and policed between and among Black men.[29] Such codes set the standard for speech, dress, thinking, and being. The young men identified some standard codes or rules for how they were to carry themselves as "the young men of Urban Prep," such as how they used "sir" and referred to one another by their surnames, as well as by learning poems like *Invictus*, a signature practice among Black Greek lettered fraternity members. I recognized these codes from my own experience at the school. Adult Black men modeled these codes, and the young men policed one another.

These codes, however, are dictated by norms of heterosexuality and hegemonic masculinity that easily work to marginalize young men attending Urban Prep who do not easily fit within these established cultural norms. During my time at UP, there was little discussion by the administration or faculty about the unique opportunities and challenges a single-sex schooling environment might create for the young men's healthy racial and gender identity development. And very little from the young men's discussion reveals the school's efforts to support their critical thinking about the implications of their social location in the gender and sexuality social identity hierarchy. These young men admitted to having some difficulty figuring out how to perform their gender identity. In a follow-up discussion with the young men, one of them described differences in masculine performance as "personality" differences. He went on to say that if you had a "different personality," you either left Urban Prep or were peripheralized in some way. The freshmen year was awkward or tough in part because these young men were adolescents figuring out how to *be* within this new community of very diverse Black men and boys. It makes sense that the dominant forms of masculinity they saw would be the forms of masculinity they would adopt in order to fit into the collective identity Urban Prep was aiming to establish.

Like Dancy, Tony Laing found in his study that for those young Black men who attended an urban single-sex high school, brotherhood created a sense of inclusion, on one hand, because of their shared racial identity, but, on the other hand, it proved to be exclusive based on school norms that valued dominant heterosexual gender performances.[30] Gender is a social construction, which means, like race, it is not rooted in one's biological sex. A young man will likely decide how to carry himself based on models of masculinity normalized as "right" or "good" in the local school context to avoid being othered. Educators have some responsibility, especially in a single-sex school, to foreground, expose, and embrace diverse performances of gender and masculinity. Doing so would help impressionable young men and boys appreciate other men and boys who may look or behave differently. It would also disrupt social hierarchies that subordinate young men and boys who do not project dominant norms of masculinity.

The intersections of race, gender, and class in the single-sex schooling environment emerged in the young men's reflections and also, subtly, in the data. Explicit attention to these connections are especially important in single-sex spaces if educators are intentional about disrupting heteronomativity, sexism, toxic, and bipolar masculinities in the Black community.[31]

The Urban Prep Way: Rewards, the Creed, and Prides

ZOOM IN

The dinner conversation had grown quite lively—with some help from the beer—as the young men began recalling how Urban Prep recognized and rewarded them for their achievements.

QUENTIN: One of the things I really loved about Urban Prep was that they rewarded you for being successful. That's one thing I really appreciate about them. A lot of black men on the news today are either on the news about a killing they've done or something like that. I found it very interesting that Urban Prep rewarded success. The other thing I really loved was the gold tie thing. The reward that you got for doing really well in the class.

Jeff: Yeah, the incentives. That helped us a lot. We actually got rewarded for doing good. The first time they rewarded someone was when the whole Pride got iPods and $100 gift cards for doing good academically. The incentives helped a lot.

REGGIE: Everybody wanted to have fun, and everybody wanted gift certificates. Everybody wanted this. It was cool, because you'd go crazy when you see other people receive the gift, it's like, "I could have did that, I could have got that." I was one of those persons.

Distracted by something Quentin was showing Antwan on his cell phone, Reggie paused midthought and asked, "What y'all lookin at?" Quentin flashed his cell phone and asked the group, "Y'all see this video?" Damani, irritated by the interruption, barked at Quentin in a most teacherly way, "Don't be rude. Show us in a minute."

REGGIE: I realized a lot about life and reality and [the adults giving out the rewards] are not going to be in college with us. [The college professors] are not going to say, "Oh, if you make this, you're going to get this." It was no more of that.

WINSTON: At Urban Prep—oh man, I definitely amped things up. I remember after the semester was over, we had Mr. Anderson, Mr. Whitfield, and other teachers, those guys up on stage. Summer time coming around, and these cats are giving out iPods for grades. I was like, "What?" Evan Johnson got the iPod Classic, and I was like, "My parents are not going to buy me an iPod, get out of here." I wanted it, or I wanted something like that. This stuff like that, it was that incentive factor. It definitely gave incentive. I thought that was wonderful because you've got to sort of—When you have students who are just children, people, kids of that age just in general, you've got to sort of give them that sort of sense of incentive. It was all those sort of things, that incentive factor: "I believe in you. This is because I believe in you. Here, you've been doing well." You're not working for nothing.

Giordano's was filling up. The men commented on how loud the place had become since they first sat down. It didn't bother them, though. They were enjoying one another's company. "Pass the pitcher!" squawked Quentin. Reggie, clearly deep in thought, pondered Winston's last comment and remarked that, having now graduated from college, he has a more mature view of the rewards system and its utility for cultivating young men's intrinsic motivation to act in ways that produce the most favorable outcomes for them.

REGGIE: Okay, yeah. I just thought once you got used to everything as far as receiving stuff, you get tired of people telling what you should be doing, "You need to do this, you need to do this, you need to do this." Well, I should be knowing myself what I should be doing. If you don't do what you're supposed to do in high school, you won't go to college, and you came here [UP] to go to college. You might have some type of mentors in college that push you through college, but it's not guaranteed. It's not. Like, now, I really don't have a mentor, so there's nobody pushing me. I'm pushing myself, and that's why I say to myself I'm glad I did not continue on with that mentality.
WINSTON [*nodding*]: It's like, okay, so what are we here for? We're being rewarded for keeping the image together. No, I'm just kidding. But I don't know. Like, it could be viewed as that as well. I don't want to say it's like a—it wasn't like a bribe, by no means . . .
ANTWAN [*interrupting*]: I remember being in Community and Mr. Whitfield called me up and talked about all the work I did without being paid. He said, "Come on up and get your iPod." Everybody was like, "Man, next time you're doing some work hit me up." I realized my junior year, don't do it for that, do it for yourself, because when you get to college it's not going to be like that.
WINSTON: Mr. Green, who was only there for one year, and then they let him go, only because he was the only teacher that actually rewarded me for things, like the simplest things. But it felt good, because it felt like Urban Prep was always punishing us for things. He would just reward you. He would reward me just for being me because everybody else in that class didn't really care. The most simplest of tasks that everybody else had the hardest time doing, and so when I would do it, he would make an announcement about it and reward me for it. I would get embarrassed about it, but, at the same time, it felt good because it was like Urban Prep was always telling you what you did wrong, and this rule and that rule is going to do that, so now we can't do this anymore.

Glen remembered being reprimanded by Urban Prep's school leaders for not nominating his students for a reward one week. He thought about the benefits and drawbacks of the school's practice of rewarding and incentivizing students and asked the group what aspects of the school culture they found to be particularly valuable.

JEFF [*with his hand on his head, as if trying to remember something he'd misplaced*]: What was it called? What was the thing that we—the Urban Prep Creed. Yeah, that was one part of my freshman year that definitely stuck with me throughout high school up through college. The Creed, the mission statement, and all that stuff definitely stuck out for me. Like, I still say some of the Creed—I don't know the whole thing, just some of the lines, like not letting obstacles stop me and stuff like that. So yeah, definitely. It definitely worked well to have that Community in the morning. Whether you'd say, "Yeah, the Urban Prep Community in the morning set the foundation for the entire day"—there were some days where I'd kind of say the Creed and not really feel what I was saying. Other days, I would say those words and really mean them, and it would help me.

QUENTIN: Yep. I still think about that every day, especially the last sentence in the Creed saying "we are our brother's keepers." That's really helped me out a lot, because I look out for a lot of people. That's the type of person I became over the years. I just want to look out for people and make sure everybody is on the right path and making sure everybody is doing what they're supposed to do. There's just a lot of lines in the Creed that I still live by today. Yeah, just the Creed. That's like the main lesson that still stick with me.

ANTWAN: I also feel like the motto—you know, telling the students and having us repeat that "We Believe," you say it enough times, you eventually believe it. You start to live it. It's good.

JEFF: Looking back on that now, it was a subliminal message. Because once you start saying something every day for four years, you start to believe it. Sometimes even when I didn't believe, I saw myself doing stuff that I really wouldn't have saw myself doing for people I didn't know or something. I think it was subliminal. They didn't tell us to be our brother's keeper. They didn't tell us to be college bound. No, we were saying it to ourselves. We weren't saying it for no one else. We were saying it for ourselves. Just looking back on that, I see that that has subliminally affected me as far as being exceptional, resilient, because it has something to do about being resilient, our brother's keeper, accountable to our families, making an impact on the world, just those different things that stick with me today. Our mottos, Creed—you never fail, because you never give up. Those type things. That's really what prepared me for college the most.

Damani then challenged the young men, asking them, "Who remembers the Creed? Like, who can recite it right now from memory?" They looked at one another around the table and then, beseechingly, at Glen. Through nervous laughter, Glen said, "Don't look at me! I didn't go to Urban Prep; I just taught there"—to which Damani countered, "And helped write the doggone Creed!" Together all the men around the table began, "We Believe. We are the young men of Urban Prep," managing to stammer their way through to the end, and not butchering the lines too badly. To celebrate the achievement, Antwan poured himself another glass of beer, finishing off the pitcher. Jeff asked the group whether they kept in touch with members of their Prides. Antwan offered, "Sort of, mostly through Facebook. We don't talk regularly or nothin'." The other young men nodded in agreement. Glen picked up on that and asked them what the Pride meant to them while they were in high school.

WINSTON: With my Pride, in general it was about understanding the purpose of a structure, understanding the purpose of what it is to take care of one another, the "I am my brother"s keeper" component of the Creed. It was good. Especially having a dude like Mr. Dickens just like leading the Pride, it was phenomenal, because he's a part of a fraternity, and he knows and he understands those things. He went to [a HBCU in the South]. He understands those structures, the structure units, what it's like to be in all-male situations.

ANTWAN: We had a Pride competition thing going on. At Urban Prep we did have Pride competitions, but inside of our Pride, we had our own little competition. Pride competitions. Those were fun. Fun things to look forward to.

JEFF: My Pride leader, he was, to a lot of us in the Pride, the father that we didn't have at home, because he taught us about things that his father taught him. He didn't talk to us in a father's perspective. He talked to us in a son's perspective, as how we should go about life and some decisions that we should make and shouldn't make. He explained a lot of things to us, broke it down to our level so that we can understand. He was just down to earth with us.

He wouldn't sugarcoat a lot of things. He told it to us how it was. That helped me out earlier on a lot too, because I know some people who don't get those lessons earlier on. By the time they actually learn it's too late, and they either did something stupid or something like that.

WINSTON: They would reward Prides and stuff like that for grades, but it was interesting how some of the people who had the Pride leaders who had the most difficult classes, they would always get the better grades because their Pride leader was like the history teacher, the class that everybody was failing.

JEFF: It motivated us, that little brotherhood that we created earlier on. We learned that brotherhood from our Pride leader, Mr. Dickens. He taught us about being there for our brothers because our Pride was mainly our family. I felt like I was at school more than I was at home. It was 8:30 to 4:30. Sometimes I went to school earlier for sports and sometimes I stayed late just because I didn't want to go home. I could do my homework at school. I just felt like that was my home. Pride was my second home. In school I was closest to my pride leader.

ZOOM OUT

Urban Prep aimed to create a structure that included mechanisms for making its students feel important and valued in school. This was important for earning students' trust and getting them to buy into the Urban Prep mission of preparing them to be successful in college. The counterstory's composite characters—Jeff, Reggie, Winston, Quentin, and Winston—connect popular narratives of Black men in society to Urban Prep's practice of acknowledging and tangibly rewarding its students for doing the "right" thing. The UP rewards structure seemed to be effective for incentivizing these young men to meet the school's standards for behavior. Yet, these young men also wrestled with the conflict they felt about the ways that the rewards systems may have had an adverse effect on students' development of an intrinsic motivation to perform well academically. Having been out of high school and in college for at least four years, these young men recognized the tension between incentivizing young people to do their best work and cultivating in them an expectation that they will always be rewarded for demonstrating strong effort, when that is not the way the real world works. Still, the school, cleverly, got its students to say, and subsequently internalize, the Urban Prep Creed. *Believing* in these young men's potential to be academically excellent was a driver for UP's professional philosophies and practices. Participants in this study noted how, over time, they began to believe all of what they were saying. As Jeff remarked, "It became subliminal." With the recitation of the Creed, they engaged in a daily practice of talking to themselves, as opposed to only adults talking to them, about their futures and the possibilities of the type of men they could become.

In her ethnographic study of street culture and schooling, Lory Janelle Dance found that urban-dwelling Black and Latino men need to *feel* heard, cared for, and acknowledged in the school environment in order to optimize their participation in school.[32] Students need to have a voice, but, more consequentially, they also need to be treated in a way that communicates to them that their voices matter in the academic community of the school. At Urban Prep, much of this was accomplished by learning and reciting the Creed every day, and through the communal bonds established in the Prides. The school's strong commitment to regularly acknowledging the young men's accomplishments also made the young men feel important and valued in the school community.

Dance's work corroborates the scholarship of Joseph Nelson and other scholars on the importance of "relational" schooling environments that emphasize the capacity, creativity, and brilliance of young Black men and boys.[33] In such environments, a premium is placed on establishing and maintaining strong student-teacher relationships.[34] UP's daily Community is important for establishing a relational environment, and also for reinforcing the 4 Rs (respect, responsibility, ritual, and relationships). It's also the time when rewards are handed out. The young men gather in their Prides, and the whole school recites the Creed. Evidence from Derrick's and my interviews with the young men suggests that Urban Prep was effective in establishing a structure that helped these young men think differently about themselves and each other.

Just as Antwan pointed out, saying "We Believe" every day had an important impact on these young men's visions of themselves, who they were and who they could become. Saying the Creed reminded them of their academic commitments and the limitless potential they possessed—*but* to a predetermined end: graduating from high school and going directly to a four-year college or university. After all, the third line of the Creed promises that the young men are "college bound." This aim was the point around which all of UP's work orbited. Nonetheless, the Creed, Prides, and rewards system were structural aspects of the school that set the stage for establishing a culture of "academic success." It was the daily interactions with adult Black men that seems to be the feature of Urban Prep's practices that had the most profound influence on these young men's conceptions of what it means to be(come) a "successful Black man."

Stakeholder Interactions with Adult Black Men

ZOOM IN

All the talking and laughing had slowed down the eating considerably. "Eat up," Damani ordered, pointing at the two remaining pies sitting untouched on the table. The discussion about Prides organically transitioned into a conversation about the important relationships Reggie, Jeff, Winston, Quentin, and Antwan had developed with so many adult Black men at UP. Quentin started by commenting on how at UP he got used to having more men teachers than women teachers.

QUENTIN: Urban Prep was definitely a lot more influential because I was around a bunch of male teachers. I was used to the female teachers who would play the mother role in the classroom. I was just used to having a whole lot of female teachers. It was just adjusting to all male teachers, with occasional female teachers, but learning from not only the things we have to study in classes but some of the life lessons they had to teach as well. That was kind of what made learning at Urban Prep different.

ANTWAN: Academically, it was a bit more challenging, because I felt like I had women teachers in elementary school who nurtured me to getting good grades. It was more like a mother-child relationship.

QUENTIN: I didn't have a father figure in my life. I never had a big brother. I had a cousin. He was like kind of like my big brother, but he wasn't always there. He went off to college, and stuff like that, so he wasn't at home all the time. Those teachers, they kind of served like a father figure or older brother figure. That's probably why I decided to play football and played basketball and things, to surround myself around those other male figures just to see how it is to have a big brother or see how it is to have somebody, a male role model in your life. I used to think, "There's a *successful black man*." There was a type of guy that I seen, you know, in high school that really pushed me to be more successful and be a successful black man, more than anything, because that was basically all that I was surrounded by.

WINSTON: For me it was interesting because they were my first male experiences. But it was interesting because I had never been around men like that all day, every day, because I lived in a house with mostly women. All of my teachers in grade school were mostly women too, and a lot of people in my family were mostly women. To have a predominantly male atmosphere for me was refreshing, because I got tired of being around women all the time. It was fun, but at the same time it was weird, because I always had the impression that men were these hard people who didn't understand and took no bullshit for any means.

The table erupted in laughter at Winston's spirited declaration. Glen asked, "Is that what y'all thought of me?" With a hint of a smile, Antwan responded, "No comment." Glen leaned back in his chair, realizing that he may never get the answer to that question. Reggie, picking up on this exchange, commented on his perceptions of the Black men he interacted with during his time at Urban Prep.

REGGIE: They were real. They kept it real. They didn't lie. They gave personal testimonies. Down to earth. They kept it 100. They didn't sugarcoat anything. "I'm going to tell you how I feel." It's "Either you're going to like it or you're not." They shared their failing times. They said where they are now. The difference showed.

QUENTIN: They pretty much were my mentors, my support group. They knew what I wanted to do. They were more than just "teachers" to me. I did well in these classes because I had some type of relationship with them other than just being their student. They were willing to talk with me on a personal level and on an academic level.

REGGIE: That's what I like about them. I needed somebody real. I don't want nobody that's going sugarcoat anything. They [were] pushers.

Perplexed by Reggie's use of the word pushers, *Damani asked him to explain what he meant.*

REGGIE: Pushers—that's what each young man at Urban Prep needed, because we all come from different backgrounds. Some of us might share the same story. Everybody needs that pusher in their corner. That's what I would say 95 percent, 90 percent of the teachers did. They were pushers. I didn't grow up with a male figure in my life. I wish I did. But once I got to high school, it was, just—they taught me how to be a man. I'm not saying I don't know how to be a man, but I was in the process.

QUENTIN: I felt like some people were too strict. But them being strict, they kind of pushed everybody to become a better person. Because if you didn't have that strict person in your life, what would you be today? Or how would you handle yourself today if you didn't have anybody that would tell you no?

Damani surmised that a pusher was an adult who the young men perceived as being successful who not only held them to high academic expectations but was firm and encouraging. This was likely someone who was, in pedagogical terms, a warm demander, someone who pressured students into working hard without making them feel like a failure when they did not meet the expectations.

QUENTIN: Mr. Boston and Mr. Young, those were, you know, family guys. They had families, also had jobs. I just say they're successful as to where—and I mean by "successful" is having no worries financially, family is good, and just stuff like that. They helped me, you know, see that image is somewhat everything, and your first impression on someone, it could be the last, so always make sure it's the best. These guys always came to school sharp, all the time, fresh ties, fresh shirts, you know. These guys getting and doing paper [colloquial term for money or cash] and, you know, getting all successful. And they were always fresh. That always helped me, you know, keep my self-esteem, because you never knew when these guys would come with an opportunity to talk to the camera or, you know, do this interview or take these pictures, or something like that. So, these guys really placed that successful image in my mind, what a successful Black, educated man looks like. So, that's what I really got from them.

Quentin was especially vocal about his interactions with Black men at Urban Prep. At one point, he spoke so passionately his voice started to quaver when talking about the influence these men had on his life.

QUENTIN: Again, I think that they taught me a lot. They taught me how to become a man, how to handle myself in situations, when it comes to getting slowed down by the cops and things like that. It was a lot, but I think that they played a big role in my life. I felt like they were like that male role model that I wanted in my life, everybody that may have been successful in their own type of way. I felt like, "I can get on their level if I just keep on working hard." They were, like, a big influence on me. I just want to get to that point, because they pushed over the years to try to get to that point. I just want to get there.

Sensing that he may have been dominating the conversation, Quentin leaned back in his chair. The other young men picked up the conversational thread and also shared how Black men teachers leveraged their influence in order to earn students' respect, particularly for legitimizing the merits of a college education, and to emphasize what they believed to be important lessons about being Black and male in America.

JEFF: It was African American history, or something like that, I believe, or world history. It wasn't the topic so much that I liked; it was the message the teacher was trying to send. Everything he tried to warn us about and tell us about, like, being Black and being in America, like all the stuff that happened in the past and what's going to continue to happen to us coming up. Once I got to college, I definitely started seeing it a lot more. Some of the values that he wanted to instill in us. Yeah, just for his lessons, his values, life lessons that he gave us is why I really liked him.

ANTWAN: Another person that taught lifelong lessons was Mr. Young. He taught the first history class. He did it in chronological order. He taught about Olmecs, ancient African civilizations, and stuff like that. It all related to me. In grammar school they only teach you Harriet Tubman and slavery. But in Young's class he went underneath that. He taught me who Mansa Musa was, he taught us about the pyramids, he taught us about the Olmecs. It was just a whole different learning experience for me.

QUENTIN: That's why I enjoyed that time at Urban Prep. They looked out for me. That's why I appreciated their role in being my teacher or administrator, because they were willing to listen, willing to talk, willing to help out. I'd get good advice and guidance toward what I'm supposed to do. Dr. Williams was really helpful placing me into a really good summer program based on my academic success each year and just making sure I was doing what I was supposed to do. All the other teachers were making sure I was understanding material in the classes and I was doing okay. It was that personal time they took making sure I was doing okay and I was doing fine in the class. I really appreciate their time.

ANTWAN: I also remember Mr. Jones. He told us the story about all the girls he was messing with and how big of a freak he was. He said he had caught something and how scary it was. He was basically telling us to be careful and watch who you're hanging with. It was just a bunch of social stories. In Community, I remember when Mr. Boston used to teach us lessons everyday. He would talk to us about "pick your battles" and not being the tough guy all the time. That helped me learn that sometimes with school you can't always stick to the book.

Surprised at the young men's candor, Glen and Damani exchanged glances. Teachers never know the impact they have on a young person, so it was affirming to hear their former students' reflections.

QUENTIN: I can honestly say, without the relationships [with Black male teachers], I wouldn't be the person I am now. Mr. Griffin, he was my coach. He was there for me on the field. He believed I had potential both with football and academics, so he kind of pushed me to be the best person I could be on both sides. But I knew if I didn't do well in class, I couldn't play football, so he taught me to keep my grades up. Mr. Perry, he was there for me as well. I went to church with him. Whenever I needed to talk to him, he was there to talk to me. Mr. Davis, he did his best to have a pretty close relationship. He was always there. If I needed anything, he was like, "Just come ask me. I'll help you out." I mean, I had summer classes that I had to take. He actually paid for them, which I thought was nice for him to do, because I really need those classes and he paid for them. I just thought it was a real great deed that he did for me.

ANTWAN: In high school, me and my dad were not close at all. I did not like the sight of my dad. I couldn't stand him. Sometimes it felt like I didn't really have a dad. I really never got a chance to see him. Mr. Jones being there, he kinda replaced—he didn't replace my father, but he played that role that I needed, so that I didn't completely go off the deep end or do whatever. It was important to me to be able to have somebody to talk to.

WINSTON: Being in a place like UP really did help, because they had a lot of resources, like having a guy like Mr. King heading the place and knowing he's got connections like an El station.[35] He knows he's got connections, like a flight plan, I guess. He just knows. Being able to use those connections to make it work for creating a school and helping other students and other young men see that, "Hey, if we just put the hard work into it, then you too can have these things or be comfortable in your career structure and things like that."

JEFF: They just let me be myself. They knew the potential that I had. They forced it on me. They forced it on me. [*Pauses to find the words.*] But they didn't actually *force*—they weren't on me about it. To clear that up: they told me that I had potential. They saw things in me that I didn't see in myself. That helped our relationship to get pretty strong in high school.

REGGIE: I believe, like all the relationships I established in high school—I think the relationship now, today, is like respect. I feel like my teachers in high school respect me more as a man because they know that I'm out here trying to make a difference. When I went back and spoke at my high school, it was like, "I'm glad that I took a chance on this Reggie kid because it worked out." They could look at me now and see that I was trying hard, so I think it was, like, respect. I could see myself being successful. I could envision myself in that position.

JEFF: They were genuine. You could tell it was a genuine relationship. Especially that first class . . . with us being the first class. I'm not sure if that was what it was because, you know, I can't really compare myself to other high school students. But our teachers genuinely cared and walked us through, you know, freshman year, sophomore year, junior year, and through senior year to make sure we were engaged in class. And, like, if you showed them that you cared, they cared. At the same time, they weren't about to try to pick somebody up that didn't really care.

ANTWAN: As a group, you could tell they wanted us to be successful. Each teacher was different, but as a group they all cared. They all wanted us to do well. They made sure that if we were struggling with something, that we had the resources and the help that we did need to succeed, whether we wanted to realize it or not. Some teachers were stricter than others.

At this point, Glen spoke up. "I must say, I did feel like working at Urban Prep was a calling. It was something truly special, and you all are reminding me just how special of a time in my career it was." The men smiled. Signaling the waiter, Damani ordered another pitcher of beer. No one seemed to be in any rush to leave, even after an hour and a half of dinner conversation.

JEFF: All of Urban Prep teachers cared, definitely. All of our teachers cared. They were there for us. They supported us. They wanted to make sure that we were doing good. They wanted to make sure we were grasping this information. Well, some of them were. For the most part, most of them were. I'd just say they saw the potential that I had and they stayed on me. I didn't like it because they knew I was doing the very minimum. I didn't like it at the time. I do realize now that they were just trying to help me in the long run.

ANTWAN: I realized that people weren't out to get me, regardless of how I felt at the time. People were trying to help me. And that's hard to understand coming from where I come from and transitioning to an environment where people really want to help you. I come from a [home] environment where people are tearing you down, so it's hard to believe people want to help you.

JEFF: Those relationships were good. You know, my dad was in my life. They were other Black men that I could model myself after. They showed me that there are Black men out here that genuinely care about other Black men and want them to do well in life or whatever. Prior to that I hadn't really been around this many Black men that were Black teachers or Black men that cared. Just being surrounded by that and those particular men, just them trying to help as much as possible, that relationship really meant a lot. It meant a whole lot. It was like an extra support system. A good support system to have.

WINSTON: Going to Urban Prep, it was like, "Wait a second. These cats kind of have feelings and they express those feelings." We would be really confused that they would snap our photos in class because they cared. Our impression of men was that they just handled their business.. I didn't understand the intricacies of an older male/younger male relationship until I got there . That was a very positive thing, but it was interesting. The teachers, I felt they actually cared about what you thought, and, even when you failed, they didn't beat you up about it, which was good. I never felt bad for doing something that I wasn't supposed to do.

JEFF: Mr. Young, he was a Pride leader. He was a great mentor when I first came. It's funny, when I first got to Urban Prep, the very first day of, like, our summer school session, he made me step out of line because I didn't have a tie on. I had to go on stage, and they almost sent me home. I'm thinking in the back of my head, "Who's this nigga about to get me kicked out the first day of class? Dang!" Afterwards, it was all love. Like, he genuinely cares about the upbringing of young black men. He showed that everyday, or whatever, through his long, boring speeches, but you could tell that it was a message much deeper in what he was saying. He instilled that definitely. In terms of change, it was that sense of care, it was that sense of understanding.

ZOOM OUT

It is clear that these young men viewed interactions with their Black men teachers and other adults in the school as overwhelmingly positive. These teachers' transparency and effectiveness in communicating with, and relating to, students in ways that translated care to these young men are noteworthy.

When UP opened its doors in 2006, there were only two individuals on the faculty who were not Black men. This meant that these young men went almost a full day without seeing anyone other than Black men. Entering Urban Prep as freshmen and regularly interacting with several different Black men who reflected dominant conceptions of success impacted the way these young men learned to see themselves. After all, these Black men teachers were the physical manifestation of the messages and values that the young men were reciting every day in the Creed. They were "exceptional—not because [they] say it, but because [they] work hard at it." They were examples of "living honorably" and never giving up, as evidenced through the many stories they shared with their students about the complications that being a Black man in America may pose for upward mobility. If the young men of Urban Prep were to make going to college a reality, believing was only one piece of the puzzle. They also needed regular, ongoing exposure to a portrait of the "success" that they were aiming to personify. These adult Black men were just that for their students.

Any attempt to more fully understand the significance of these young men's interactions with adult Black men in determining their education trajectories means drawing attention to the intersection of race with young Black men's gender and sexual identity development. A recurring theme in the young men's commentary about becoming "successful Black men" is the portrait of Black men who are married to women, who build a family with a wife, and who comport themselves in ways that align with hegemonic forms of masculinity. Patricia Hills Collins, in her classic article constructing the role of family as a privileged example of intersectionality, demonstrates how examples like the ones espoused by the young men work to reproduce White, dominant notions of masculinity and heteropatriarchy.[36] This "traditional" family structure also naturalizes masculinity as a form of authority that is performed as tough, and without emotion. Comparably, the young men admitted to feeling bewildered when their Black men teachers expressed emotion and were willing to share those emotions with their students. This says something about the way the young men think about manhood and masculinity.

Urban education researchers tend to explain the academic failure of young Black men and boys through isolated analyses of race *or* class. Missing from this discourse are intersectional analyses of race *and* class with sexuality and gender. Joseph Nelson, Garth Stahl, and Derron Wallace insist that the field's preoccupation with the "boys crisis" (the persistently low educational achievement of boys socially constructed and positioned as Black around the world) has led education researchers and practitioners to isolate understandings of boys' education into unitary identity categories.[37] Nelson and colleagues argue that this type of research analysis is limited in its attempt to explain the paltry educational outcomes for boys of color. This is because such analyses center either on race or on class instead of on the intersections of race *with* class or *with* gender and sexuality.

Of course, what the young men did not say is just as important as what they did say. Given the diverse challeges threatening young Black men and boys' academic achievement, improving their educational outcomes must include intense discussion about the ways a school environment potentially invisibilizes queer youth. This is especially pertinent for young Black men and Black boys, considering that far too many fully grown Black men continue to be critiqued for failing to fight for the justice of Black women and Black queer people.[38] As Brittney Cooper points out, "Uninterrogated masculinity is a violent enterprise, period."[39]

Studies show that a schooling environment, especially in a single-sex school, which fails to be fully inclusive is ripe for incidents of bullying, victimization, and gendered harassment.[40] These environments limit education attainment and engagement among students who identify as lesbian, gay, bisexual, transgender, queer (LGBTQ), as evidenced by their higher rates of truancy and dropout, lower grades, and/or exhibition of other maladaptive behaviors.[41] A lack of intention about emphasizing, honoring, and explicitly naming the diversity within Black manhood along the contours of gender and sexual identity too easily confounds efforts to render *all* young Black men visible in the school community.

Findings from the UPCPS indicate that Urban Prep's effectiveness hinges on cultivating the bonds of brotherhood among students and adults in the building. However, the counterstory raises questions about the ways the social network these young men developed at UP worked to center race and heteronormativity at the exclusion of other diverse expressions of Black manhood and masculinity. Brotherhood means very little if you feel excluded for not adhering to the brother code, even if you never outwardly express those feelings.[42]

I agree with Lance McCready and others who argue for diverse and progressive masculinities that (pro)actively reject essentialist notions of Black boyhood in the making of "successful" Black men.[43] The framing of *crisis* to explain the present state of Black boys' education suggests they are uniformly burdened by an identical oppression that threatens their educational attainment. McCready's work on Black male queer youth suggests that the term *crises* (plural) is more appropriate, since the factors impeding young Black men's academic success are myriad.[44]

> Cultural differences accorded to intersections of race and class with gender and sexuality, collide at particular times, in particular contexts . . . they create different kinds of crises for boys in school. For some boys the crisis reflects discrimination based on gender non-conforming behaviour which could be read by peers or the teacher as a sign of being gay. Other boys in the school environment

> might experience discrimination based on class background read by teachers and administrators as their neighbourhood of residence. Still others might be gender conforming, but experience discrimination based on their perceived race and record of academic achievement.[45]

Founding faculty members had many discussions about the ways that we needed to organize the schooling environment so that every student realized academic success. Nonetheless, at one of our first meetings as a full faculty, before Urban Prep opened its Englewood campus, I overheard a few of my Black male colleagues say, "I hope we don't have any gay boys at this school." I was jarred by this. I considered bringing it up with the school's founder, but I felt extreme apprehension. I did not want to be othered by my colleagues or viewed as a troublemaker by the school administration. I did not have the courage at that time to push back against what I felt was a dominant point of view among my peers.

For queer and gender nonconforming youth, not being fully accepted by peers or adults or the lack of representation in schoolwide discussions of Black maleness can have severe consequences on their persistence and engagement in school. Often these young people suffer in silence, not ever wanting to stick out or draw attention to themselves or to the oppression they may be experiencing. Although UPCPS was a study of a small cohort of the school's first graduates, I can't help but wonder if any of the 30 percent of young men who leave Urban Prep before finishing high school do so because the school environment is assaultive to their sexual or gender identity. And I also wonder what the young men who identified as queer who did complete high school at Urban Prep had to do to mask aspects of their personhood in order to fit in and avoid harassment. Being Black and from a low-income family alone is the crisis that McCready and Nelson and colleagues reference. Being Black *and* poor *and* identifying as LGBTQ complicates further the discrimination and marginalization urban youth may experience in school.

Furthermore, these young men differentiated between their women teachers, who they described as "pampering," "nurturing," in a "mother" role, and the men teachers, who were "tough," "father figures," "pushers," "sergeants." This positioning is consistent with prevailing views of Black men as disciplinarians, role models, and father figures.[46] Ed Brockenbrough and several others have done important research on the complex intersections of race and gender for Black men who teach in both single-sex and coeducational school settings.[47] This work underscores how conceptions of manhood as tough and womanhood as softer and nurturing reify patriarchal norms in schools.[48] For Black women, discussions of race tend to center men, while discussions of women's rights in opposition to patriarchy tend to center White women's issues.[49] This leaves them to experience a particular form of oppression that is altogether different from that of Black men.

We did not, as a founding faculty, have serious discussions about shared meanings of manhood and masculinity. Nor did we consider the ways that the schooling environment may have been marginalizing to women and LGBTQ persons. Alternatively, these young men's frequent references to the many ways that adult Black men modeled and taught them about "what it means to be a man" do suggest that there was a standard, dominant conception of gender and sexuality in the school. This conception did not acknowledge, much less affirm, gender nonconforming or queer young men. Members of UP's first graduating class had little interaction with women teachers during their first year at Urban Prep. One Black woman teacher who started orientation with the founding faculty was asked to leave before the school year began. A second Black woman left midyear because she was frustrated with what she perceived to be incongruities between espoused school values and the pedagogical practices of her (Black men) colleagues and superiors. She was replaced by a third Black woman teacher. The only other Black women in the building were UP's business manager and the women who worked in the school's main office. There were few opportunities, at least in their freshman year, for the young men to engage in substantive conversations around manhood and masculinity that were not limited to discussions of heterosexual relationships and the heterosexual family structure.

Attending to the ways race mediates gender and sexuality identity development would have likely better informed *how* adult Black men at UP discussed the barriers these young men would face as they moved along the education pipeline to college. Identity represents a "temporary attachment to subject positions," where our own actions and the social forces that surround us call us into a particular social location.[50] Identity is fluid and strongly influenced by dominant discourse in a local context and by interactions with individuals in positions of power and authority. Given how these young men tended to hold their Black men teachers in such high esteem—and the plausibility that there was little discussion about, or few references to, sexual orientation and diverse representations of Black masculinities—it is reasonable to infer that these interactions likely posed barriers to determining a form of "successful" Black manhood that best complimented their racial, gender, and sexual identity development.

Conclusion

Urban Prep intended for its school environment to affirm the Black male identity, but it did so by centering race and class in the school's design. The school has taken great care in developing a culture and climate that treats Blackness as an asset to young men's preparation for college. The school has actively worked to counter the damaging impacts of poverty on the young men's access to education opportunity through various means, such as by guaranteeing every young man the use of a Macbook. This is important for bolstering students' academic self-efficacy and for getting them to "believe" they are college-going material.

Other blind spots associated with attending to issues of gender and sexuality are cautionary. This discussion is not meant to diminish the work of Black men at the school. Rather, it is intended to raise our collective consciousness about the ease with which issues centered on concepts of manhood and masculinity, for instance, get muted or overlooked. This can only increase young Black men and boys' academic vulnerability, not eliminate it.

Teachers do not come into a school necessarily knowing how to oppose the dominant notions of success that undermine the dreams and ambitions of diverse youth. Nor are they always well versed in addressing issues of gender and sexuality in their interactions with Black boys. Professional learning communities and opportunities to think broadly about the issues of justice facing different student populations are key. Discussions of race isolated from discussions of (dis)ability, religious affiliation, sexual orientation, immigration status, language, and so on will minimize a school's effectiveness in meeting the needs of an increasingly multicultural US public school population. Justice is a multifaceted, multidimensional project that requires the participation of every single member of a school's constituency. We all must become "woke" in order to further disrupt the failure of public schools to provide a free, appropriate, high-quality education to all young people.

4

UP Years 3 and 4

Preparation for College

Glen and Damani were comfortably ensconced in the warm coffee shop. It was getting late, they knew, but their conversation kept stumbling onto new and interesting revelations about the implications of race and racism on teaching young Black men and boys and adequately preparing them for college life—areas both their scholarship focused on. Not just an academic dialogue between two professors, there was also a shared appreciation of the evening's fellowship. In reflecting on the dinner table conversation, they marveled at how seven Black men—a couple older, the others several years younger—had gathered in celebration of a bond that would last a lifetime. With deferential acknowledgment, each had admired how his brother had overcome life challenges to achieve success in higher education. It had been a blessing, they agreed. Glen remarked that the joyful laughter and good-natured teasing "felt like moments to just be, *without the fear or consequence that our Blackness may cost us our lives . . . these moments are fleeting."*

It was indeed a happy counterpoint to the shrill news of Black deaths that filled print, television, and social media. But Glen and Damani acknowledged that celebrating their own and others' achievements couldn't make them forget that driving or walking or laying down with your hands up or standing still minding your own business while Black *could "justify" unlawful assaults. At various times during the evening, the men were painstakingly conscious that gatherings like this one were no longer available to Michael, Trayvon, Tamir, Jordan, Freddie, and so many other young Black men and women whose life circumstances so closely mirrored their own.*

> I guess the first two years it was about adjustments, making adjustments. The last two years I was aiming, I was achieving goals.
>
> **REGGIE**

In a society saturated with negative depictions of Black men, the media attention given to Urban Prep has been valuable for shifting, and even erasing, some deficit narratives and perceptions of young Black men and boys growing up in urban spaces. There are few places I go where, when I mention the name Urban Prep, people do not get excited. They have likely read or viewed one of the many news stories about the school. The Black Lives Matter movement, as well as the ever-increasing assault on Black people and communities of color writ large, necessitates stories like the ones these seventeen young men told. Such stories not only counter pervasive, damage-centered social constructions of urban Black youth, but they also provide hope that American society can change, that it can one day be different than the one our ancestors inherited. A different America from the one where Black people were viewed as three-fifths human, controlled at the pleasure of White settlers aiming to accumulate massive wealth no matter the human toll.

I find it perplexing that so many US citizens exhibit outrage over a football player's refusal to stand for the national anthem while at the same time keep silent on issues that affect millions of their fellow Americans, such as the dismantling of public education in predominantly Black and Latinx communities, destruction of land to build the Dakota Access Pipeline, the repeated attempts to discontinue or gut the Affordable Care Act, and the failure of the government to hold White men accountable for taking (Black) lives they swore to protect. Of course, many of these issues are not new; they just have greater visibility thanks to camera phones, Twitter, Facebook, and myriad other social media platforms.

It is in this climate that education practitioners teach, design curriculum, and create learning experiences meant to prepare young Black men and boys to face a world that builds more barriers to success than pathways to opportunity. This chapter considers the messages these young men received about going to college. It also examine their perspectives on the college preparation they received during their last two years at Urban Prep, including the quality of instruction, access to enrichment programs, and overall academic support provided by members of the school community.

"We Believe . . . We Are College Bound"

ZOOM IN

The young men were finishing up their second slices as Glen began passing the third round. The conversation about the young men's interactions with mostly Black men teachers during their first and second years at UP led them to reflect on ways Urban Prep was completely unlike other Chicago high schools. As members of the very first graduating class of the very first public, all-boys charter high school in the United States, these young men had a unique perspective on this. They had observed and experienced many of the school's growing pains and, in the process, developed a critical sensibility towards UP. These young men had also been the subject of intense scrutiny as supporters and critics of the school watched to see if Urban Prep would make good on its promise to get Black boys out of Englewood and into the ivory towers of higher education.

WINSTON: We knew that we were Black males, and we felt like commodities. We felt different from the other high school kids, despite that sometimes we didn't act different. We knew we were expected to be greater and that people would extend their hand out. It's kind of like a double-edged sword, because then you always expected somebody to help you.

QUENTIN: I know, for me, toward my junior year and my senior year, I was counting a lot. I was, you know, doing a lot of interviews, and I was doing a lot of picture taking. So that's what really motivated me. And you know, going to college, I felt like I had a lot of people watching.

WINSTON: I don't want to say we were caged. Okay, we were definitely caged in. Okay, we wasn't animals, but there were a lot of limitations put on us, and I think that was because they were afraid that if they allowed too much freedom, certain things would happen instead of understanding that it was a high school. It seems like there was a lot of focus on publicity and, you know, what the outside saw of us, and having time away from actually doing work. We were putting so much time toward going on field trips or were getting interviewed, and we'd have cameras coming in and we'd have this coming in, and "your uniform needs to be prepared because the mayor is coming."

ANTWAN: I assume more time was being put into the look rather than the actual students toward the end. It was just like, "Okay," for us looking at that. And plus they had, of course, their favorites. They had students that would just like get pulled out of class. Sometimes I would get pulled out of class to do things when I knew I should have been actually in class trying to learn something. I should have been in class rather than them taking pictures or running errands and students getting excused absences for having to go to a luncheon or doing things like that. I think that definitely took an effect on some of the ones that were chosen to do those. But at the end, of course, it was up to the students to actually be proactive in what they were doing. But sometimes you lose the way if you don't, if you are not focused.

GLEN [*breaking in*]: That's why we were always saying, "Stay dedicated, committed, and focused," Antwan. It's hard to stay on top of everything, especially as you get older and have to shoulder more and more responsibility.

WINSTON: It was a new school, so we knew everybody who owned it, who was downtown. We knew everybody. Those people would have a very different attitude from the teachers, which is why we felt that most teachers were getting fired, or just left. We didn't know, man. It was like every year there was somebody gone, and it wasn't really hard to build relationships with people, but we just took it for what it was. We knew that every day we'd come to school someone [a teacher or student] might be gone. Or every semester you're not guaranteed to see people's faces. Especially freshman year. That's when they kicked out the most people. Freshman year everybody was leaving. We were like, "Hey man, this person could be gone the next day," and we wouldn't know. We would talk about it. We was like, "Man, I don't think so and so is going to be here next week." Sure enough, the next week they [a teacher or student] wouldn't even be here.

Damani noticed that Jeff and Reggie were on their phones and barked, "Get off your phones!" The young men chuckled. It reminded them of the times Damani would scold them during the Black history course he taught at UP but how he would always end with praise: "You all have gone from teenage boys to college educated young men. We are so proud of you. People everywhere are proud of you!"

ZOOM OUT

A visit to the "Newsroom" page on Urban Prep's website nets a substantial number of reports and news pieces about the school. Not surprising, most of the stories featured are positive, even inspiring, such as the interview by ABC News 7 with Urban Prep alums who were mentoring and helping younger grads get through college.[2] But some are less happy, like the January 2017 *Chicago Tribune* piece titled "Prestigious Urban Prep Not Immune to Violence," about the eighth UP student killed since 2014.[1] This article is just one example of how Urban Prep is viewed by many as a "prestigious" high school in part because of the attention it has garnered for helping each of its graduates gain admission to a four-year college or university. But, just as a 2016 *Huffington Post* article insinuated, the haziness around what a 100 percent college acceptance rate indicates about the quality of the school's academic programs is a growing concern.[3] This concern is raised by many who are interested in the factors that produce the school's success, especially those educators in traditional public schools who aim to be more effective.

To that end, the coverage Urban Prep has received from popular media outlets has been met with mixed responses from researchers, education practitioners, and those on the front lines of urban education in Chicago and elsewhere. Some criticism, like that from Chicago Teachers Union past president Karen Lewis, has centered on the boast of "100% college acceptance" with little evidence of instructional effectiveness, which fuels false narratives that suggest Chicago charter schools are outperforming Chicago public elementary and high schools. This, at a time when hundreds of families are being dislocated from their neighborhood preK–12 schools, with those buildings slated to house a growing number of charter schools.[4] Another source of contention is how often a 100 percent college *acceptance* rate becomes conflated with a 100 percent college *enrollment/matriculation* or *persistence* rate for UP graduates. Tim King has admitted that UP does not make such claims about its graduates' college enrollment or persistence, yet the school does not provide the rates of enrollment/matriculation and persistence for its graduates, a metric that is important for assessing the value added for UP students' preparation for college.[5] Researchers, too, have fallen victim to misleading news reports. Anthony Mitchell and James Stewart, writing about the "efficacy of all-male academies," note that UP received major media attention for achieving "a 100-percent college enrollment rate."[6] This claim is likely based on a 2011 report they cite published by theRoot.com that is simply not true.[7]

The dominant narrative of the school's success can be misleading if it does not attend to other indicators of academic quality, including understanding the utility of single-sex schools for closing achievement gaps for young Black men and boys. Diane Halpern and her colleagues point out that when student attrition rates between freshmen and senior year are computed, graduation rates for UP and other traditional Chicago public high schools are comparable.[8] This is the reason Derrick and I only included in the UPCPS young men who had started high school at Urban Prep in 2006 *and* graduated from the school four years later, in 2010. Others object to characterizations of single-sex schools as *the* answer to Black males' academic failure, and/or they assert that there is just not enough evidence available to confirm such a claim.[9] Data from the 2015–16 Illinois Report Card reveal that Urban Prep's Englewood campus had a 94 percent graduation rate, but only 16 percent of the school's graduates demonstrated evidence of college readiness.[10] This is alarming because it casts doubt on the overall quality of the school's academic programs nearly a decade after its opening.

Indeed, given the excessive media attention the young men of Urban Prep have received, it makes some sense that the UPCPS participants would describe themselves as "caged in," "different," unlike other high school kids and say that the school was putting "more time in the look rather than the actual students." UP was a new school focused on getting Black men to college, no matter the cost. Take, for example, the impressive fifty-three-second *Now This News* video posted to Facebook on May 7, 2016. This news clip, titled "100% of Seniors at This All-Black School Are Going to College," has been shared more than 500,000 times (including by Urban Prep Academies) and has had almost thirty-one million views.[11] The video tells a compelling story of how Urban Prep took a group of "economically disadvantaged" Black boys and, "for the seventh year in a row," helped 100 percent of its graduates get "admitted to four-year colleges or universities." The video touts the school's rigorous curriculum, small class sizes, and devoted teachers. A Facebook post by Urban Prep Academies "sharing" the video reads:

> What would happen if the 10 million people who watched this video about 100% of our graduates being admitted to college each year gave Urban Prep $1? We'd be able to provide a high quality college prep education to over 1,200 students for a year; we'd be able to give college scholarships for all of our seniors; we'd be able to continue to support our alumni to help them get through college; and much more. Help us celebrate 100% of our seniors being admitted to college by watching this video and taking action to support them . . . Thank you for helping Urban Prep students as they continue changing the narrative through college and life. #WeBelieve #10AndChange #ChangingTheNarrative #Donate

This video, and the subsequent post by Urban Prep Academies, calls into question the ways that urban youth are exploited to propagate capitalist gain and wealth accumulation by private entities. Missing is an easily identifiable system of accountability, which might include annual reports that demonstrate accomplishments and areas of improvement. Such a system is important for evaluating the fidelity of school operations to achieve aims set forth in their charter *to be a school that serves the public.* Raising money from the public and not demonstrating evidence that the service provided is indeed improving outcomes beyond college admission is confounding. There are variables that enable one's long-term academic success worth noting.

But what the media says, the public believes, and the dominant story is that Urban Prep is doing a superlative job of educating young Black men and boys. The metrics and/or benchmarks by which the public might assess the school's effectiveness, however, need to be more clearly established. A statement like "We knew we were Black males. We were commodities" should raise suspicion. It is a call to look deeper and probe further. The public has very few options for determining a return on investment in Urban Prep Academies. The school is soliciting funds based on a storyline that grabs at the emotions of those serious about improving the education experiences of young Black men and boys, but there is almost no publicly available data about the college persistence, retention, and completion of its graduates. From what evidence can be found about the school's academic programs, like the data found on the

Illinois Report Card or a 2011 report published by the school, the academic benefits of attending Urban Prep do not appear very favorable.[12]

Thinking more broadly, the problem is not necessarily the heart work or good intentions of Tim King and others working to improve urban education for young Black men and boys at Urban Prep Academies. Evidence from the UPCPS does suggest the school was effective at getting these young men to "believe" they were prepared to graduate high school by exposing them to college as an option and presenting them adult Black men with whom they could build substantive relationships. The issue is why the public is okay with this school being touted as exceptional without having any evidence to corroborate its effectiveness, and why that same energy and effort is not given to the good things happening in Black schools all around the city of Chicago and across the United States. The media positions UP and its young Black men as special and extraordinary, which says something about the ways that young Black men and boys are imagined in the mainstream. The intense attention the school has received has also had an impact on the way these young men view themselves, their perception of the ways UP treated them, and the messages they internalized about college going from adults at Urban Prep.

Therefore, it is important that their story is told. These young men's perspectives, the corporatization of public schooling in US cities, and the lack of evidence specific to UP's pedagogical effectiveness should cause all of us to pause and consider the long-term impact this school—and now others like it—is having on its graduates.[13]

"We Are Dedicated, Committed, and Focused"

ZOOM IN

It was getting dark outside. The restaurant was filling up with more patrons. None of this mattered to the men, each of whom was completely enjoying good food and conversation. Loud laughter erupted when Antwan, mocking one of the school's two founding principals, stood up and declared, "We are dedicated, committed, and focused" in his best Mr. Whitfield voice. This line from the Creed was an exhortation that adults could regularly be heard repeating in class, Community, Prides, the lunchrooms, and hallways and at activities and events. It was a call to remind the young men of the personal qualities required to earn admittance to, and later graduate from, a four-year college or university. This was part of a very clear message from day one that the young men of Urban Prep were college bound.

WINSTON: I feel like we kinda didn't have a choice. From the moment you got to Urban Prep, they talked about college. Like day one, they were preparing you for college. I'm thinking, "Who wants college? I just got into high school! I'm just trying to get over the fact there ain't no girls here and you telling me about college." It was kind of like Urban Prep's mission. It was great, but it hit you really hard, really fast. There was no ease-in.

QUENTIN: They talked about college a lot. It was the main focus, to get everybody to college. They talked about it, but some teachers, they actually talked about the wrong parts of college, like the whole partying aspect of college, and they didn't really focus on the academic part of it. There were teachers that talked about college a lot, like Mr. Chris. Every single day, every time we went to his class, he talked about college, "If you do this, you're not going to do well in college," and all that stuff like that. Sometimes I would just say, "I'm, like, here, in high school. I'm not in college yet."

REGGIE: If I'm not mistaken, that's the only thing that they were preaching in high school every day, that's what they were talking about—college. Mr. Davis, he'd come in every blue moon, and he'd tell us that we're going to college and we're not trying to get you to college but through college. I always tell people that I always thought college was a fairy tale. You graduate high school and then you work. But they talked to us about going to college and finishing college, and you'd have more options. So, I *believed* in it, and I just stuck it out.

QUENTIN: Yeah, the main goal at Urban Prep was—well, they say "We Believe." I had to believe in myself before I could believe in anything else and, of course, I believe in myself . . .

WINSTON: [*interrupting*] They gave us the tools. We got the tools, but it wasn't like, "Okay now if you go and visit this place, that you do this. Okay, let's walk over together and let's do this together." It was never like that. It was to a sense of, "This is what it is, this is what you are going to face. And if you ever face this situation, this is what you need to do. This is the office. These are the people that you need to know."

ANTWAN: I don't know how traditional high schools work, but from what my friends—not friends, but acquaintances or people that I talked to in the After School Matters program [an afterschool program founded by former Chicago First Lady Maggie Daley] they would say there was a college prep track [at their high school] but it was optional. At Urban Prep, college prep was part of our curriculum. Urban Prep was going to push college to you 24/7 no matter what. "Even if you don't want to go to college or don't like college, we're still going to push it as an option." They didn't just let you say, "Here, here's your diploma and maybe you can go to Job Corps."

JEFF: I always thought, though, college isn't for everybody, realistically. But they used to kind of throw it in people's faces, like, "You need to do this, or it's just not going to work for you," or "You need to make sure you're doing this." But everybody's not built like that. I do feel like students, when they came to Urban Prep, some felt as if they were being forced to go down a route that they didn't necessarily want to go to. Urban Prep, in a sense, was a big control, or they tried to be real controlling over some of the students. They had the best intentions at heart, but I think they could have probably did it in another way. I don't think it's fair.

The young men hinted at the pressure students felt in relationship to UP's college-going mission. Damani was interested in Jeff's comment that some UP students felt like they were being forced in a direction "they didn't necessarily want to go." He asked the young men what their teachers, or other adults in the school, said that convinced them that college was the right path for them.

WINSTON: They pitched the words "You can study abroad." I'm like—man, I'm trying to get to these things. It's all like placing those things before me, that these are things that you can get to, so now you've just got to put the work into getting to those places. It's climbing that academic ladder.

QUENTIN: Yeah, like I said earlier, I felt like they were trying to use the partying stuff to try to get us to college, but they weren't talking about, like, the academic part of college. College is fun. I mean, it wasn't a bad thing to talk about it, because they are still trying to get us to go to college, but that was the wrong way to try to get us to get to college by telling the whole party aspect of college. That's what they emphasized the most. And graduation. You know, I wanted to hang with Mr. Becker. To hang with Mr. Becker, I had to graduate from college. So, when I graduated from college, then that was the first person I would go and hang with.

ANTWAN: I received messages that a lot of black men didn't go to college. That going is a good thing. That going to college would keep you out of trouble. It would help you improve your life, improve your community. Of course, there's more money in going to college than those that did not go to college.

QUENTIN: I do remember there was a question of diversity and how race played a part, being a Black man in White-dominated universities. I do remember some conversation that we had about making sure that you work just as hard as the students there because you're there, you have to stand out and make an example and change the stereotypes that people have of Black people in general in these White universities. There was always discussion about being the only Black person in college classes.

ANTWAN: I use Mr. Dean for an example. Considering the fact that we were a predominantly Black, all-male school, he was just telling us some of the stuff that we had to face coming into college. Overall, all the teachers were talking to us about the things that they had to go through in college.

QUENTIN: Yeah, for some adults, those stories definitely made me feel like I was able to do anything I put my mind to because they did it too. I was able to do it myself. Just looking up to them as examples. These are adults who went through the same kind of challenges and hardships that I went through, and how they overcame them.

REGGIE: Seeing how we [the UP academic community]value it [going to college] as a goal, with people coming after me, I wanted to give us a good name for our skin color. This was from everyone. The teachers and the whole administration. "That's the beginning of growing up." "It's the beginning of life." "It's the best time to take opportunity, take risks." I needed to see the benefits of being a student in college.

JEFF: Those were the messages that we got, honestly, on the regular. It's like, you know, "You got to be successful." It was vital that I got a degree. I felt like it was embedded in the things that Urban Prep taught us. It was implied. No one ever told me that per se. It was implied in all of their ways and everything. "You need this paper, a degree." So yeah, that's what it was.

These were some of the same messages Glen and Damani had heard about college when they were high school students on Chicago's South Side. They were anchored in such meritocratic values as working hard to earn one's due reward and conveyed a sentiment familiar to every man at the table: college was a way out.

ANTWAN: You didn't necessarily hear this from teachers, but just from hearing everything else and talking with students. [College] was a way out. It was the way out of your current environment. No matter what it was, whether you were in a happy home with well-off parents or you weren't. College is one of those ways to do it. Whether you're going to go to college for sports or academics. Either way, it was a goal to become a better person, to get away from whatever situation you were at that you didn't want to be in anymore. It was a goal that somebody showed us, explained the importance of it, the purpose of it. Something that you really didn't have any option not to do because it was like, "If I don't go to college, if I don't take this choice, at least try for it, then what am I going to do?"

REGGIE: Yep, you make your own way. How you treat yourself is what you're going to get out of it, and it's nobody's fault but you. You make your own mousetrap for yourself.

JEFF: The message that I got at the time was if you want to get out and try to be successful, you need to go to college. That's basically what it was. It was like, you see what's going on in Chicago. You don't need to be here. Graduating from high school and going to college is your way out. That's going to be your way into a new life. That's going to be a way to get your family where you want them to be.

ZOOM OUT

Some degree of postsecondary training is increasingly important for youth of color from impoverished backgrounds.[14] Preparing these young men to attend college is a laudable ambition, but insisting that college is the only postsecondary pathway to "success" for poor youth of color is problematic. This is especially true when that insistence can create another layer of marginalization for young people whose talents and passions don't immediately align with the aim of enrolling in a traditional four-year college or university immediately following high school.

Urban Prep's college-going message was delivered primarily by Black men who the young men admired and respected. It was a message that these young men internalized. Their notion of college going centered on liberal values, with messages that suggested that, in the long run, race doesn't matter if you work really hard. At face value, principles of meritocracy and race neutrality make sense, but they contradict the lived realities of growing up in communities where hard work does not necessarily earn you a livable wage and where doing the right thing does not always mean you're exempt from harassment by police. These young men demonstrated dedication, commitment, and focus simply by going to school every day despite numerous stressors in their home lives.

As these young men disclosed, members of the Urban Prep leadership, faculty, visitors to the school, and other professional staff presented college as "a way out," as a way to improve their lives. At the very least, they were told that going to college would allow them to escape threats to their physical and psychological well-being. I heard similar messages as a high schooler, and I admit to having used these same messages to motivate my own students during my years as an urban educator—"Make something of your life. Go to college. Get away from here!" However, this message confounds an ethos of community uplift, and responsibility for others in the village—the network of social support. The work of legitimizing the benefits of a college education must extend beyond merely convincing urban youth they need to simply escape their neighborhoods. Again, it is not the message of going to college that is problematic. It's the implication that obtaining a college education requires one to disassociate from loved ones and disavow the cultural knowledge acquired having grown up in the "hood."

But the messaging around college going was just one step in UP's creation of a college-for-all school culture. The next step was ensuring that the young men's coursework and academic experiences would prepare them for college-level work.[15] The young men revealed, however, how Urban Prep did not succeed in truly being a "college for all" schooling environment, despite its stated aim. Making sure its students were college ready while at the same time growing the school, setting the tone for its culture, and arranging high-quality culturally responsive learning experiences no doubt impacted the efficacy of UP's efforts to adequately prepare each of its graduates to contend with the rigors of college-level coursework.

Coursework, Rigor, and Academic Expectations

ZOOM IN

"We'd like to box the rest of the pizza," Glen told the waiter. The men were leaning back in their chairs, stuffed. But they were still enjoying one another's company and weren't ready to leave. All of the talk about college-going messages prompted them to reflect on the various aspects of their academic preparation for college—the courses, the activities, the enrichment programs. They even had some ideas for how Urban Prep might improve in this area.

QUENTIN: It was two or three classes that I felt like, "This was an easy A. Why am I in this class?" When you got to exam period, that's when it got challenging. They put their foot into the exam period. I forgot how the process went, but during the five weeks when you have to do classes, the material wasn't all that rigorous. I could have done it in the classroom and been done with it, and had no homework. It was work I was doing in my spare time. It wasn't work that was supposed to challenge me. Those are the things I felt like were impeding my success academically.

WINSTON: Yeah, a lot of things we were taught at Urban Prep were kind of the same things that were taught at grade school in terms of getting ready for the next level. I don't remember it being challenging, to be honest. I felt that I was prepared for high school mentally, so I didn't have to take it too seriously.

QUENTIN: I feel like all the things that we learned, somewhat, was a waste of time, because I really didn't have to use it in college. College is really based on networking and doing interactions with people. I just thought it was tedious work. I felt like some stuff we didn't have to do. I felt like we're just doing stuff just to pass time, and that's one thing that I don't like. I don't like to do stuff that I don't really have to do. I felt like it's a waste of time.

WINSTON: It was not the inability to do it, it's just the content of it all and how to approach it. They definitely held our hands to a certain extent, and that was good. But you've got to hold our hands with the right supplements put in place. That was probably one of the biggest things that I wish that could change, and it's one of the things that, literally, I want to talk to them about putting into their curriculum. I did like honors geometry, or something like that. You've got to have a system, or set in place a system, where things, like, stick for you.

That's really important. I think there was only one class between my junior and senior year—well, my senior year I had one class that I feel like was actually challenging, and that was AP, I think, a literature class. That class definitely was—we got challenged and we were able to identify what we struggled in, and the teacher actually tried to assist us individually on where we were.

ANTWAN: Yeah, I took AP English. Doing that put me in the mind-set for college a little bit. The rigor. The work was more rigorous. That helped me for college. It also helped me to go ahead and knock out my English courses, requirements that I needed for my major, early. I actually got to skip a couple English classes because I got the AP credits for it. For math, just the critical thinking skills that I needed for my specific major helped a lot for college. I was taught enough math at Urban Prep to do well.

WINSTON: The curriculum was never easy. I feel like it was challenging from a sense, but it's almost like when you have a challenge but they don't allow you to actually *experience* the challenge. [*Pauses to scratch his head and think about how to articulate his thoughts.*] Having now completed college, I can say this: it would have been so key having a philosophy course, or having a small sociology course, or something like that. It would have gotten us prepared to just be able to read and take in that sort of information, like case studies and stuff. I would understand how to read a sociological study, or understand or see the importance of those sort of things. We wouldn't be stuck on this Walter D. Myers–esque understanding of, like, reading, this basic sense of reading.

"Wow, Winston!" Damani said. "That is a strong critique." Winston gave a Kanye shrug, and the group roared with boisterous laughter.[16]

QUENTIN: It wasn't until my junior year when they started adding honors classes and AP classes into the curriculum. I feel like if there were a lot more classes that had this rigorous level, more college preparatory at Urban Prep, I feel like that would prepare a lot more Black males [for college] and help with them stay in college. I felt a little prepared with taking precalculus or honors algebra, and English literature. Classes like those prepared me for college-level courses.

JEFF: Well, the AP classes that I took in high school, and reading that kind of English literature, and just really having the academic success that was really crucial to the work that you do in college. Meeting people, networking, etc., that might also be important.

QUENTIN: A lot of students couldn't get into those classes because of their GPA. You had to have a certain GPA to even get into those AP and honors classes. I think that placement shouldn't be that limited. I feel like everyone should try to find a spot in some type of AP class and have a lot more variety of AP classes or honors-level courses for students at Urban Prep, so when they get to college they will be a lot more prepared.

WINSTON: If there was a college-level course, those teachers showed no leniency. I like the challenge that some of my favorite teachers took, or some of the really good teachers took, with the material. Taking certain exams would be a lot harder, because that teacher was that good in their curriculum. I think the teachers who were the most challenging are the ones who handled the curriculum very well, the ones who were looking out for the students' interests in the classroom. And also some of the teachers I remember who were there trying to put a life lesson into it as well, making it relatable to someone's life.

Damani noticed that Reggie was fidgeting and exhibiting annoyance at Winston for dominating the conversation, as everyone knew Winston tended to do. But Winston missed the social cue and carried on with his assessment of UP's academic program.

WINSTON: We were given the amenities of a Mount Carmel [a well-funded private high school on the South Side], but without the price. You were expected to be Mount Carmel–style students, but you didn't have to make the same sacrifices or pay the same price out of pocket that they did. The expectation of what the bar was set at and where we were at was different. It was almost like Urban Prep didn't meet you where you were. You were just expected to be there. I think most teachers understood that. That's why most teachers had a very compassionate attitude toward students.

QUENTIN: They shaped me to where I knew that nothing was going to be given to me, no matter who I was, you know, what I did. You know, things still had to be worked for no matter who you were. When I got to college, that helped me a lot, because these professors don't really know me. Well, they didn't know me at all. The only thing they knew of me was my name and that, uh, there was work that needed to get done and my charm wasn't going to get that A, or that charm wasn't going to get me that grade I needed to pass when I had to take it over. So, you know, the teachers helped me in a way to where I know I really had to work to get what I wanted.

ANTWAN: I felt like I was the kid in class where they saw something in me to get me to reach up more. When I got to Urban Prep, it was more like, "Hey, get your work done or you're going to fail." It was a different learning experience. In grammar school, like I said, it's like being pampered. It's like they're babying you and you're being spoon-fed the information.

WINSTON: My English teachers impacted me the most though, because writing was my escape for stuff. I didn't even know I was a good writer until they made me write all the time, and I was like, "Damn, this is a lot of writing." Then they would say, "You're really good." It really hit me when they compared me to Richard Wright. Yeah. When my senior history teacher said, "You're like the next Richard Wright," I understood it. I just smiled, but I was just like, "That's interesting." I remember reading some of his books, and I was like, "Oh I guess that is a compliment."

The conversation was now very animated, energized. Glen, wanting to capitalize on this momentum, nudged the young men to share their perceptions of their teachers—"Don't mention names, but tell us about the characteristics of teachers you most disliked *in high school."*

WINSTON: I disliked teachers who weren't diligent enough taking into account all the students. All the students had some life situation. Since most of the teachers understood this, not everyone is going to be a good student, and you have to work with some of the students that were at Urban Prep. Some of my favorite teachers were able to understand this, and the classroom wasn't so chaotic. The ones I disliked also let the class be chaotic and let some students do whatever they wanted to do. I understand you want to have, like, a cool, relaxed classroom with your students, you want to keep the culture of your classroom. You put the nature of yourself within your classroom, and you can do that. But if you can't set the disciplinary tone as well, then maybe teaching just ain't the thing for you.

QUENTIN: Like I mentioned earlier, a teacher who wasn't taking into account the curriculum. They would give us easy work like it was elementary school, like we didn't understand what we were doing. Dumbing down the material so everyone could understand it. I feel like that impeded my progress.

WINSTON: It was weird how Urban Prep worked. It was more so like you didn't have to be smart. You just had to know how to do stuff. It wasn't about being smart at Urban Prep. It was about saying, "I need this to get done. Now how can I get this done? I probably need to talk to this teacher. Maybe stay after school for thirty minutes. The teacher is going to give me this extra work and I'm going to do it because I don't really want us to fail."

The young men agreed that they didn't like teachers who they perceived as having low expectations. They preferred teachers who were tuned in to what different students needed, who did not subscribe to the one-size-fits-all model of teaching.

ANTWAN: I feel like Mr. Weber, he challenged us the most. He challenged me the most. He just made me feel like he cared. He cared enough to help me develop these writing skills, the communication skills, stuff like that. And he also gave us positive criticism, you know what I'm saying? If you don't have somebody giving you that positive criticism, then they don't really care. People will see you doing wrong or they'll see an error and they'll say, "Fix this." He did more than that. He showed us and told us and he went more in-depth.

QUENTIN: Those are definitely the ones who helped me prepare a lot more for college. They taught their classes. If there was a college-level course, they showed no leniency. There was some leniency with the material and with the grade. I like the challenge that some of my favorite teachers took, or some of the really good teachers took, with the material. The ones who were looking out for the students' interests in the classroom, and also some of the teachers I remember who were there trying to put a life lesson into it as well, making it relatable to someone's life.

JEFF: Academically, the teachers that really challenged us, it was like, "Life doesn't care about your feelings today. You still got this work to do."

REGGIE: All these teachers had a kinda—they just believed. They believed in me. They just kept pushing and said, "You might not get it this time, but you can get it." Even you two [*looking at Glen and Damani*], you both kept pushing me—even when I didn't want to be pushed but I needed it. They gave me personal advice. Like, Ms. Simpson taught me that I couldn't be a perfectionist because it was stressful, and I needed that. They taught me that not everything I put out was going to be right. I might not have it all the way right the first time. They helped me really improve, find out a way to get a task done the right way. I carried that with me in college. There were numerous times where I didn't have it done the right way and I had to rewrite or ask the question differently. And it was all right. I just had to find a way to get through that.

ANTWAN: As a group, you could tell they wanted us to be successful. Each teacher was different, but as a group they all cared. They all wanted us to do well. They all wanted us to do well. They made sure that if we were struggling with something, that we had the resources and the help that we did need to be successful, whether we wanted to realize it or not. Some teachers were stricter than others. As a whole, they were cool. I liked them a lot.

WINSTON: I think I appreciated the qualities [of the teachers] more than the actual educational experience I had. The qualities, as in more of, like, the maturity that I gained there. It's like you are going to have the struggle, you are going to have the challenges, you are going to have the different obstacles that you are going to face. But okay, what am I, as the teacher, giving you that can influence you enough to be that motivator or to inspire yourself to go and do what you should be doing. I don't want you to just feel inspired during class, where I'm going through the information, but I want you to feel inspired outside the class when you are doing the work.

ANTWAN: It made me want to get into my studies more. It made me realize that all it takes is that one push to unlock the potential in someone. It made me change my perspective on teachers as a whole. The grammar school that I came from, they were only there to get a paycheck. The teachers at Urban Prep, it was teachers who came from where I came from. In my post–high school experiences, it made me think about teachers more critically. It made me wonder if this teacher can relate to me. Why am I not getting this, that, and the third? Will they take time out to make sure that I get the lesson? Will this lesson relate to who I am? It made me realize that every teacher is not going to be as nurturing and challenging as I had in high school, because they were doing stuff that they wasn't even getting paid for, most of them at least.

ZOOM OUT

These young men's experiences in college underscore the importance of having access to a group of educators in high school who both cared deeply and challenged them academically. From their time at Urban Prep, these young men recognized the importance of developing key academic skills (study skills, writing, reading and comprehending complicated texts), acquiring content knowledge, and building a social network.

The young men claimed that their Advanced Placement (AP) courses were the most challenging and, for that reason, the best high school classes they took in preparation for college. Most notable in this discussion, at least four years out of high school, was the value these young men placed on high academic expectations and on having access to the necessary support to reach those expectations.

Furthermore, these young men's reflections suggest that they greatly valued teachers who demonstrated a willingness to go the extra mile. They valued authentic learning experiences with activities that were relevant to their real lives, experiences that helped them more deeply understand the subjects they were learning. They described good classrooms as being disciplined and places where students had boundaries, and the workload made them feel like they were being productive or that their time was not being wasted. They valued teachers who were encouraging, affirming, patient, organized, and well-prepared.

The young men had conflicting points of view about the quality of the school's academic programs. And data specific to indicators of academic success at UP's flagship Englewood campus does suggest that there is some need for improvement in this area. For example, none of UP students fully met or exceeded expectations for performance on the Partnership for Assessment of Readiness for College and Careers (PARCC) assessment, as compared to 26 percent of CPS students and 34 percent of students at the state level. Moreover, UP had a *no* freshmen on track to graduate in 2016, as compared to CPS's 64 percent and the state's 82.4 percent.[17]

Clear and consistent across these young men's reflections is their unyielding desire to be *seen* by educators as smart and worthy of receiving the most demanding learning opportunities the school could make available to them. This includes what the teachers say to students, how they say it, how they organize instruction and the classroom, and the learning opportunities teachers make available to young people. Overwhelming data underscore young Black men's academic vulnerability as demonstrated by their overrepresentation on measures of school failure and underrepresentation on measures of school success.[18] These trends center on the failure of schools to establish learning environments that compel young people to put forth their best effort. What these young men's narratives indicate, and other research literature confirms, is that young Black men do care that they receive a high-quality education, even if their actions are not immediately read that way by the adults standing in front of them.[19] It's not that young Black men and boys do not want to be engaged in their learning; it's that they may not trust the teacher, or the classroom is too "chaotic", or they do not see themselves fully represented in the curriculum. These aspects of the learning experience matter for strengthening their education outcomes.[20]

Extracurricular Enrichment, Programming, and Academic Self-Efficacy

ZOOM IN

While Damani stepped away from the table to take a phone call from one of his daughters, the men compared their experiences with different summer programs that UP's college counseling department, led by Mr. Phillips, helped them find. Glen asked Reggie, Jeff, Quentin, Antwan, and Winston whether they believed these outside programs helped prepare them for college.

QUENTIN: They were like classes, but I didn't see them as classes, or I didn't see them as extra work. I knew I could rely on those programs to make me feel better. I liked to write little short stories. It took my mind off of the challenges that I was going through in classes. I did, like, a weeklong program. It was basically mostly on leadership skills. And there was also a six-week program at Syracuse that I attended. That somewhat gave me a big idea of what college is like, because I was on a campus for six weeks. I was on my own for six weeks.
ANTWAN: What I enjoyed most was the college trips. I got a lot of opportunities for internships going out for Urban Prep to different places. That was really cool. That made things a little better. I applied at Urban Prep for the

Google internship. I got that. I was able to go to DC as a page for the House of Congress. I got to go here and there. I went to LA, New Orleans. Field trips to represent Urban Prep—those were pretty cool.

QUENTIN: Not all the students at Urban Prep were eligible for summer programs. They were only getting preparation through classes. Even if they didn't take their classes very seriously, they were missing out on their preparation for college-level courses. I know with the summer UP programs, I was sitting in classrooms, college-level classes, for a month or so at other universities. I had a lot of preparation. A lot of students didn't have it all. I think that was the only thing they had to help students prepare for college.

ANTWAN: Like I said, I got to go to DC as a congressional page. I got to go to Google as an intern, where I first got introduced to computer science. Being a page, I realized I didn't want to go into politics. The internship was great. People were cool. But I realized that was not for me. Politics was not for me. That helped me. I went to the University of Chicago for a class after school. Can't remember what it was, but it was cool. Those type of things helped build my character, helped me become a little bit more outspoken and developed my personality. They were rigorous internships, too. They forced me to have to think on my feet. Forced me to get used to things I wasn't used to. Situations I wasn't used to. Really forced my critical thinking. All of that. I was one of the three Black guys on my Google internship. That was a whole other experience being isolated in California with a whole different lifestyle. But it was good, being introduced to that. When I got to college, I wasn't shocked. I wasn't surprised.

QUENTIN: I went to a lot of programs in high school that really taught me a lot about college. They taught me how to, you know, live on my own, because I wasn't with my family. I was there for, like, months, like two months, a couple of weeks, and I was taking college-level classes and things like that. It kind of taught me how to handle myself in college before I actually got to college, like getting up on my own, sitting in a college classroom, developing relationships with professors, and things like that. Just living on my own and just living that college life.

Damani returned in time to hear the men talk about how valuable these summer enrichment programs were. During his time at the school, he worked with Mr.

Phillips to make sure that the school placed as many young men as possible in various extracurricular activities and programs each year, so he was gratified to hear that it had such a positive and lasting effect. He asked about other UP activities and programs the young men believed helped them to become ready for college.

QUENTIN: There was extracurriculars that helped influence your major decision. If you knew you wanted to go into engineering, you did SWAT [Students Willing to Assist with Technology], or if you knew you wanted to do sports, you played football. If you wanted to be a journalism major, you were on the newsletter. I don't feel like it always really *prepared* students for college, because they all didn't cater to what you were trying to do in college. Those were just what you were doing through our high school to fill time. You enjoyed doing them. There needs to be a lot more programs like summer UP, though.

WINSTON: I'd say the Ambassador Program. I remember at some point with that we got to lead the "Seeing Is Believing" program [informational tours and sessions for prospective students]. That was so awesome, because there were some folks that came all the way in from London to sort of check out the school. It was definitely number one, I would say. The Ambassador Program, that sort of helped me, because like I said, it is seeing where life can take you, or meeting all these different people, go to do this, go to do that. Like I said, all those things, they helped me see what was out there. Being an African American male from the neighborhood of West Englewood, and Englewood in general, there is accessibility, but only within that sort of structure, what's inside of that square. Being a part of those programs helped me step outside the box.

REGGIE: I feel like I came in more prepared than a lot of other students [at the small elite liberal arts college he attended]. I'd done a lot of internships and stuff like that. People would ask, "How did you know how to do this, and how did you know how to do that?" I was like, "I did it in high school." They'd say, "You guys did all that in high school?" I was like, "Wow, I went to a good ass high school!" The things I learned in public speaking class and test prep, those things really added up—a lot. Now when I have to speak on campus, I'm not nervous—well, just a little bit. But I'm able to give speeches and give presentations and I feel really good about it. All of that is based on being prepared by my high school.

QUENTIN: It's just crazy when I say this, but it was the last sport I actually got involved in—I'd say it was track. I just felt like my coach was a strict coach. He was one of those people that he made sure your grade is on top. He was like, "You're not going to participate in this meet if you're grades aren't up to par." I felt like that kind of shaped me to do the best that I could.

REGGIE: I would also say the college tours. I really took those to matter. I really did. You spoke to students that was going through a situation that you're not going through at that moment but that can be you in the next three, four years. It was a good insight on how college is, what you're about to get yourself into, how to prepare yourself for the real life. I took that with me.

JEFF: What I enjoyed about being at a college prep high school is I got to see what college things would look like, because I feel like that's the definition of college prep and being in a college prep high school. Exposure to a life that I never knew existed outside of my community.

WINSTON: Yeah, like becoming a young man, and having the opportunities that we had to go off and go out of our neighborhood. I really liked that. I didn't really have those types of opportunities on my own. Things like that. Yeah, I think it was the opportunities that I really enjoyed the most about the school.

QUENTIN: I didn't realize it until I got to college how relevant some of the courses at Urban Prep and some of the extracurriculars at Urban Prep were relative to my college experience. For the extracurriculars it was all about—well, I guess what I took the most out of it was leadership development, being a leader and learning to work with others. Those extracurriculars I did at Urban Prep definitely played a role in leadership development I've taken to college. For classes, I guess the most relevant thing I took from that to college was just how to study, how to work hard, how to push through material that I didn't understand, how to relate it to my life in general.

ANTWAN: We had to apply to like twelve colleges, and I got accepted to seven. That was big. That was cool just knowing that schools wanted me, and all I had to do was sign on the line, get that financial aid, and I was gone. I was putting in after hours, we get out at 4:30 and I was still there at 7 or 8 p.m. I was going hard. I think it was one or two times that Mr. Phillips had to drop me off because I was there still filling out application forms. I remember I filled out thirteen out in one day, and I gave them to Mr. Phillips and I was like, "Here."

JEFF: Mr. Phillips, he used to always tell us, "I'm trying to get you all out there with these White people." He would always tell us that. He definitely got me out there with those White people. He put me in with a couple programs at the University of Chicago. Got me connected with several programs. So just him and his will and his drive to want to see us do good made me want to do good.

Damani chuckled, "I'm going to have to give Mr. Phillips a call and let him know how much y'all appreciate his work!" Glen nodded in agreement.

REGGIE: To be honest, I really don't think Mr. Phillips got a lot of credit for the things that he did. He had—I don't know how many straight years that he had 100 percent graduation rate at Urban Prep. But I felt like he don't get the credit that he deserve. Like, he put in a lot of work, a lot of hours. He put in a lot of work, a lot of hours trying to get people to jump into college, reading all the applications and reading all the essays before they send them out, having to call about ACT scores, and things like that. He should be like the main focus, because he's the one behind the scene making it all happen. So I felt like he just—I don't know. He don't get the credit that he deserve as a person for his job at Urban Prep.

As Reggie finished his comment, the waiter moved in to clear their plates. "Dessert, anyone?"

ZOOM OUT

By exposing its students to college campuses, internships, summer academic enrichment programs, and extracurricular programs, Urban Prep created a strong college-going culture. Daily interactions with college-educated people who looked like them and who had similar backgrounds, regular discussions about college life, and the college pennants and banners lining the walls made college feel attainable to these students. Urban Prep's founding college counselor, Mr. Phillips, also played a significant role in curating this school environment. The young men spoke of his diligence in finding summer enrichment opportunities. He made sure that the right opportunities were presented to every young man, and they acknowledged the important role he played in ensuring that each UP student applied to and was admitted into a four-year college or university.

Conclusion

There is a tension between drawing attention to work being done to improve the lives of urban youth and unknowingly contributing to prevailing deficit discourses about them. The conversations Derrick Brooms and I had with these UPCPS participants four years after their graduation from Urban Prep were indispensable for better understanding the potential shortcomings and blind spots in the school's efforts to prepare its graduates to be successful in college (graduate from a traditional four-year institution of higher education). Through their candid commentary, these young men offer up a cautionary tale for urban educators everywhere: serving the public, and garnering its support, means being transparent about the efficacy of the work.

Any inadequacies in these young men's academic preparation for college were overshadowed by the strong, confident belief in their ability to achieve postsecondary success. Students value teachers who challenge them intellectually.[21] For instance, holding young people to high academic expectations regardless of the distress one perceives that their home life may be causing them is perceived by students as a form of care, and it is hard for students to learn from teachers who they believe do not care about them.[22] Likewise, cultivating a young person's belief in themselves and then making sure they have the necessary wraparound support of multiple adults in the school building who also believe in them, is an important step in the right direction for opening up doors of possibility.

That is not enough, however, if those possibilities have been too well defined *for* young people as opposed to *with* young people. Young students of color, like their White counterparts, should also have the chance to dream out loud, to imagine a future that may or may not include college. The teacher's job is to equip them with skills to pursue those dreams, not to reproduce in students their own thinking and ways of being. In their comments, the young men emphasize that every young person deserves to be seen, celebrated, and made to feel special. This sort of recognition should be evenly distributed across schools and neighborhoods; it is not reserved for the privileged few who happen to attend one or two schools deemed "exceptional" by the popular media. We all must be vigilant in our efforts to find the good stuff happening in every school, in every school district. And then we must document and share that good news widely.

There are good things happening in urban education. But first, we must assume—*believe*—that there is good work happening. I am confident that, if queried, every school leader or teacher could find some evidence of a positive impact they are having, or will have, on young people over time. As Tim King asserts, "Either you do or you don't"—we must *believe to see,* not see to believe.

5

College Transition, Persistence, and Completion

"I better get going," Damani said, looking down at his watch one final time. "It's almost midnight. How is it that we've been sitting here talking for two and half hours already?" They packed up, squared away their tab, and suited up to face Mother Winter.

It was bracingly cold outside, and a light snow was falling. But Glen and Damani barely felt it. The excitement of the evening, of their reconnection with each other and their former students, had lit a fire in them. They recognized the need for stories of young Black men who were beating the odds to achieve great things, of young Black men who were persevering. They understood the potential these stories hold for helping to disrupt mainstream deficit discourses about the academic achievement of young Black men and boys. They understood how these stories of resilience would better equip schools to (re)imagine an antiracist, anti-oppressive schooling environment that affirms and celebrates diverse forms of Black manhood. They believed that these stories could help the public understand the role and function of a high school in subverting anti-Black schooling practices and putting young Black men on a path to postsecondary success, regardless of what route—college or career—they eventually choose to take.

Outside the coffee shop, they shook hands before heading in opposite directions toward their cars. "Give my regards to the family, and safe travels back home." "You too!"

> College was the biggest reality check for me, though. High school for me—I was very sheltered. It was very, very sheltering. There were also times when I feel we were overcoddled, because a lot of the processes we weren't aware of, the whole college process. I still don't know what traditional students have to do to apply for college. All I know is that it's hard and it's difficult . . . We never felt the gravity or weight of reality in Urban Prep, because everything was done for you. They always hired somebody to take care of this stuff for you, but we never knew what the stuff was. Going into college—for me, it took a little bit of adjusting.
>
> **WINSTON**

This chapter describes dominant themes in the young men's transition into college and their persistence through to completion. The counterstory continues with their adjustment to college during their first couple years on campus and is followed by a discussion of some of the obstacles they faced as they matriculated through college and the factors they believe helped them overcome numerous personal setbacks. This chapter reveals lessons the young men learned that may be important for improving Black male college graduation rates. Finally, the study turns to the participants' candid reflections on what they believed to be the differences between them and their classmates who did not complete college, and the consequences of a one-size-fits-all approach to urban schooling.

The Transition into College

ZOOM IN

Since Glen and Damani were paying for the meal, the young men took advantage of the opportunity to order something from Giordano's Sweet Endings menu. Glen was impressed that, after the heavy meal and multiple pitchers of beer, these young men still had room for chocolate layer cake and s'mores pizza. As they perused the menu, he turned the discussion to their experiences transitioning into college. Damani jumped right in.

ANTWAN: My transition into college was cool. I would say that my transition, socially, was great. I've gotten used to being in different situations and making friends. Different places and making friends. I would say that I didn't manage my time the way I should have. Looking back, if I had a choice, I would do some things over. Just the way I managed my time.

QUENTIN: My transition to college was, as far as the academic standpoint, it was pretty smooth. I was never a 2.0 student. I was always around a 2.5, yeah, the 2.5 range, all the time. I was never looking to, you know, be that academically excellent all the time. But my thing was, basically, controlling myself and not really messing myself up. But the transition from the work, you know, was pretty easy. It's just mostly about controlling myself, being away from home. That was basically it.

WINSTON: My transition to college was more so socially focused. That's pretty much it. It was a scary time because it was the first time being away from mom for that long. And I was the second oldest. So it was like, "Is he going to be the first one gone?" and "How long will they all be gone?" I spent a year at the community college. The first two years were tough. It was tough academically, and me trying to find my spot, because socially I was doing fine. That was probably my biggest patch.

JEFF: My transition was very bumpy. It's crazy because I went from an all-boys school to the university. Coed dorms. Parties every weekend. Alcohol all over the place. Parties. Staying up late. No rules. My transition that first semester—shoot! That first and second semester, that first year of college, was just me trying to figure out what I'm about to do here, or whatever, at college.

ANTWAN: I was open and submissive to a lot of things like parties and stuff like that. And then, again, I was trying to balance and manage the schoolwork at the same time. So, I was just trying to get my footing and get that fantasy out my head. I was just finding myself. I was free. Girls were coming over and spending a night with you—I mean, they were *spending the night with you!* I didn't know how to conduct myself, especially coming from an all-boys school.

REGGIE: I didn't know what I was getting into. I just knew I was going to school. The only thing I was worried about was waking up in the morning. For some reason it wasn't that much work; it was just general ed classes. A lot of chances to get to know each other, networking and stuff like that.

Reggie's comment was all but lost amid the laughter over Antwan's exaggerated statement about women "spending the night" and the off-topic comments and recollections that ensued. It took a while before the conversation got back on track.

ANTWAN: I don't think I had many concerns. I was more excited. I was just ready to go. I was ready to escape all the violence, all the financial home troubles, and just escape all the BS. Just anxious to start my own life. I was ready to start the next chapter. I think the transition was fairly smooth. I wasn't even thinking about graduation. I was just thinking that I had freedom. I was just looking at the incentives, like girls and a job.

QUENTIN: I wasn't studying enough. I still watched too much TV, so I had to eliminate a certain amount of things. I had a social life. I was involved with two or three organizations on campus already. I didn't eliminate the organization part of it, but I just eliminated probably a party or something like that. Spent more time on the weekends going to the library, looking over reading materials, doing it with someone else so I wasn't doing it alone, seeking the resources that I was given. Using the resources to my advantage. It was just a huge adjustment period where I needed to make sure I maintained my spot [at the university].

Quentin's admission about not "studying enough" struck a chord with the group. They all had something to say about the academic challenges they faced during their early college years.

JEFF: You know, I wasn't really prepared. I wasn't entirely prepared for college-level work. I wasn't ready for the amount of work that I was about to get hit with. I wasn't ready for how the work was going to come. I wasn't ready for particular terms that were getting dropped on me. I wasn't ready for a lot of stuff. I didn't study like I needed to study. I wasn't taking work as serious as I needed to be, partially because I was in my whole "I'm free" type stage, you know, freedom. So that's partially to blame on myself. That was my first-year transition. Paying for it. Academics. Staying on point so I don't get kicked out. And that was it, really. I wasn't really worried about anything else.

REGGIE: I thought I was prepared, but I wasn't. I had certain things I knew, but there was some things I just wasn't ready for. I wasn't good at studying. I learned how to study. I learned my own process of studying. I wasn't good at getting up for eight o'clock classes. I had to learn how to get up—ain't nobody going to wake me up! How to do homework when it's due, not last minute. I learned a lot. I learned how to do homework before it's done so I don't have to worry about it, and that gives me more freedom.

WINSTON: Just piss poor. First year, first semester, I took a stats class, and that just, like, bent me over backwards right there. It was terrible. I failed that fantastically. It was a fantastic fail. I really didn't know what I was doing. I had all the books and everything. They cost me a grip. Barely used any of them—one of the biggest scams in America, to be honest. And that was the thing, I just wasn't ready. I don't think I was really applying myself to what it is to study for that. Like I said, in high school it came to me, it was like clockwork. It was fine for me, it was all fine and dandy, and it was great.

JEFF: It was just me trying to get adjusted to studying, getting my study habits on point, my work habits, task management, my time in order. I had to figure out what type of student am I going to be. What type of person am I going to be in college? What type of person am I going to be known for? It was a rough transition period, but it worked out smoothly.

ANTWAN: I *felt* very prepared. I still didn't know what to expect, but I felt prepared. But I looked at things different though. I feel like the schools everywhere in America is held to a low standard. I have friends from Japan and all over the world, and the way they think is just so different than us. If we had the same things around us and we could learn different languages—they say that's when you learn most, while you're developing. I feel like we're getting cheated. I feel like we're learning things in grammar school and high school that won't help us in the long run. We should learn accounting and how to run a company and real real-world stuff that will help us be successful in the real world.

Glen and Damani knew that Antwan was often misperceived as aloof, even withdrawn. They knew him to be quite an observant and intuitive young man and, at times, even quite the jokester. In his strong statement about learning "real-world stuff" they saw a different side of him, a new confidence and assertiveness. Glen could see how going away to college had helped him grow and mature.

ANTWAN: I did what I always do. Whenever I'm challenged academically, I work—I don't learn from a teacher. For me, I learn better from reading the book, like a textbook, and doing problems and examples. Go over some examples and [go to class] to hear the finer details that you might miss in the book, and have a question or two to ask. Other than that, I did most of my learning myself in my room or at the library. That's how I operate. That's how I overcame my challenges. If I had a challenge, I would just take more time out to go over the information. I would be staying up late.

WINSTON: Transition-wise, I felt prepared work-wise. I didn't feel prepared structural-wise. I didn't know who to talk to. I felt like Urban Prep tried to prepare you for the work, and will remind you that you're not ready for college-level work but will not remind you of just the basic survival skills. You just had to already have those survival skills going to college. A lot of people who went out of state realized that they didn't have them. Urban Prep made it feel like everyone's college experience would be kind of the same. The transition, it was a major struggle, because there were some things that in high school that you kind of get by with, but there are things that in that transition you find out, no, it's not okay, and I will get caught, and it's just not going to happen.

JEFF: I didn't really know what to expect before I got to college. I was still kind of waiting for that first day to see what it would be like. And, most importantly, I knew I'd have to seek out new sources. I thought I was ready, but I found out I wasn't. I actually had to see what other people were doing and mimic what they were doing just to try to be successful. I saw other people taking notes, so I took notes. Even though I took notes, I didn't read them. I didn't read them because I didn't see that. I only did what I saw. I thought that in my mind—Somewhere in my mind I thought if I took the notes I'd be okay. I didn't do nothing after that, after taking notes. I didn't go back and read them, I didn't rewrite them try to understand and highlight what I didn't understand.

Antwan was about to speak when Reggie halted the conversation. "Wait, I gotta take this call. It's my great-aunt. But I want to hear what you're about to say, Twan." While he took his call, the young men asked Glen and Damani about their families and what they'd been doing since Urban Prep. The two discussed what it was like to earn a PhD, their lives as college professors, and the difference between teaching high school and college. After about ten minutes, Reggie came back to the table. "My bad. Thanks for waiting, bros." Antwan then resumed the conversation by further clarifying the difference between his imagined college life and actually going to college and living that life.

ANTWAN: For me—I can only speak for myself. I feel like if I was just more ready for the responsibility and free time, if I—I didn't know, man. I just realized how [to get stuff done]. I don't think I took everything as serious as I needed to. Freshman year was really easy. Sophomore year was like, "Ok, now you're really in college." I don't think I was ready. I was ready class-wise. Academically-wise I was ready. It wasn't that I couldn't do the work. I just wasn't ready for the college experience. Just going, seeing colleges was cool. You know they're there, they exist, what they look like. Actually *being* in college is a whole different thing.

Building on this point, Glen asked them to talk about what actions they took to overcome some of the difficulties, academic and otherwise, that they had during the transition.

ANTWAN: I hung out with a bunch of upperclassmen. They taught me a lot. They taught me what college was about from their first experience and things they dealt with. They talked about their classes and their grades and all the things they did bad, what teacher and classes to take, how to beat the system when I needed to—just basic college guidance.

WINSTON: So, like, if I had a problem with my writing, I had friends who were majors in English. They helped me. I'm on the newspaper. I struggle, but I have people to help me, and so I'm not afraid to actually ask for assistance, because that's the point where you fall, if you are too prideful to ask or to admit that you need help. You're not going to grow if you don't admit that you need help. Taking that opportunity to actually ask for assistance, take advantage of the tools that the school has, and utilizing it to the fullest abilities and whatnot.

JEFF: I was in a couple of organizations my freshman year. Minority Leadership Group, that's what it was. Just a group of minorities on campus I used to meet with every week. Discuss stuff. Discuss issues with the police.

REGGIE: At the freshman orientation I met this young man named Ron. We stayed in the same dorm. I stayed on the first floor, he stayed on the fourth floor. And we grew from there. We're still friends. And we helped push each other. We became best friends. Our families know each other and everything, and that's something I cherish about our friendship. Yeah, we held each other accountable. I went to him and I just let everything out. Once I let it out I was able to breathe. I felt like it was a new beginning. I just breathed. I feel much better than I ever have before, really. I can say that. Yeah. He had his mother. They were very good. Even though she was a single parent, she did what she had to do, just like any other type of mom. He wasn't feeling how I felt. I was dealing with a lot of family stuff in college.

Damani then posed the question, "So how did Urban Prep help with this transition, guys? What would you say it contributed to your adjustment to college in your freshman and sophomore years?"

JEFF: I think Urban Prep in general kind of set up the tone for what I wanted to do when I got to college. Just, you know, the whole system of black males succeeding. That's something that I saw Urban Prep doing with all black students, so when I got to college that was the first thing I asked them, I was like, "What's a group you know on campus that's full of black men trying to do something?"

QUENTIN: Yeah, I relied a lot on Alumni Affairs at Urban Prep. The Alumni Affairs was definitely supportive of making sure I performed better in classes and making sure I maintained my spot.

WINSTON: I received financial support from Urban Prep one time, just the mental and spiritual support from family and church members just telling me to keep going. I would say besides helping me that one time, very little. It's not their fault, they've reached out. Once I was done with Urban Prep, I just wanted to be done.

ZOOM OUT

For four years these young men had recited the UP Creed, and they did indeed "believe." They believed that they were prepared for college life and all the experiences to follow. There was not much in the interview data to suggest that these young men were necessarily afraid of the obstacles they might face in college.

Having attended a college prep high school, they believed that all that they'd heard and seen about college life in high school would mirror their actual college experience. It was the reality of managing their newfound freedoms responsibly, negotiating their time effectively, balancing a social life with studying, identifying important campus resources, and acquiring the life (or "survival") skills necessary for sustaining academic success that was most taxing for these young men early on in their to college transition.

It was in their first year of college that they came to understand the stark differences between the messages they had internalized about academic achievement as young Black men and the realities of new and demanding academic expectations. Considering the extant literature on Black men's adjustments to racist campus environments, I expected these young men, many of whom attended predominantly White institutions, to have more to say about adjusting to racist campus environments.[1] Interestingly, though, most of these young men did not describe their transitions in terms of feelings of racial and/or cultural isolation. The stories they did have of racism were not the moments of "surprise" they disclose. This makes some sense considering the strong racial socialization these young men received from adult Black men at Urban Prep.

In their study of Black male undergraduates' college transitions, Shaun Harper and Chris Newman's describe students' "surprise and sensemaking."[2] The young men in their study who had "seamless starts" in college were most enabled by their strong "academic and social preparation." Conversely, those who experienced the most turbulent transitions felt "academically underprepared." The high-achieving Black male collegians who transitioned smoothly emphasized that their high schools had managed to simulate the college academic environment, which prepared them for the rigors of college curriculum and life.[3] Moreover, Harper and Newman contend that young men with strong preexisting networks and access to precollege programs or first-year college transition programs are also much better prepared for the social challenges of the transition into college. Robert Palmer and Estelle Young and others also confirm that preexisting relationships have a substantial influence on assisting underprepared Black collegians to become academically successful in their early college years.[4]

Furthermore, the transition to college represented a newfound "freedom" for the young men. Urban Prep always described its students' futures by placing college at the center. Also, external factors beyond the control of these young men, such as their family income or overexposure to street violence, restricted the ways they expended their agency. As a result, the young men had very little space in their lives to dream, to create, or to imagine a future different from the strong messages they'd received about going to college from adults at Urban Prep. So the experience of feeling "free" in college was new and invigorating. College was the first time they felt truly able to make decisions of their own volition, with few external forces manipulating, constraining, or controlling those decisions. It was the first time they got to determine who they wanted to be(come) and the life they wanted to live without the noise of the South Side, their families, or Urban Prep.

Self-determination represents the opportunities young people retain to exercise autonomy over their own actions, decisions, and desires, aside from the control imposed on them by external factors.[5] Autonomy is not the same as agency, which centers on one's active decision making; autonomy is the freedom to make those decisions. Until they enrolled in college, these young men had little autonomy in determining how they would subjectively interact with the social world. Neighborhood conditions in the young men's childhoods, and the struggles brought on by poverty, influenced what they could and could not do growing up. They did not have the autonomy to venture freely into certain neighborhoods in the city, to wear certain clothes, or to engage fluidly with certain individuals in their neighborhoods.

Compounding such restrictions outside of school, Urban Prep was similarly restrictive to the young men's autonomy. From day one, the school dictated how they were to behave, dress, and interact with one another, adults, and guests to the school. The school determined for them that college would be their expected end, and thus, everything they were told to do in high school was intended to get them there. They were also provided a model of "successful" Black manhood that they were strongly encouraged to emulate. At fourteen, boys were socialized to become the "young men of Urban Prep." Many of their UP experiences centered on making them men and preparing them for the difficulties faced by Black men in America.

But lost, or neglected, somewhere in the shroud of good intentions was the fact that these young men were still boys. They were adolescents who, at an early age, were being remade into the image of young men. This too often occurs in a social world where Black boys are already imagined as grown-ups far sooner than White children are considered adults. Unlike White youth, young Black boys (and Black children) do not get to enjoy a childhood with the freedom to dream and self-determine.

Michael Dumas and Joseph Derrick Nelson contend that Black boyhood has been rendered "unimagined and unimaginable."[6] Black boys are too often envisioned in the mainstream as adults and are subsequently treated as such by the criminal justice system, as just one example. Their innocence is snatched away, and others, like the police officer who killed Tamir Rice, feel justified in handling them like adults. Moreover, Black boys' interactions with authority outside of school even cause them to begin adultifying themselves. This is a protective mechanism necessary for preserving their own dignity. There is much research that suggests the ways young Black boys have been adultified in school by educators.[7] Most poignantly, Ann Arnett Ferguson demonstrates how schools make Black boys into criminals. She points out the significant impact they have on creating, regulating, and shaping Black boys' identities.[8] This adultification significantly impedes opportunities Black boys have available to them to just *be*—to play without inhibition, to create, and to live freely in the moment. James Earl Davis underscores this impossibility of Black boyhoods when he insists that even in early childhood, schools too often "ignore [Black boys'] aspirations, disrespect their ability to learn, fail to access and cultivate their many talents, and impose a restrictive range of options."[9] Childhood is the time when young people begin self-determining, but this time seems to be cut short for Black boys as society and schools place more and more restrictions on their bodies.

This is especially true in "college for all" charter schools proliferating in predominantly Black and Latinx school communities. These schools are established under the guise that they are providing better schooling options for young people and are organized to minimize occasions for Black youth to self-determine.[10] Yet these environments feel restrictive and controlling. Urban Prep is no exception. It used most of the time available in a school day to catch the young men up on the academic and social skills administrators and faculty thought would prepare them to be successful in college. This, and all the eyes watching them as the first graduates of the school, imposed on the young men in this study tremendous pressure to perform academically without giving them the space in which to practice acting out the fullness of who *they* wanted to become and the passions *they* wanted to pursue. White supremacist logic requires that Black bodies remain under control; institutions must determine *for them* where they go, what they do, and how they act. But this is not just about what White people do; Black educators are also complicit in such a system.[11]

An important aspect of the freedom of self-determination in the first year of college for these young men had to do with the autonomy they felt in taking back control of their own bodies. Many of them were not strangers to trauma. Feeling safe—not having to navigate the common risk associated with the urban environments where they were raised—made the transition to college one they looked forward to and then enjoyed. The freedom of being on a college campus because of their own desire and aspiration to live in the moment and figuring out for themselves how their bodies would be maneuvered in this new space were tremendous benefits of going to college. That is not to say that in one broad stroke issues of racism and other invisible threats on the college campus vanished, or that they were not aware of their social location in this new shared collegiate space. My assertion is that their college transition afforded them a greater awareness of the control they now had over their own bodies, and that awareness felt new, unfamiliar, liberating.

The young men's reflections on the freedom they felt once they'd managed—or survived—the transition into college raise questions about how it impacted their UP classmates who couldn't manage the transition, who did not complete college. I wonder how this newfound self-determination allowed some young men to, for the first time, disavow their choice to go to college and to leave their neighborhoods. Given how strong the college-going culture was at Urban Prep, it is not outside the realm of possibility that there was a cadre of young men who felt manipulated—maybe by the school, maybe by their families—to go to college. Others may have gone only to avoid marginalization at Urban Prep for choosing an alternate postsecondary pathway. Either way, these young men's revelations about their transitions to college are quite instructive.

Obstacles and Roadblocks to College Completion

ZOOM IN

Dessert finally arrived. After a few bites, the sugar kicked in and reenergized the conversation. The men resumed their tales of the numerous pitfalls and obstacles they faced—and overcame—in college. Finances, family drama, academic probation, personal health challenges—all of these, at one time or another, posed very real threats to them achieving their higher education goal.

QUENTIN: I always worried about how I was going to pay for the next semester. You know, that stressed me a lot, how I was going to pay. And, uh, with me being homesick, you know, wanting to come back home was there too. That's where I really stressed myself a lot, about, my freshman year, how I was going to pay for it, because I know my mother couldn't afford it. So, uh, that was my only thing, how I was going to be able to afford to do this all over again.

REGGIE: My biggest fear was staying in school. Everyone pushes the issue of money is going to be the issue for school. That's a number-one issue with school, money, and I was afraid. They pushed it [at Urban Prep], teachers. Everybody had their own issues to be back in school. It's always a money issue.

ANTWAN: I would like to have gotten to have graduated in May with the rest of my class, on time. And I was homeless. I didn't have a meal plan. Didn't have my tuition paid, so I couldn't register for classes. I was going around talking to everybody, the president, the head of the departments, everything like, "I got nowhere to go. My aunt dropped me off. I'm trying to finish."

JEFF: Sometimes it was getting back and forth to college. I didn't have a lot of money to pay the bills, and for taking trips back and forth during breaks.

ANTWAN: So, I lost my scholarship. My GPA dropped below a 3.0. One year I didn't have the money to be at school. I couldn't take out the loans or anything like that for it. Mr. Thompson, he's in the math and science department. I was talking to him over the summer. Calling people, trying to figure out what I can do. He actually found me money for my tuition and for housing. Him and Miss Martinez, they definitely looked out for me, keeping me in school so I could finish up. Besides that, my aunt, she's been a big help. She let me store all my stuff that I'm not using at her place. After classes started, we eventually got some money so I could register for classes. It was like, "Cool. I'm in school now. I'm going to take my classes." Still didn't have a place to stay for a little bit after that. Eventually I got some money, found a place I could stay off campus. God was working. Everything worked out.

Financial challenges posed a formidable threat to these young men's college completion. Glen remembered seeing one of his former UP students, one of the young men's classmates, working at a local Walgreens the fall after his graduation from Urban Prep. When Glen asked him why he hadn't enrolled in college, the young man said that he didn't have the money. But money wasn't the only obstacle.

REGGIE: Freshman year of college was the same as freshman year of high school. That's when I was dealing with finding out who my biological father was. Then I took the semester off. I put myself behind. And I'm not faulting anyone. I did it myself. I blame myself. I don't blame no one else. It's okay, because everything happens for a reason.

JEFF: I was living so far from home. I was leaving a lot of things behind. My sister was sick at the time. I didn't want her to pass while I was gone. That was a big concern of mine. Those were my main concerns. She actually didn't pass until that break I took. Getting back into college was, I felt, a turning point in my life, because before then I had health problems with my back and everything. I just felt like everything was just at a downward motion. It started to just plateau for a while.

WINSTON: I had to leave college for a year, I had go with my tail between my legs and tell Mr. Wright and Mr. Davis [a UP college counselor and founding teacher] and those guys that were in charge of that department, "Hey, they just kicked me out of school, what do I do?" After a while, Mr. Wright, he hits me up, he like, "Yo, what's going on? What are you up to? What are you doing?" I'm like, "To be honest, Mr. Wright, nothing, but I want to get back into school. I don't like just sitting here. I don't like not doing anything." He came back to me not even probably a week later with several options for me. He helped me pay, even to get my transcripts from my last school. He pulled together the funds to pay for book loan fees and things like that.

JEFF: Going back to school was a new chapter in my life. I felt like there was still hope for me somewhere. I still have time to be successful and make something of myself, being able to support my family, my parents, anybody that I can who might walk in my path. I feel like everyone who's come to my life has been there for some reason. There's a reason everyone was in my life. I'm learning more to not try to understand the reason they're there but to take advantage of the time that they're there, while they're there. I'm taking advantage more of the opportunities that I have. Sometimes I didn't know what to do. That's when I got that phone call giving me an option. I got an e-mail giving me an option of things I could be doing. I feel like I'm real fortunate to be given the opportunities that I've been given. It didn't cost me a lot of money to get those opportunities. That's basically it.

WINSTON: Yeah, I left for freshmen year like, "Yo, I'm going to get it in four years. Boom! In and out. I'm going to have opportunity, come out on top, it's a wrap." It didn't happen. When I got kicked out the first time, I was definitely discouraged because I felt like I let a lot of people down. It's because of being involved with all those things, being on MSNBC, being on NPR, CNN—all of those things, saying all those things on the air. All of those people, they all had a sense of belief. I had to finish.

It was clear that these young men gave a lot of thought to what failing would mean for their families and all of the people who had invested in them. But life happened. And when it did, the young men had to decide what they were going to do and who they could call for support. These stories of persistence were further examples of the resilience and community cultural wealth instilled in these young men on Chicago's South Side, that they took with them to college. Quentin was inspired at this moment in the discussion to say more about what he perceived to be Urban Prep's role in his college persistence.

QUENTIN: And I'd say Urban Prep really got me far, because it was their conversations with me about financial aid and admissions. They got me in the door. And if I hadn't really gotten that help to get in the door, you know—it was stuff that my mama didn't know how to do, and that my aunts didn't know how to do, because they never experienced it.

WINSTON: I would just get random Facebook messages. "Hey, how's it going, Winston? What is you up to?" Or, "I heard this, I heard this. What's going on?" I'm like, that's perfect. I haven't talked to you myself, but here you are reaching out. It's a network. It's all still a network. To be honest, I don't know of anybody in any other school whose teachers or professors, or ex-teachers, will reach out to them and be like, "Hey, what's going on?"

REGGIE: Without Urban Prep I would not be in school. I don't know where I would be, quite honestly. I don't know where I would be.

JEFF: That's definitely my backbone—my mentors and my family. I mean, totally my family. They set the tone. They really set the tone. Urban Prep definitely set the tone for what it means to go to college. Stay in college, graduate, and do your thing after. You know, they check in on us or whatever from time to time. I get checked in on every once in a while to see how things are going with me. I need to ask for some money or whatever, but they've done their part. I don't know how, but they're there in a sense, I guess. I don't want to say that Urban Prep as a whole, but particularly teachers have played their part.

ANTWAN: A couple of times, I needed help in paying the rent due to me being unemployed. A person from the alumni office helped me out a couple of times in my freshman year with talking to my professors. Mr. Wright has helped out too. He even reached out to one of my professors. He couldn't really do much, though. Still, Mr. Wright did a lot to help. When I was going through my whole scholarship ordeal, losing my scholarship, he came down there, actually, to talk to some people for me and a couple other students that were in school with me who didn't end up graduating. He definitely helped out a lot, connecting me with people, finding out who I needed to talk to.

JEFF: I had to make changes that forced me to drop out and everything. I wasn't going to go back, but Mr. Dickens actually contacted me and asked me what I was doing? I told him, "I'm not in school right now." I wanted to go back to school. I wasn't thinking about going back to school where I was going at the time. I knew I wanted to do something, but I didn't know how to go about doing it because I was—I felt I tried to do stuff on my own, independently. That's when I found out that I can actually ask for help. I don't have to be ashamed about asking for help.

QUENTIN: Like, I could have simply sold drugs. I could have simply, you know, stole or robbed somebody for the money that I really needed. But instead of doing that, if I really need it for positive things, [the adults at Urban

Prep] would give it to me out of their pockets. So, I really didn't have to go do nothing stupid to get it, because, you know, like, I asked for it. So, I asked for something that I could get, instead of going doing something stupid and regret it for the rest of my life.

The seven men recognized in each other's stories just how much they had in common specific to the various obstacles they had overcome and the shared values and internal motivators that enabled their college persistence.

ANTWAN: Just like when I failed that class three times. That last time I took it, I passed it—finally! I didn't give up. I kept going to tutoring, and I kept getting help. I learned not to get caught up in the social life, and to just put first things first. Just get my work done.

QUENTIN: I just had to, you know, basically, have faith. I pin most of my worries on my faith and just, you know—God sent me here for a reason. So, if He's going to take it from me, I guess it wasn't meant to be. Or, you know, if He had me stay here, it was meant to be. So that's all I left with Him.

REGGIE: I studied more. I actually talked to people in my classes more. I asked for help. I went to tutoring. I took everything very serious because I had been through dropping out of school for a semester, and that's something I don't want to go through again. Like I said, I really don't care about not graduating on time, as long as I get what I came for.

JEFF: No, staying in college was all me. The high school, I credit them for getting me in the door. That's what I felt like. That was their job. It wasn't their job to—I don't feel like it was their job to get me *through* college. It was their job to get me in the door and make that entrance as easy as possible, that transition as easy as possible the best way they knew how.

QUENTIN: I also had to realize how many resources we had on campus. Just asking for help. My adviser, she actually introduced me to a lot of resources that was on campus and having mentors in college and things like that. And just asking my family for help if I needed help. I felt like that really helped me when it came to college and just overcoming those challenges and opportunities. Whenever I needed help, I'd go out there, because they're willing to help you. But some people, they're scared to go ask for the help. And then when they're scared to ask, they end up failing, and things like that. And, you know, mental support, motivation, you know, it was having—It was my mother's plan to go to college, and I was my grandma's first grandchild to go to college. I had a lot of pressure from that.

Glen motioned the passing waiter for the check. "I know we've got to get ready to roll, but I have just one more question. What else—what other factors were important in helping you get through college?"

JEFF: I wanted to be in [a Black fraternity], and I knew you needed a certain GPA, so I started focusing. I got my schedules together. When you plan on taking a nap. When you plan on eating. When you plan on working out. When you plan on going to study hours.

QUENTIN: That's the last thing. If I dropped out, I feel like I'm going to let a lot of people down, especially at Urban Prep, because they had so much hope in me.

JEFF: My sister! Because even though she was dealing with breast cancer, she still went to school. She got a degree. It was a certificate or something for dental assistant or something. Just seeing her, everything that she went through, and basically just overlooking that to still get what she wanted, that was really influential, because that was the only person that was close to me who went to some type of college.

ZOOM OUT

The young men's primary roadblocks to college completion were financial, academic, and personal in nature. Concern for their family members' health and well-being, as well as their own internal conflicts, took a toll on these young men during their college years. Jeff described how difficult it was to manage the demands of school and at the same time deal with his sister's failing health, and Reggie spoke of the emotional toll of learning the identity of his father. Such obstacles and distractions are not unfamiliar in the literature on Black male college persistence.[12] Many of the young men who participated in this research study described themselves as having grown up in a low-income family and as having few people in their personal network outside of UP who were college educated. In this regard, Urban Prep played an important role in providing and instilling values that the young men would need to complete college, such as "dedication, commitment, and focus." These values are not easily measured, but they are just as important as a young person's book knowledge.

The young men's regular, ongoing personal interactions with, and exposure to, college-educated Black men while they were in high school helped foster their self-determination in college—after they decided that they were committed to finishing their undergraduate degree. Moreover, the school provided its students with a safety network of financial, emotional, and counseling support that the young men relied on to navigate a number of personal setbacks. Urban Prep's Alumni Affairs Office stands out as an important component in the school's design. It supports the school's aim to provide its graduates the necessary provisions needed to help them complete college. As these young men indicated, much of their engagement with UP faculty and counselors after high school was social. The young men valued the kinship they'd developed with these adult men and women and made numerous references to former teachers and other UP-affiliated persons who kept in touch. The work of individuals in the Alumni Affairs unit to advocate for the young men and help them solve problems, like how to pay for school, also contributed to these young men's college persistence. This engagement, however, does raise a concern about the sustainability of such a department as the number of UP graduates on its three campuses continues to grow. And, certainly, given the financial duress urban school districts like Chicago Public Schools are under, it certainly does not seem feasible for such a model to proliferate at traditional neighborhood high schools.

It's important to remember that these young men were a cohort of UP's first graduates who were now college graduates. There were no alumni from Urban Prep on their college campuses for them to network with. Research confirms that peer networks, or "peer pedagogies," strengthen Black students' college persistence.[13] The young men in the study recognized how important a social network of Black men was for keeping them in school. Jeff, for example, insisted on finding the Black men's group on campus during his early college transition. Now that there have been more graduating classes, UP is utilizing its alumni base to augment its efforts at supporting its graduates' college retention and persistence.

Young Black men's academic preparation for college, including their participation in precollege or summer bridge programs, should begin as early as middle school.[14] Also, access to adequate financial aid and resources and a network of generous, supportive relationships can enable them to respond productively to adverse personal life events.[15] These factors help determine who finishes college and who leaves without a degree.

Terrell Strayhorn, Royel Johnson, and Blossom Barrett's study of young Black men confirms that struggles in their childhood prepare them for struggles they may face later in life.[16] For the graduates of Urban Prep, the resilience they began developing as young boys, in part because of mama's struggle and their own struggles to safely navigate the South Side, were essential in strengthening their resolve to complete college. These young men had something to prove—first to themselves and second to the world. They decided, as part of their self-determination, that they would finish college despite any number of obstacles in their path. They persevered through various setbacks, which included getting kicked out of school and later returning to finish. They learned to identify campus resources that would enable their academic success and cultivate peer and mentoring relationships that buffered other social barriers to their college completion.

To Finish or Not to Finish

ZOOM IN

An uncomfortable silence had came over the group when Glen asked, "What do you think are the differences between you and your classmates who did not complete college?" Jeff and Winston leaned back in their chairs. Reggie looked away from the group, out into the crowded restaurant. Quentin adjusted his baseball cap lower over his eyes. As soon as he asked the question, Glen felt its weight. These young men knew what it felt like to be exceptionalized, to be seen as different from their other Black male friends and family members. They were reluctant to set themselves apart from their Urban Prep brothers. After a few seconds of silence that felt much longer, Quentin responded.

QUENTIN: I just felt like I have more motivation than them. Like they probably don't have that person in their life that pushes them to move forward.

Like I said, I grew up—I saw people go to college. I saw people graduate from college. Like, some people didn't even have that. They don't want to do it because, I don't know, they probably think like it's a waste of time. But I saw it first-hand. I just felt like it was just the motivation I had in my life.

REGGIE: They just didn't have as much support as I do.

WINSTON: If I could tell them, I'd just tell them to go back to the source, because the source [Urban Prep] is there for you. I was telling this to another student, and it was just like, "Look, if you want to get back in school, you've got to want to get back in school, because Urban Prep will help you. Why do you think they flood our inboxes with these "Come to the alumni winter gathering" or "Hey, take this survey?" It's because they care, and they're gathering the data. They're gathering these things to see where you're at, because they meant the mission not only to help us get into college but also to get through it.

JEFF: My family. And just wanting to finish. I don't want to be another dude that tried to get his degree and it didn't happen. So just the mind of just finishing and getting that college degree so I can come back and, you know, say I did it.

QUENTIN: So many people telling me that, "Quentin, I want you to go to college. I want you to succeed." My family and at Urban Prep. They probably didn't have that, and they probably just had Urban Prep to do it, and that probably just wasn't enough for them. They probably just felt like Urban Prep was on their back. They find that Urban Prep would be irritating and things like that, but it's just motivation, motivation that they didn't have, and I thought I had it.

JEFF: Like I said, everybody has a different story. Everybody comes from different areas. So some dudes, you know, you try to be on your books, but you come home and you got a dope dealer there. You got a gang-banging brother. You got an uncle that's got drugs all out. But you got your friends that you mostly around that's selling drugs, and you thinking, you know, "Why am I in college?" That's what they're thinking. That's the mind state. "Why am I in college? So I can get *this* money? When I got friends on the block making more money, you know, than some teachers or my parents, or whatever." I had to battle with that my freshman year, honestly. Just like, "Dang! I'm in college, trying so I can make money." But it's dudes back at home that said,

"Forget school," and they making racks. They using it wrong, but they making money. Just that support system, that environment. Yeah that's what it is, environment, with some people. Definitely the environment with some people.

The waiter brought the bill, allowing the young men to retreat from the slightly uncomfortable conversation for a moment as Glen and Damani reviewed it and produced credit cards. It was interesting how this part of the dinner discussion sharply contrasted with the rest of the conversation. Antwan finally weighed in, subtly shifting the focus back to how individual choices most determine one's educational trajectory.

ANTWAN: They've lost sight of the goal, of the whole plan—like the Creed and everything we fought for and put our time in. They lost sight. I'm not saying I was perfect through it all, but in every situation I still had it in the back of my mind to stay up and not fall off track completely to where I can't get back.

QUENTIN: If they really wanted it, they could have made a situation like what I did. So, the only thing about it is that I felt I really wanted to, you know, graduate from college. I had a point to prove. I really wanted to prove that point, I mean, because I graduated from college.

WINSTON: Also, some of them, they probably just don't want to get it [a degree]. They probably went away to school just to say like, "Hey, I did it, I tried it, it ain't for me," but that's because they're not putting their mind to just saying, like, "Hey, I actually want to try." Some of them would say, "I'm not about going to take out money for nothing." I definitely had to make this work for me.

REGGIE: I don't want to sound like too up there, too clichéd or anything, but only the strong survive. If you want something and you're itching for it you'll make it happen. I feel like that's something I have over a lot of people. My family issues where I come from, that pushed me. That was my pusher. My family was my pusher. My family situation was my pusher. I put myself through counseling. I was afraid to go.

WINSTON: I'm going to put it as bluntly as I can: they don't get it. It's just that mental maturity. You've got to understand that you've messed up, and it's okay to go back and say, "Hey, I failed. Hey, it didn't happen the way I expected it to be."

The young men's tones started to shift away from the apologetic as they thought more about what separated them from other young men in UP's founding class who had not completed college. Their body language even changed. No longer leaning back in their chairs, or slouching over the table, they sat up erectly as they expressed themselves confidently, even assertively.

REGGIE: Everybody can succeed, but they had to take the initiative to show the professors that they wanted to stay. But *they* didn't. It's really on them! I got that letter [of academic probation], I could've easily balled that letter up and went right back to partying. That's as easy as it is. They had a choice. In life you have a choice—you have *your* choice. And they chose not to. And, I'm sorry for them.

WINSTON: I had a little vision and direction of where I was going. Not to say they didn't, but it's kinda hard, and opportunities are pretty slim to get places without a grinding mentality.

JEFF: You just got to be hungry. I learned you got to be hungry out here, or whatever. You know, I'm not going to say that I'm the most hungry person. I'm doing everything I need to do, but I know I'm doing good enough or whatever to where I'm not about to be one of these leaves blowing in the wind.

WINSTON: I just realized that school is what I wanted to do. Obviously, for whatever reason, they decided that school wasn't the best choice for them. I can't say that makes them lesser people, because we all have to live with the consequences of our choices, good or bad. I believe that this just wasn't the opportunity that they felt would prepare them for work. No matter how many opportunities you miss in life, there's always another one around the corner. That's why when I see people who don't have anything in life, I used to think that I was just blessed all the time and I would literally have anxiety about why I have so many good things happening in my life.

JEFF: I have somewhat of a vision for where I see myself future-wise. I'm more of a long-term thinker, as opposed to a lot of my friends, my classmates, who are not in school now. Their views are real narrow and just trying to look at how to get money right now, being successful right now. I'm looking more at long term, because I want to be able to make a family that I never had, and get them opportunities that I've never had. That's what any parent would want to do for their child. My Dad always told me his job isn't complete until I'm doing better than he's doing. He don't feel like his job is complete until I surpass what he's done. I just have that mentality for my family-to-come, in the future.

The waiter returned with the checks—"Thanks for joining us this evening, gentlemen," he said as he started clearing the table. Although it was time to go, the conversation had picked back up, the young men's hesitation had subsided. The more they thought about it, the more adamant they became about the significance of intrinsic, rather than extrinsic, motivations for their college persistence.

WINSTON: There are some people who struggle, but there's a very select few people who just struggle all the time and just can't seem to catch a break. What helped me to be more comfortable receiving the stuff that I receive is knowing that everybody has the same opportunity. They just might not want to take that one. A lot of my reasoning for staying [in college] is not to make Urban Prep proud. It's for me to accomplish the goals that I have set for myself. I appreciate them for being used in a good way as a positive influence but at the end of the day, it's about, "What does Winston want, and how hard is Winston willing to work to accomplish the goals that he has set for himself?" That's how I see it.

ANTWAN: I just feel like they ain't seek the support like that, 'cause it's out there.

WINSTON: For people who aren't in school right now, the difference is just I saw school as something I wanted to do, and they saw school as something that they didn't want to do or couldn't afford, or whichever. I feel like, again, a lot of the ones that I heard of—because I honestly don't keep up with their information—but the ones that I heard of [who didn't finish college], unfortunately I wasn't really surprised. I wasn't surprised that they weren't in school, because those were the individuals that were being carried through high school. And so at some point, again, you have to let go of the hand, and they can't go to school with you.

The waiter returned with the boxed pizza. The men pushed back their chairs in a move to leave. Quentin put on his coat, preparing to face the winter waiting outside the restaurant. Damani, noticing that he hadn't participated much in this part of the discussion, asked, "Quentin, what would you say is the biggest difference between you and other guys who didn't finish school?"

QUENTIN: I don't know. The biggest difference between me and those guys is that they probably are working full time now to make ends meet. Their life scenario is different than mine. Maybe they financially couldn't afford college, so they had to work it off for a while and then go back. I don't think that their mentality is much different from mine. I don't think that they're not as smart as I am or anything like that. I just feel like their life scenario is just different from mine. They didn't have the same opportunities that I had, so they had to work with whatever they had.
ANTWAN: Yeah, but you can't make excuses, you can't talk about the block, because it's people dealing with those issues. And if you wanted to be in college, then you would. They don't want it. Like, for me, this was it. I don't see nothing else. And that's how you have to do it. Treat going to college like you ain't got no other obstacles. But, then again, you don't know their situation and stuff like that. I wish them boys the best.
WINSTON: You have to be proactive. If this is not something that you want— You have to personally want it. If you don't want it, you are not going to be able to stay. You have to be active in your learning.
ANTWAN: At the end of the day, I don't think there's anything different— there's nothing different between us. I feel like I might just know myself better or more than they do. Or it could just be that I'm more motivated to do this. Or it could just be that I don't have as many distractions in my life as they might. I can never tell you without talking to them. Like, "What happened? Why are you not here anymore?" Because it's not like I got the finances either.

The men walked away from the table and toward the door. Damani said, "I'm so glad y'all took a little time to hang with us old guys." "Speak for yourself!" Glen joked. "In all seriousness, fellas, this has been great. Reconnecting with you guys has been good for the soul."

Outside the restaurant, in the cold Chicago night, the men shared goodbye handshakes and hugs before heading off in different directions. Glen and Damani watched them go and then began their slow walk south on Michigan Avenue.

ZOOM OUT

These young men's views about the differences between them and their classmates who did not finish college reflect the tension between a philosophy of success based on individual merit and one that is rooted in a greater sense of communalism. Black educators have always insisted that education work for the collective advancement and uplift of *all* Black people.[17] This orientation grows out of concerns over the imperatives of preparing Black youth to face the harsh social, political, and economic realities of living in an anti-Black society that privileges White interests and cultural norms. As such, an important principle of Black education has been to teach young people "community"—how to think with others, to appreciate and find ways to lift each other so that every other person in the community finds success.

Individualism and competition are mainstream, capitalist ideologies that run counter to more Afrocultural learning orientations centered on cooperation and verve.[18] UP's rewards system, for instance, reinforced Eurocentric conceptions of success in its focus on competition and individual achievement, even though it was intended to increase students' motivation and engagement. Disentangling an individualist philosophy from one that is more community oriented requires school leaders to recognize that there are numerous structural, social, political, and institutional forces that significantly impact the achievement trajectory of poor students and students of color. An orientation that centers self in the pursuit of postsecondary success also fails to sufficiently acknowledge the creativity, passion, and agency that young Black men and boys bring to the classroom before they're ever told that college is a postsecondary option.

My experience working at Urban Prep, considered alongside these young men's narratives, suggests that Black adult stakeholders (teachers, school leaders, board members, founders, families, staff, etc.) care deeply about the holistic well-being of the young men Urban Prep serves. The organization of the school—the 4 Rs, daily recitation of the Creed, Prides, Community—support this claim, and the young men's testimonies confirm it. These educators take actions similar to the ones taken by Black teachers in the late nineteenth and early twentieth centuries who taught in segregated southern schools, schools where Black students consistently reached their highest potential.[19] Educators at UP are "dedicated, committed, and focused" to building community among the UP student body, staff, and faculty, and school officials emphasize being a "brother's keeper" so that the young men graduate with a great fondness and respect for the brotherhood they develop with other students and adult Black men educators at Urban Prep.

While the brotherhood was important for getting them through high school, the participants in the UPCPS conceded the centrality of independent decision making and intrinsic motivation to their college completion. Many of the young men's comments about their classmates who left college, remarking how leaving may have been their own fault for not being "hungry" or "motivated" enough, imply that completion is chiefly a function of personal will. Reggie, Winston, Quentin, Jeff, and Antwan persisted because they wanted to complete college; those who fell short did not want to complete college. It seems simple: it is up to the individual to determine how and to what degree he will engage with school. The social network—the brotherhood—is only important to the extent that the young men utilize it to bolster their own academic pursuits.

This way of thinking points, once again, to the tremendous agency exercised by these young Black men. But it also makes me wonder, beyond the scope of this study, about the utility of this network for those other young men from UP's founding class who never actually wanted to attend college, or who got there and self-determined that college was not the right choice for them. Did the brotherhood mean as much to these young men? Did they receive the same level of moral support from Alumni Affairs as young men in the UPCPS claimed to have received?

Prior knowledge of these young men and their families leads me to further contemplate how adult stakeholders at Urban Prep selected or identified specific students in whom they invested special support. The young men mentioned the ways that certain voices tended to be more heard, and valued, in the school, and others less so. Winston was particularly vocal in sharing his view that young men with higher grades and more positive relationships with adults in the building tended to get more academic opportunities, rewards, and incentives. So I wonder how UP faculty and staff decided who they would advocate for and to what degree they would follow up to ensure that a young man stayed enrolled in college.

In *Up from Slavery,* Booker T. Washington insists that success is not measured by what one accomplishes but, rather, by what obstacles one has overcome to achieve those accomplishments.[20] Accomplishments include, but are not limited to, graduating from college with an undergraduate degree and beginning a career. Interrogating the ideologies undergirding these young men's conceptions of success is important for better discerning the motivations driving their decision making and the contributing factors that positioned them to achieve success in higher education. Specific accomplishments do not say much about their journeys. Rather, it is a deeper understanding of their journeys (and those of their classmates who did not persist through college) and the process of accomplishing their goals, that is most revealing. The counterstory is instructive for educators committed to ameliorating opportunity gaps and creating learning environments that significantly reduce barriers to every young person's ability to envision their future selves.

Importantly, the best version of their future selves cannot be detached from the place(s) where they grew up or from the people in those communities who have had a noteworthy influence on them. The young men's visible discomfort in articulating this position points to larger tensions between their ideology of success and their cultural roots on Chicago's South Side. They felt extremely uncomfortable being exceptionalized, or viewed as better than their classmates for having completed college. It was awkward for them to think of themselves as smarter or superior because they finished their degrees. How is it that these young men could put so much emphasis on the significance of their own decision making and willpower, yet, at the same time, not want to be perceived as being exceptional? This tension is rooted in a struggle they felt internally to give up part(s) of who they are, their identities as young Black men from the South Side—whatever that means to them—in order to find "success."

This gets to the core of Black educators' failure to acknowledge how our own educational philosophies are rooted in the matrices of oppression we have effectively navigated to become formally educated.[21] A school like Urban Prep, with all of its media attention and celebration, implicitly sends the message that its students are being molded into *better,* or model, Black men who are not lazy, who do not make excuses for their lack of success or access to opportunity—beginning with a faculty full of respectable, "good" Black men these young men could emulate. I was present for early conversations among the UP faculty, Tim King, and the school leaders when we collectively imagined the impact the school might have on the young men and families it would be serving. I do not remember discussing anything like Carter Woodson's call for Black educators to consider how what they do in service to Black youth could reproduce the logic of the oppressor.[22] And there was minimal conversation about how our schooling practices and policies might work to oppose dominant local, place-based social and cultural norms students brought with them to school. We were driven by a fierce passion and sense of purpose. We absolutely believed in these young men, that they could become whatever they wanted to become. When drafting the Creed, for example, we didn't spend much time examining the ideologies underscoring the pledge to "live honestly, nonviolently, and honorably." We never asked, What does living honorably mean for *these* young men in *this* local context? What does living honestly and nonviolently mean in a largely xenophobic, Christian, ableist, homophobic, patriarchal society? We never gave thought to how we were defining and using the language of exceptionality. Yet, this really needed to be interrogated. It mattered how we used this language in our work then to establish the cultural norms of the school. These would be the values our young men would adopt.

Emerging out of this is a dilemma facing any educational institution serving predominantly Black youth: Should we teach Black students to maneuver *within* an oppressive system to achieve success, or is the crux of our responsibility to teach our students to imagine ways they can remake that oppressive system altogether?

Conclusion

These young men struggled with the fear that becoming "successful" (going to college) meant losing friends and family who may not be college educated. They also struggled with imagining themselves as middle class, further distancing them from who and what are familiar. Even in my own experience, becoming more educated has made relating to those who raised me and loved me incredibly complicated. It has been difficult having to develop certain habits in order to facilitate my own educational and professional career trajectory. As the quality of one's life changes, so does that individual's tastes and worldviews. Sometimes this is too hard for family and long-time friends to fully comprehend. It is not their fault. It is not my fault. But it is the fault of an anti-Black, racist society that values credentials over credibility, competency, dependability, and integrity. And even then, for Black people, those credentials still can't save us.

This is not a critique of Urban Prep as much as it is a critique of an education system, and a society, that privileges certain ways of being over and above diverse others. Many Black educators, and those educating Black youth, feel the pressure to make our kids fit in, because "it's just the way things are around here." It is important for us to start to think a little differently about concepts of success and what we as educators can do to prepare urban youth to achieve it. A bend toward justice requires encouraging resistance to the status quo and other structures that place limitations on young people's expressions of their full humanity. This requires some courage and some risk taking, but the future of this country depends on us figuring it out.

6

Reimagining the P–20 Education Pipeline for Young Black Men and Boys

with Derrick R. Brooms,
Associate Professor of Sociology,
University of Louisville

The narratives produced from the Urban Prep College Persistence Study appropriately contextualize the factors that most influenced these young Black men's education trajectories to and through college. Analyses of these young men's stories reveal a plethora of noncognitive and institutional factors that enabled them to stay "dedicated, committed, and focused" in achieving their education goals. These young men's indomitable determination to be successful, their agency to act in ways that support their goals, the numerous lessons they learned and internalized after attending Urban Prep, and their access to a strong social network were key factors enabling them to ultimately complete college. Their narratives add appreciably to the ways we might think about and approach urban schooling, and encourage us to think more critically about improving the opportunities available to young Black men and boys as they move along the education pipeline.

Anti-Blackness and Structural Impediments to Young Black Men and Boys' Academic Success Along the P–20 Education Pipeline

There is no strengthening or fixing an already broken P–20 education pipeline. This "broken P–20 education pipeline" is the range of violent, dysfunctional, culturally assaultive schooling environments and educational experiences young Black men and boys (and other culturally diverse youth) endure over the course of their pre-K through high school education, as well as in any postsecondary study in formal school settings. These are school cultures and pedagogies that consistently fail to appreciate, acknowledge, account for, and/or appropriately respond to diverse students' interests or curiosities, cultural diversity, and/or learning styles/preferences.

Suggesting that contemporary public education, especially in high-poverty communities serving racially, ethnically, and linguistically diverse youth, can simply be "strengthened" indicates a disavowal of the original intention of US public schooling to subordinate non-White people to a permanent working class.[1] Furthermore, refusing to concede that today's public education in urban school settings is *not* meeting the needs of all Black (male) youth—in light of voluminous evidence of persistent opportunity gaps and the widening of achievement gaps—implies a belief that public education institutions are performing in just the ways they were imagined (with the intended outcomes intact). And believing that today's public education system *is* working places the burden of responsibility for Black students' academic underperformance on the students themselves (or their families), implying that it's because of where they're growing up rather than the public schools they're attending.

Education as a social institution needs to be *reimagined* as something entirely different. This means reenvisioning the aims of schooling in segregated communities of color ravaged by decades of neglect. This work hinges on firm institutional commitments to actively disrupt the systemic inequity felt by every member of the school community. A first step might be learning to center the most marginalized students in institutional policy making and practice. These are the students who are multiply subordinated, individuals who daily experience forms of oppression unique to the intersections of race with multiple other social identities (e.g., Black Muslim queer woman).

Reimagining education begins with contemplating the pain and suffering Black people endure just by virtue of being Black and living in America.[2] Because anti-Blackness has had such a profound impact on the ways that Black people have historically experienced public schooling, it is necessary to recreate education and thus improve outcomes as students move along the education pipeline by honoring, extending, and affirming Blackness *explicitly*. This includes preparing young people to reject dominant social and cultural norms in formal school settings so that their own cultural ways of being are regularly honored. Recognizing the implications of anti-Blackness on students' schooling experiences demands that educators individually and collectively reflect on how well-intentioned pedagogical practices and policy exacerbate and/or exploit Black youth, their families, and their communities.

Anti-Blackness in American Society and PreK–12 Public Schooling

Anti-Blackness represents an active, not passive, disdain for Blackness and Black cultural aesthetics in the public imagination. Its study is motivated by questions of Black suffering, and it has been understood in scholarship as the impossibility of being simultaneously Black *and* human.[3] Anti-Blackness led White colonists to enslave Africans and transport them to the Americas to occupy a permanent laboring class. Anti-Blackness explains the numerous attempts in US history to erase Black people's contributions to White America's accumulation of wealth in every industry, from music and entertainment to medicine and engineering. This history gives little to no credit for the ways their ideas and inventions have enriched all of our lives.[4] Anti-Blackness undergirds the government's practice of mass incarceration, such that Black people remain state property long after the end of slavery as a legal economic institution.[5] In effect, throughout US history, Black bodies have been objectified, rendered as the property of others—intended to never be viewed as deserving of basic human rights.

Anti-Blackness also constructs the Black body as inherently problematic. That is, to be Black automatically means being broken and in need of repair or disposal. This perspective is important for understanding the way that contemporary public urban education for Black youth has been, in a word, unfit. It also provides a framework for critiquing the efficacy of contemporary urban education reform for Black youth growing up poor in major cities. College has *not* been the great economic equalizer for far too many of America's non-White citizens, as evidenced by persistent wealth inequalities for Black college-educated Americans.[6] Nonetheless, "college for all" elementary, middle, and high schools continue to dominate the urban education reform landscape.

The concept of anti-Blackness is a particularly useful lens for evaluating Urban Prep. Because of the way that success gets imagined at Urban Prep, the school's claim to "changing the narrative" is anchored in reimaging Black male bodies. By doing so, the school endeavors to shift the public's schematic reference of young Black men and boys. For example, UP is very closely associated with the image of young Black men in shirts, ties, and black blazers. Why is it that the mainstream public excitedly celebrates a Black man in a suit and tie but is aghast when that same Black man wears a hoodie and sagging jeans? Why don't White men or Asian men in suits (or hoodies) garner the same response? Anti-Blackness gives us a way to think about this cognitive dissonance. Changing the way young Black men are viewed by the public does very little for eradicating the problems of White supremacy and anti-Black racism behind such problematic depictions. Instead, such imaging and popular discourse about UP continue to exceptionalize these young men by reifying the "good" Black man image and dominant conceptions of "success." Urban youth who dress in suits and ties, look studious, and attend a prep school are not threatening.[7] Such "good" young Black men and boys do not threaten public safety (they won't thieve, plunder, and pillage) or the expansion of the White supremacist US nation-state, seeing that they, in some ways, benefit from its existence.

Because anti-Blackness is active—always in motion and operation—pushing back against the anti-Black imagination means actively affirming that *all* Black lives do indeed matter. Studying Black educators, Black social movements, and other contemporary justice campaigns gives educators and institutions the skills, language, history, pedagogical conventions, and knowledge needed to disrupt the decades-long failure of public schools to provide an adequate education to Black youth. The vision and work of Black educators like W. E. B. Dubois, Carter G. Woodson, and many others provide the ideological scaffold necessary to begin this work of remaking education for Black youth as we know it.[8] In addition, it is necessary to stand in solidarity with social movements that raise the public's consciousness about present-day trends in state violence committed against Black people, such as #BlackLivesMatter.[9] Remaining silent is a form of complicity. Taking a position draws attention to the problem and shows active support of the struggle for basic human rights. And disavowing anti-Blackness in education includes foregrounding the ways that Black people's fight for freedom from racism and White supremacy is closely tied to struggles for land sovereignty and the fight against cultural erasure by Native Americans and other Indigenous peoples of the Americas (e.g., Standing Rock #noDAPL). This work of reimagining is also anchored in educators' resistance to the propensity of education practice to (un)intentionally or (un)consciously devalue or "invisibilize" acts of brutality endured by people of color in the United States.

Ultimately, schools must find a way to become *Decidedly Black,* to establish or organize themselves to cater specifically and explicitly to the needs of Black youth, families, and communities. It is these individuals who articulate and give voice to those needs. Becoming Decidedly Black might be a small gesture, like providing Black students attending a predominantly White school their own time and space each day or each week to convene with one another and other Black faculty members. Or it could be a big gesture, like an entire school being designed from the ground up with Black youth in mind. Becoming Decidedly Black represents a philosophical and intellectual orientation intended to move Black youth from the margins of education practice and policy making to the center.

Tensions of Becoming Decidedly Black: The Case of Urban Prep

Urban Prep is close to being Decidedly Black. Much of what makes UP almost Decidedly Black begins with the school's justified beliefs about, and knowledge of, young Black men's brilliance and possibility. These beliefs and knowledge ground the school's philosophies, policies, and practices. UP's founder is a Black man who grew up in Chicago. He established a school for Black boys who presumably reminded him of himself. This school was purposefully and thoughtfully designed to expand access to education opportunity for young Black men and boys specifically by putting them on track to gain entry into higher education. The thought that higher education is valuable for improving one's quality of life is directly connected to Tim King's experiential knowledge and that of his colleagues who helped author UP's charter. Moreover, they imagined that helping young Black men and boys to get admitted to college would help shift dominant deficit perceptions of them.

The school's motto, "We Believe," demonstrates the confidence UP school stakeholders had in their students' capacity to be academically successful. Believing was the engine, the chief driver, of the school's success in helping each of its graduates earn admittance to college. That believing was explicitly about these young Black men, their abilities and their promise and potential. That believing was so strong that the young men featured in this book even started believing in themselves in ways they had not before attending Urban Prep. They not only made it to college, but most of them have now graduated and are giving back to the communities that gave so much to them. All the school's practices and policies centered on the concept of "We Believe." This motto is not passive; it is a daily, active decision by Urban Prep teachers, families, administrators, and other adults to communicate to its students their extraordinary value and worth.

Yet, important tensions emerged in these young men's narratives that call attention to the significance of *what* educators believe about Black male youth and Blackness to establishing institutional arrangements that are in some way Decidedly Black. Educators must interrogate *how* such beliefs or confidences in young Black men and boys' abilities get taken up in institutional practice and policy. In other words, while it is essential to counter anti-Blackness by actively and purposefully centering Blackness in the practices and organizational structure of a singular institution, it is equally necessary to attend to the ways a school's work/ideologies improve or exacerbate the suffering of other Black people within and outside of the school building. At Urban Prep, Community, the 4 Rs, the Creed, and Prides cater to the humanity of its young Black men students. But these design elements do not explicitly challenge anti-Black constructions of people on the South Side or acknowledge diverse possibilities for the young men's future.

In the present neoliberal market context, it is necessary to question the fidelity of UP's priorities for doing little more than producing Black male bodies with middle-class values. To become Decidedly Black, a school's actors must examine what they are doing to enable young people to make their own decisions about what postsecondary pathways they will pursue in an anti-Black society. The research evidence from this study indicates that these young men had very little space in school to self-determine or dream of and make decisions about the futures they wanted for themselves, a space without external factors controlling the limits and setting the boundaries of those decisions. Rather, the dominant message was that they *had* to go to college after high school. This implied that college is the great equalizer, and those who do not go to college don't care about education or becoming successful.

There is also little evidence that Urban Prep did anything to disavow prevalent negative views of Black students attending traditional neighborhood high schools. In fact, it benefited from such narratives when recruiting these young men to be members of its first class. UP's "100%" success story, meant to "change the narrative" and solicit the admiration of the public (and the money of wealthy donors), was in fact validated by mainstream deficit projections of Black communities and poorly resourced urban schools.[10] The charter's popularity was propped up by anti-Black depictions of urban schools as failing. This is evidenced, for example, in the school's "Background Information and Preliminary FY11 2011 Data Findings," a report of school data that makes unfair comparisons between Urban Prep and other CPS schools.[11] Even though these types of comparisons are widely accepted, this practice does little for disrupting the deficit perspectives and perceptions of urban schools serving predominantly Black and Latinx youth or the stigma attached to them. Anti-Blackness makes this practice perfectly acceptable.

Because there are numerous social variables that directly impact teaching and learning processes in the local schooling context, it is unfair to base claims of effectiveness on faulty comparisons between schools. Certainly there is work to be done to more effectively educate diverse youth who are growing up in segregated, densely populated, economically disenfranchised communities of color. However, the widespread public press Urban Prep has received diverts attention away from gains made in traditional neighborhood public schools in the city, which further worsens the public's views of these schools (and the students they serve). As Urban Prep is being heralded as an answer to urban education, what happens to Black youth attending Chicago's Harper, Englewood, and Robeson high schools?[12] Who believes in them? And what responsibility does Urban Prep have to negotiate its political capital to benefit other Black youth, thereby alleviating the suffering of all Black people in the communities where their campuses are located?

Furthermore, while Urban Prep continues to proudly boast its "100% college acceptance" rate, the public is distracted from the expectation that the school produce stand-alone evidence of its instructional effectiveness year after year. If a school's successes can receive this much popular press, its misgivings and areas of improvement should also be made readily available to the public. Urban Prep is a public school; this means that it is in service to the public, even if it is run privately. Its designation as a charter is not the problem; it's how that privilege gets used that raises questions. What does it mean that 100 percent of the young men get accepted to college when 100 percent do not matriculate into the freshman year of college or complete college, much less even graduate high school? Knowing about and learning from UP's successes *and* failures can be instructive for improving the practice of urban education for all young people.

One of the UPCPS participants remarked, "Urban Prep, in a sense, was a big control, or they tried to be real controlling over some of the students. They had the best intentions at heart, but I think they could have probably did it in another way." But becoming Decidedly Black is not about control or manipulation; it is the practice of bottom-up community organizing so that the will of the people guide the practices of the education institution. Decidedly Black education institutions must prepare their students to recognize the systems of inequity that maintain the oppression and marginalization of Black people. It's not enough to do service *in* the community. Educators must be about doing service *with and for* the community by finding ways to create systems in community spaces that will sustain efforts to improve the quality of life for all the Black people in those communities.

As the UP grad noted, Urban Prep is the result of good intentions. But good intentions are too often more tied to emotions than to evidence-based factors for disrupting the material impacts of anti-Black racism on the schooling of Black youth. Education stakeholders can and must do better in pushing back against anti-Blackness and, in the process, in countering the forces that structure how committed educators do the work of improving outcomes for Black youth. Imagine what it would mean if a school like Urban Prep prepared its students not just to go to college but to, as Woodson suggests, change the world as they find it?[13] This would be qualitatively different than simply preparing them to occupy an inequitable system.

Moving Forward: Improving Young Black Men's and Boys' Academic Outcomes in the Local School Context

No one stakeholder group is responsible for Black male school failure. Yet, the education institution does play a key role in expanding or restricting access to education opportunity for this population. Aside from the young men's own agency, resilience, and power to self-determine, data reveal three approaches a local preK–12 or postsecondary school can take that might improve outcomes for young Black men and boys regardless of education context: addressing notions of success, developing a school culture, and building relationships.

Addressing Notions of Success

How the concept of success is imagined, discussed, measured, and negotiated in a school can have important implications for policy and practice that improve or impede education outcomes. Educators must commit to meaningful conversations and activities with individual young men around the meaning of success. They must co-construct a vision of success specific to each young man. This helps avoid the tendency to essentialize all Black (male) youth.[14] Articulations of success should flow from the bottom up rather than from the top down. For example, the teacher who says, "I do what I do because I want my kids to be successful" must interrogate how well their construction of "success" aligns with their students' definition or vision of success.

Moreover, discourse about, and research on, Black males is underinformed by these young people's own worldviews and meaning making. Young Black men and boys experience education settings differently depending on their intersecting social identities (sexuality, gender, class, ability, etc.). Thus, co-constructing visions of success centers on the importance of including their first-person accounts of life in school, of developing the practice of bringing

Black males' voices into the institution's decision-making process. Young men are not just bodies subject to schooling influences. They are co-creators of knowledge whose perspectives can work to significantly improve their schooling experiences—*if* adults are listening. Additionally, reimagining a more robust concept of success *with* young Black men and boys allows them to transcend static expectations of who they can become and what they can accomplish in their futures. Complicating how one thinks and talks about Black male school success begins with knowledge of the *who* (What makes young Black men and boys feel happy? What makes them sad? What gives them anxiety?) and the *how* (How do young Black men and boys in this school learn best? What topics or academic disciplines excite them? How are they seeing themselves represented in the schooling environment?). Taken together, such perspectives can provide an alternate viewpoint for determining the ways that school might be a site of Black suffering. These viewpoints might also help disrupt dominant notions of success that tend to be rooted in White, heteropatriarchal, middle-class, Christian values.[15]

Finally, redefining success with Black male students necessitates that educators notice the ways young men resist deficit framing of themselves, including how they reject being treated poorly by school actors. This is especially true in underresourced neighborhoods, where many students perform well in spite of anti-Black schooling conditions.[16] These are conditions that make young people feel like they are perpetually being held in contempt by adults. They actively oppose deficit perceptions of classroom-level opportunity gaps such as teacher beliefs in color blindness. This raises fundamental questions regarding how well equipped adults are with regards to appropriately interpreting young Black men and boys' resistance as productive. Listening closely to their stories may be a step in the right direction.[17] Education research on young Black men and boys must bring these students' own actions and decisions to the forefront of analysis so that we better appreciate their resistance, resilience, and persistence.[18]

School Culture

A school's culture should expect and celebrate academic rigor. Researchers note the importance of a demanding academic atmosphere during the secondary school years.[19] Pedro Noguera asserts that too many Black males are excluded from rigorous classes and prevented from accessing educational opportunities that might otherwise support and encourage them.[20] And while Ebony McGee finds that when a young man is determined to achieve, not even the lack of access to academically rigorous learning experiences can stop him, this still renders young Black men academically vulnerable, especially when or if they decide to matriculate into an institution of higher education.[21] Culturally responsive and sustaining school cultures that offer academically rigorous learning opportunities must be a priority.

Yet, academic preparation alone is not enough. The young men who participated in the UPCPS matriculated to college despite disparities in their academic preparedness. What put them there first and foremost was the confidence they had in their capacity to leave the familiarity of the South Side to enroll in and complete college. This was something very few of the young men had seen anyone else accomplish before them, other than the adult Black men with whom they interacted at Urban Prep. A school culture that rewarded and acknowledged these young men daily and challenged them to self-affirm through recitation of the Creed contributed very positively to their academic self-efficacy.

Institutional agents provide key forms of social as well as institutional support, especially for youth of color.[22] It behooves schools to be strategic about how they organize themselves to respond pointedly to the person-specific needs of young Black men and boys. School cultures that are inviting and uplifting provide students with multiple opportunities for them to *feel* successful and valuable. This begins with how they perceive themselves as fitting into the social milieu of the school. How they see and imagine themselves in the space influences how they will navigate the space. Black male students should achieve *because* of the school environment, not in spite of it.

Extant data about the ways young Black men are labeled, policed, problematized, and positioned as deviant are compelling.[23] Their status is complicated further by their family background and access to resources. We need school cultures that allow space for them to regularly receive love, care, and affirmation from adults.[24] More importantly, adults must *act* in ways that the young men would interpret as loving, caring, and affirming. Saying that we care about students is not good enough, especially when that rhetoric is not supported by the actions of school stakeholders or the school's organizational structure. The better educators are at building on and extending young people's conceptions of care, the better they will become at designing policies and practices that establish more student-centered school cultures.

Interpersonal Relationships

At the core of caring and humanizing the school culture is attending to the many different interpersonal relationships that make up the school community. Research confirms that interpersonal relationships are important for young Black men and boys in high school.[25] Each young man in this study discussed how his relationships—with peers, school agents, family members, and community members—were pivotal in determining how they experienced school and how they made meaning of those experiences. Relationships extend beyond the teacher-student binary. They span a broad network of individuals who create a critical ecology of support for each and every student.[26] This network of support is one that the school can work with Black male students to establish and sustain.

As Ty-Ron Douglas details in his book, young Black men and boys cultivate relationships in complex spaces such as barbershops, churches, basketball courts, and community centers.[27] Quite often, it was in and across relationships built in informal educational spaces like these that the young men in this study were able to sharpen their resilience, enact agency, and clarify their ideas of the type of men they wanted to become in the future. Among their peers, students develop their sense of self and often find solace and encouragement. And through the range of relationships they develop with school stakeholders, students come to identify their intellectual interests and their orientations toward school and maximize opportunities to develop other parts of their identities (e.g., athletics, arts).

The approaches and lenses adults in a school employ to build relationships with students should rely heavily on a few fundamental assumptions about young Black men and boys. First, assume that they want access to the best education opportunities possible but understand that they may not always trust the adults responsible for providing those opportunities. Next, assume that their behavior in school is in some way informed by the invisible factors of the school's climate and culture. Educators need to resist labeling young Black men and boys as "at-risk," "disengaged" or "unmotivated," terms that only create deficit perceptions of young Black men and boys. Instead, refer to young people who have been underserved as being "at-promise." Young people who struggle in school, for whatever reason, are motivated about something. It's up to the educators to figure out what the something is and to then build a relationship around that thing or set of activities. Finally, assume that how young men and boys choose to interact with educators in the school is purposeful, but not personal.

In this study, Black men teachers (and other Black men adults in a school) were found to have built substantive relationships with the young men. Having more Black men teachers in a school is a good thing, but they should not be relegated to the role of disciplinarian, role model, or father figure.[28] Black men offer important contributions to a young man's racial and gender socialization. Recent research posits the significant role of "othermothering" in student-teacher relationships and how Black male teachers can contribute to the schooling efforts of some Black males as "social fathers" or "community fathers."[29] Teachers assume roles as surrogate caregivers within the schooling context, paying close attention to students' personal and social development. These roles may contribute constructively, but they may be limiting.

Black men are also master teachers who add substantively to the professional learning community, whose expertise can enrich and enhance the practice of new and veteran teacher colleagues.[30] But *all* education stakeholders have a responsibility to build the types of relationships that communicate a young man's value to the school community. Young Black men and boys benefit from an expansive, extensive social network as they move along the education pipeline toward "success in higher education." Relationships with family, teachers, community people, and one another sustain them in times of need and serve them long after they complete their college degree.

Conclusion

Understanding anti-Blackness at a structural level is essential to reimagining P–20 education. At the local school level, the enduring challenge of education practitioners and stakeholders is to better understand what schooling practices and experiences work (or do not work) for improving the education outcomes of young Black men and boys in that local school context. Educators can do this by investing in efforts aimed at co-constructing notions of success with young Black men. They also do this by establishing a school culture that humanizes them and, at the same time, actively opposing deficit perspectives of Black people. Educators should also be actively engaged in facilitating interpersonal relationships among a range of individuals who are internal and external to the school. These practices go very far in bolstering a school's weaknesses and refining its strengths in service to Black students and the Black communities from which they hail.

7

Recommendations for Contemporary Urban Education Reform

None of us are perfect. We live in an imperfect world . . . Black kids have to figure it out . . . You can't pull a plug on us . . .

"MASTER P," FROM SOLANGE, *A SEAT AT THE TABLE*

As an educator and researcher, I have a keen interest in seeing that all young people have access to a high-quality public education. As a native Chicagoan, the son and grandson of Jamaican immigrants, and someone whose primary caregiver growing up has only a high school diploma, I care deeply about the affordances an education makes possible for diverse urban youth. The Urban Prep College Persistence Study had one goal: to understand how this urban charter high school functioned to support the college persistence of its graduates, all of them young Black men from the South Side of Chicago. In the study, Derrick Brooms and I set out to better determine "what works" for improving young Black men and boys' education outcomes. In rooting our research in the comments and recollections of seventeen of the members of Urban Prep's first graduating class, we learned directly from those for whom Urban Prep's successes presumably mattered most—its graduates—as opposed to learning from others about them.

The young mens' candid descriptions of growing up on the South Side, progressing through high school to become college ready, and persisting in college reveal the factors that constrained or complimented their ability to be active participants in achieving their desired goals. This research demonstrates the influence of secondary education institutions in mediating young Black men's exposure and access to education opportunity. It also foregrounds the exceptionally important role of high schools in determining a young person's educational pathway and, therefore, their capacity to use high-quality education to improve Black communities.

Contemporary Urban Education Reform—A Revolution

There are no direct, clear steps to fixing an education machine that, technically, is doing what it was designed to do. Educators and school leaders must instead completely rethink their work and the assumptions they hold about that work. There are ways to begin conceptualizing appropriate school reform efforts in local schools or in a school district. One way is to focus on becoming a Decidedly Black education institution, which means structuring the school to facilitate and reward social networking among Black boys and men (students and adults) and to regularly affirm and acknowledge their accomplishments. Reform includes talking explicitly with young men about race and racism, and about their contributions to making the world also less oppressive for women and individuals of varying sexual and gender identities.

It is misguided to think that a few generic recommendations can be the revolution that is needed, considering the failures of school reform in Black communities (and other communities of color).[1] Nonetheless, aside from the theoretical and political dimensions of reform, today's urban public schools do need some radical change. It needs to be disruptive but measured, strategic but aggressive. This vision of reform is enacted *with communities*, and is anchored in a commitment by school stakeholders who ask, "What can *I* do right now?" instead of "What will or might *they* do soon?" This is a hopefulness rooted in visionary disquietude. The reform I speak of here is one that centers on justice *for all*. It is a reform that is inclusive and specific at the same time.

Furthermore, the brand of reform I'm advancing also means pushing education practitioners to completely reconsider everything they believe to be right or normal or true or good about the teaching and learning enterprise. It's like the assistant principal in a failing Chicago school who, when asked to characterize a "good" school, said, "Off the top of my head, that's hard for me to say . . . I haven't graduated to that level of thinking yet . . . I'm used to having not [a good school]. It's hard for me to think of a good school when I've been here for so long."[2] This kind of acknowledgment is ground zero, and it will take multiple perspectives to move that thinking forward.

I am asking educators to push past their ambivalence and to move to the next level of rational contemplation of what urban youth need right now, and then to an understanding of what young Black men and boys need right now. I offer here some considerations for thinking further, beyond the findings discussed so far, about school reform centered on improving the educational outcomes of young Black men and boys, and urban youth more broadly, in various education organizational contexts.[3]

Beginning at the End: Building on Students' Perspectives

If racism is a permanent feature of education institutions, then there has to be a commitment to explicitly identifying the ways that anti-Blackness permeates our thinking about Black youth and Black communities. And if the end goal of that work is to better educate Black men and boys, then the process should begin with listening to and learning from Black men and boys directly. This speaks to the heartbeat of this book—student voice. Listening to young people seems intuitive, especially for educators, but it is far too rare that school improvement processes center the voices of its students in reform efforts. I am not talking about a student survey. I am advocating the merits of qualitatively rich one-on-one or small-group conversations that help nuance and elucidate how young men are experiencing a school environment. The conversations that anchor this study uncovered multiple truths useful for making sense of these young men's school realities. Their worldviews made clear the implications of their educational experiences for determining their educational trajectories.

Pedro Noguera has argued that it is critical to have students' perspectives inform actions taken to strengthen education reform efforts.[4] Schools that persistently fail to meet the needs of its students should not look to "well regarded think tanks or policy centers" but should turn to "students themselves."[5] Who would have better insight than the very people experiencing the school processes that one is trying to improve? This involves asking youth how they think about themselves in relationship to the school environment and the impact of their interactions with various school stakeholders. This also means taking risks and coming face to face with real problems in the school environment. Listen *through* the discomfort of what is being said to notice what is not being said.

An example of enacting this approach to rethinking how educators tackle reform or change was a conversation I had with a group of eighth-grade Black boys at a Philadelphia K–8 school. It was an effort, on the part of the school's administrator, to understand the enduring disparities in the data related to these boys' academic achievement and their high numbers of school discipline referrals. The hope was that my conversation would reveal how and why Black boys were (dis)engaging with the school environment.

The middle schoolers and I talked about how they thought teachers saw them in school and the nature of their interactions with other adults and non-Black students. The small-group setting allowed for storytelling, which then led different young men at different times to exclaim, "That happened to you too?" It was like sharing war stories about the ways they had been wounded in this particular school. These young men had attended the school since they were in kindergarten; for eight years they had been in this environment. They talked about times they'd felt surveilled or unseen by adults, and they described when and how school rules and expectations were unfair toward them specifically. They were not just describing isolated incidents, but trends in teacher behaviors at the school.

I was struck by the fact that no one had ever really asked these young men their opinions about school or about how they were feeling. I was a researcher, someone the students did not know. I was a neutral party. Also, the meeting was completely private and confidential. I made sure that the atmosphere for our discussion was comfortable, informal, and safe for them to talk freely. No one was allowed to know what we discussed or when we were meeting, except for the building administrator who invited me. But I was still surprised that no one had really talked—or *listened*—to these students to understand their disengagement from school.

After spending some time transcribing the conversation and looking over major patterns in the young men's responses, I presented the data to the school's teachers and administrators. The students' stories revealed the ways that they felt they were imagined by teachers. The young men described having to move through the school environment as if they were constantly being watched or scrutinized harshly by adults. They described mistakes they made or trouble they got into as kindergarteners and first graders that continued to haunt them well into their middle grade years. They noted how teachers would talk negatively about them year after year, which created an assaultive environment for them. They discussed overhearing stories teachers told about them, or having teachers say to their faces, "I've heard about you." These young men revealed that they felt like they were perpetually held in contempt. So how these adolescent boys chose to participate or not participate in the school was about surviving in a school environment that they experienced as assaultive, even violent. And how they chose to comport themselves in school was less about individual adults as much as it was about the environment adults had created. Whether or not their perceptions of adults in the school were accurate is not the issue; these young men's very real experiences in school are what mattered most.

Many individuals in the room were obviously extremely uncomfortable. Several said, "This can't be true," and others shut down or walked out of the room altogether. Their thinking, as evidenced by their response, actually corroborated the data. These individuals withdrew from the discomfort rather than leaning into it. By walking out, they refused to consider their contribution to the problem. Educators of color, like those in the room that day, too often shoulder the burden of trying to make the school environment better places for youth of color. Their frustrations were understandable; after all, the data I was sharing reinforced their own personal experiences at the school as well.

Even in disputing my interpretations of the data, these teachers were left *with the reality of the data*, and the burden of having to explain why the problems persist. If an educator assumes that there is nothing wrong with Black male students, then they have to examine the practices and policies of the institution to explain why, for instance, Black boys continue to be suspended at much higher rates than any other group in a school. When educators center themselves, their feelings, and their good intentions not to be racist in an effort to understand Black male school failure, they miss an opportunity to respond directly to the factors that sustain the problem(s). Alternatively, by listening, an educator creates more space in which to acknowledge students' perspectives at face value and to begin the work of remaking the institution as a place where young people feel humanized and celebrated.

Coeducational Environment vs. Single-Sex Environment

The fact that Urban Prep was a single-sex school has had various impacts on these young men.[6] For some of the young men, not having girls at the school facilitated the close bonds of brotherhood they appreciated about the school and long-lasting relationships that continued to serve them well during their college years. I think these young men benefited most from the school's motto, "We Believe," which represented one important way that the school, as a single-sex instiution, explicitly centered Black maleness. In doing so, the school's policies, philosophies, and practices hinged on "believing," supported development of these young men's will and agency to achieve that which many of them previously deemed impossible.

Regardless of whether a school is single-sex or coeducational, it is important that all students feel like they belong in the school environment. It is easy in a single-sex school environment to reinforce hegemonic masculinities that lead young men to act in ways that are destructive and violent toward other young men who they perceive to be different. This can then make the school a difficult place to learn. Any reform efforts aimed at creating a single-sex classroom or school would benefit from generating a uniform understanding of manhood and masculinity among faculty, administration, and staff. It is worth the effort to think about the ways specific students are subordinated based on their intersectional identities (e.g., race and sexuality or race and religion). Making decisions about school improvement or design based solely on a unitary social identity category such as gender *or* race versus focusing on intersectional identies such as gender *and* race will likely result in blind spots in the school's organizational structure. Furthermore, development of a cultural ethos that avoids practices and values that are unknowingly or unintentionally violent, discriminating, or offensive should be a priority.

There are other affordances of a single-sex school, such as curriculum, that are specifically tailored to the unique experiences of young men. Even these, however, should have multiple representations of Black men to ensure that the school avoids reinforcing narrow depictions of Black manhood. Moreover, a benefit of Urban Prep having served primarily Black male students was that the students had many more Black men teachers than they would likely have had in a coeducational school setting. In its first two years, Urban Prep's faculty and administration strongly reflected the race and gender of the school's students. When teaching students of the same sex, teachers have an opportunity to be intentional about either creating culturally responsive learning experiences that cater specifically to young Black men and boys or reinforcing homophobic toxic masculinities. School leaders should work to ensure that the faculty reflects the diversity of its student body and that every adult is clear about the expectations for maintaining an antioppressive schooling environment.

Charter Schools vs. Traditional Public Schools

I do not argue for or against charter schools. I recognize that charter schools are public schools that are run privately. That being said, I acknowledge the increased autonomy held by charter school operators and practitioners as potentially useful in creating schools that more acutely respond to the specific needs of their constituents—as *they* (the operators, administrators, school leaders) see and interpret those needs. There are certainly any number of liabilities with charter schools, such as the absence of transparent mechanisms necessary to assess a school's effectiveness at producing positive student outcomes. For Urban Prep, the greatest benefit of being a charter school is its autonomy. Tim King and other members of the school's founding team were able to create the school they believed young Black men and boys needed with minimal interference from the bureaucracy of the larger Chicago Public Schools system.

Much of what Urban Prep has done that is effective is transferrable to a traditional public school environment. Building relationships with students, cultivating social networks, and attending to students' holistic development have been found to strengthen young Black men and boys' educational outcomes in any school context.[7] In particular, Community is one feature of Urban Prep's design that can be feasibly transferred to a coeducational environment. Creating an all-Black male advisory group or some other male-only space in the coeducational environment could also be advantageous for improving educational outcomes for young Black men and boys. Both create a space for the explicit acknowledgment and affirmation of young Black men's various cultural identities, which can promote greater school engagement.

While the young men in the study named Community as an important space where they were publicly acknowledged for "doing the right thing," I am not in favor of a rewards system with expensive gifts. Instead, it is better to find other ways to encourage students to become intrinsically motivated. Another reform effort could be to work with young Black men and faculty to develop a litany of affirmations that represents the character, integrity, and diversity of Black male youth in the local school community.

Connecting Communities

School reform efforts for young Black men and boys must account for the cultural knowledge, language, and norms of the local community. As the young men described, community service was an important part of their experience at Urban Prep. They did this service in their Prides. *All* schools should reach out and connect with their communities. Students could identify actual problems in the community and design ongoing service initiatives that respond to them. Schools could transform Black communities by equipping young people to be critical of the problems in that community and not just provide them visions for how to escape these problems. Likewise, school reformers should be intentional about collaborating with other traditional public neighborhood high schools. There has to be a commitment to reaching outside of the school to do work that benefits all young people in a community. Think how powerful it would be if Urban Prep found ways to share its considerable resources with the local neighborhood schools that they compare themselves against.

True reform doesn't happen if the change is contained inside one school building. Replication and scalability require strong models. There needs to be greater transparency from schools that are "working." Coalitions between schools lauded as effective in closing gaps in Black students' achievements and other schools that are struggling located in the same communities hold much possibility for systemic change. This is the big thinking that may be influential in pushing back against policies and practices that maintain anti-Black institutional arrangements.

None of what I suggest here is simple. It is not supposed to be simple. The problems are not simple. But neither is anything I suggest here impossible.

Conclusion

"Black Lives Matter is our call to action. It is a tool to reimagine a world where Black people are free to exist, free to live . . . It is a tool for our allies to show up differently for us."[8] Until society comes to regard young Black men and boys as fully human, as capable of achieving and thriving at the highest levels, we will continue to experience the problem of their academic failure. This failure will not be because they don't already possess the capacity to be academically successful. It will be because of our unwillingness to notice the mechanisms that drastically minimize opportunities for them to achieve at optimal levels. The problem will persist because of our own failure to notice all of the cultural strengths and resources these young men embody and our negligence in designing academic programs around or in response to those strengths and resources.

The way young Black men and boys are constructed in mainstream society does not have to dictate how they are treated as they move along the education pipeline. Creating culturally affirming learning spaces that are academically rigorous and responsive to a co-constructed vision of success contributes substantially to young Black men and boys' academic achievement in preK–12 and postsecondary education settings. Listening to them closely and inviting them into a school's professional decision-making process will influence how they *choose* to participate in the education institution.

A young Black man's journey toward a life of fulfillment and opportunity is not solely his responsibility, or even the responsibility of one or two people. Rather, it takes an entire village of individuals who are committed to questioning their own assumptions about the work. These are individuals who acknowledge how White supremacy and anti-Blackness make the promise of equal education opportunity impossible to youth of color. Everyone in the village needs to be ready to rethink the effort needed to accomplish change in urban education. This change will positively impact all young people. The future of public education depends on the change we make today.

Appendix

Research Methods

The Urban Prep College Persistence Study examined the role and function of Urban Prep Charter Academy for Young Men in supporting its graduates' college persistence and retention. The UPCPS is best characterized as a phenomenological study that takes the form of a more narrative research approach.[1] In other words, this research project centered on acquiring first-person accounts of these young men's "lived experiences" both as native Chicago South Siders and members of UP's very first graduating class to boast "100% college acceptance." From these narratives emerge a thick description of various (inside and outside-of-school) factors that the research participants perceive to have had a significant impact on their preparation to enroll in and ultimately complete college. With the UPCPS, Derrick Brooms and I aimed to better understand the various messages, lessons, moments, and stakeholder interactions that facilitated these young men's transition from Chicago's South Side to success in higher education. Central to our inquiry was the young men's own sense making about the significance of these factors for enabling them to overcome personal struggles and structural barriers to college completion.

Theoretical Framework

Critical race theory (CRT) is a bundle of theoretical perspectives that emphasize the significance of race and racism for explaining patterns in racialized disparities. Legal scholars Derrick Bell, Kimberlé Crenshaw, Neil Gotanda, Richard Delgado, and Mari Matsuda, to name a few, conclude that social class is ineffective as an analytic variable for fully determining the multiple ways the law systematically disadvantages people of color.[2] Gloria Ladson-Billings and

William Tate are credited with introducing CRT into the field of education in their iconic article "Toward a Critical Race Theory of Education."[3] Similar to their predecessors in the legal field, Ladson-Billings and Tate argue that race and racism are un(der)theorized for their roles in structuring and perpetuating educational inequity. They demonstrate that the relationship between race and property is the battleground for educational malpractice committed against students of color, and Black students in particular.[4]

Most importantly, CRT helps disrupt and dismantle White supremacy.[5] Today, scholars across multiple disciplines apply CRT to isolate race in analyses of racialized inequality. Education researchers tend to draw on a cluster of five primary themes or theoretical propositions:

- Racism is viewed as a *permanent fixture* of American society. CRT scholars contend that race intersects, and is central to, the maintenance of all other forms of subordination and social oppression.[6]
- CRT scholars believe that *liberal ideals* prominently put forward in mainstream society—such as color blindness, meritocracy, equal opportunity, race neutrality/objectivity, and postracialism—actually work against their intention to alleviate the oppression of non-White people in the United States.[7] Scholars utilize various other CRT-inspired theories, such as Derrick Bell's "interest convergence principle," to challenge these dominant ideologies.[8]
- The disruption of all forms of racism requires a *social justice orientation*. CRT is meant to help discern evidence of racism and actively resist the systems, practices, and policies that perpetuate all forms of oppression.[9]
- *Experiential knowledge* is central to identifying, describing, and critiquing manifestations of racism in the lives of individuals from historically marginalized racial groups.[10] It is difficult to understand the reality of racism absent first-hand accounts of individuals who have experienced oppression and been disadvantaged because of their race.
- CRT scholarship is *interdisciplinary* in nature. Critical analyses of race and racism require tools of inquiry and intellectual paradigms grounded in multiple disciplinary orientations.[11]

I rely heavily on these themes to facilitate my interpretation of the young men's narratives with the intention of extrapolating their relevance to broader discourses of race and racism in urban education. CRT's application as a methodological approach helps expose the ways race mediates the education of youth who are minoritized in school.[12] In the context of *Urban Preparation,* a CRT analysis has worked to deepen my understanding of the threats and barriers to education attainment for a group of young Black men growing up in the city, an understanding that could not be derived by class analyses alone.

Studying the educational trajectories of young Black men who grew up in the US city with the third-highest population required that I use methodological tools that legitimatize the legacy of oppression impacting these young men's educational opportunities. I was most interested in the experiential knowledge that illuminated the various events, incidences, moments, interactions, and people that contributed to the young men's admittance into, and subsequent graduation from, a four-year college or university. A CRT perspective puts schools in their appropriate cultural, historical, and political contexts. CRT scholarship and other critical studies of race demonstrate, for instance, how color blindness, "false empathy," and meritocracy disproportionately disadvantage Black youth.[13] As Christopher Dunbar notes, the study of individuals who have been on the receiving end of racial discrimination and degradation requires epistemologies that value and acknowledge the impact of their racial history on the ways they are forced to navigate the world.[14]

Moreover, I contend that these young men's first-person accounts fill a tremendous gap in the extant literature on urban education. Dolores Delgado-Bernal's critical raced-gendered epistemology (CRGE) was central to how I came to understand the substantial contribution of personal narratives to the ways contemporary educators, researchers, and practitioners conceptualize culturally responsive schooling practices and philosophies. CRGE maintains that young people of color are holders and creators of knowledge, and that attention to the intersection of their race *with* gender produces the most robust representations of knowledge.[15] Knowledge is constructed through the stories we are all told and the experiences from which we derive identity and sense of self. CRGE sees all "stories as subjective and the production of knowledge as situated."[16] In other words, each UPCPS participant's narrative is his alone; but the knowledge the experiences generate are an extraordinarily valuable contribution to baseline understandings of racial (in)equity and justice for those who are marginalized because of their race, class, gender, and/or sexuality.

CRGE names race as central to shaping the cultural, political, and historical aspects of knowledge construction. The events, incidents, interactions, lessons, and/or messages the young men in UPCPS chose to share, which became the continuous counterstory in chapters 2–5, reveal new knowledge about the ways well-intentioned education reforms—such as starting a new single-sex high school—might do more harm than good (e.g., maintenance of cisheteropatriarchy, reproducing anti-Blackness, or reinforcing White supremacist logic through school policy and practice). These young men's reflections also reveal numerous social variables mediating "what works" for improving Black male student outcomes. Their reflections offer important considerations and new knowledge for overcoming structural barriers to their high achievement in preK–12 and postsecondary education.[17] Finally, their reflections also provide the field and individuals genuinely interested in public, urban education the nuance needed to adequately critique commonsense practice(s) in the education of Black (male) youth.

Participant Selection

For the UPCPS study, Derrick and I employed a purposive sampling approach.[18] That is, we selected participants based on a defined set of criteria. We wanted to include members of UP's founding graduating class—each participant having identified as a Black man—in his fourth year of college who (1) began high school at UP when the school opened in 2006 and (2) who graduated from the college prep high school four years later, in 2010. One final criterion for participation in UPCPS held that a candidate had to be on track to completing his baccalaureate degree, based on college credits earned, within six years of his initial enrollment into a four-year college or university. Six years is the amount of time originally introduced by the 1990 Student Right to Know Act that has now been adopted and used by the National Center for Education Statistics to measure college graduation rates in the United States.[19]

The research protocol had a total of forty-eight questions, some of which included between one to four probing questions to be asked as necessary to clarify the participant's response. The questions/prompts were situated under three main headings: Demographics/Background Knowledge, High School Experience, and College Experience. Sample questions/prompts from the protocol include: Describe the neighborhood where you lived in high school. How would you compare your last two years of high school to your first two years of high school? What types of support have you received since you've been in college that you believe have been instrumental to keeping you in school?

We began with a list of 88 young men who met the initial criteria for participation in the study. Derrick had access to this list because of his role as an administrator at UP from 2006 to 2010. Between the two of us, we found at least one source of contact (e.g., Facebook, parent/guardian phone number, or e-mail address) for each of these young men. We made physical contact with 25 of the 88. These 25 young men were Urban Prep alumni who, we confirmed at the time of data collection, were persisting toward completion of an undergraduate degree at an accredited four-year college or university. Of those 25 young Black men, we completed one-on-one interviews with 17. The other 8 young men either did not respond or declined participation in the study. Figures A1–A6 provide some demographic information about the young men who participated in the UPCPS.

Data Collection

The primary data for this project came from seventeen one-on-one semi-structured, in-depth interviews.[20] Each interview lasted between ninety minutes and two hours. Seidman insists that "a phenomenological approach to interviewing focuses on the experiences of participants and the meaning they make of that experience."[21] Similarly, a priority of UPCPS was soliciting our participants' perspectives about the costs and benefits of having attended the nation's first all-boys public charter high school. The young men responded to a series of open-ended questions that invited them to provide general descriptions of various lived experiences associated with attending UP and growing up on Chicago's South Side. Our interview conversations began with in-depth discussions of where each participant was raised and about the cultural knowledge they acquired navigating the space between home and school. We then discussed various aspects of their experience attending Urban Prep. Finally, our conversations ended with discussing college and the young men's post–college graduation plans. This approach provided a more holistic, ecological view of

FIGURE A.1 Primary guardianship

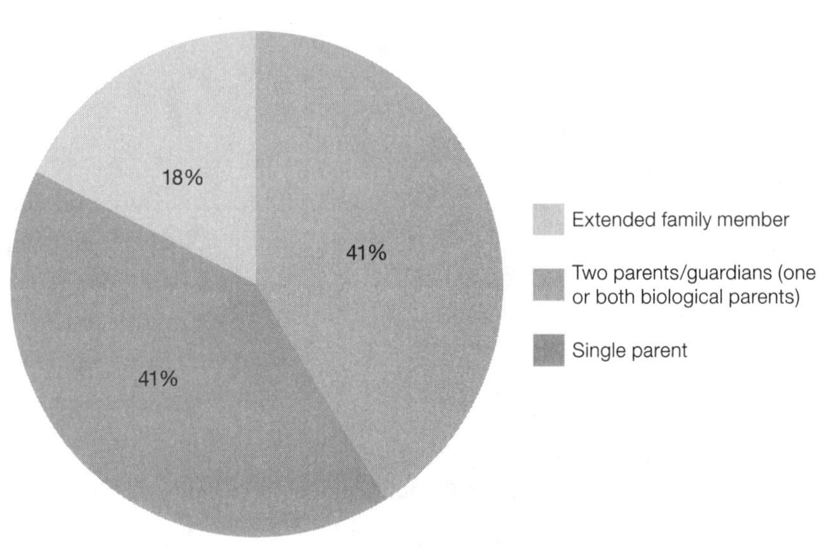

the young men's journey to college (e.g., social activities outside of school, individuals with whom they had significant social interaction in the South Side neighborhoods they navigated to attend UP, and the social experiences they perceived as significantly influencing their autonomous personal decision making). Derrick and I split the data collection, each of us traveling to various parts of the United States to conduct the interviews face to face. Five of the interviews were conducted during a holiday break when the young men were home in Chicago.

Phenomenological interviewing is a structured interview approach intended to gather experiential narrative and facilitate a casual conversation about the meanings interviewees make of their experiences.[22] It was not enough to limit our data gathering to the *what* of their lived experiences. These interviews also invited the young men to provide commentary about *why* or *how* such experiences were essential to developing the confidence to leave their South Side communities to pursue success in higher education. Much of what the young men discussed was personal; they referenced the people, messages, interactions, and events that held private, subjective significance for them as

FIGURE A.2 GPA at high school graduation

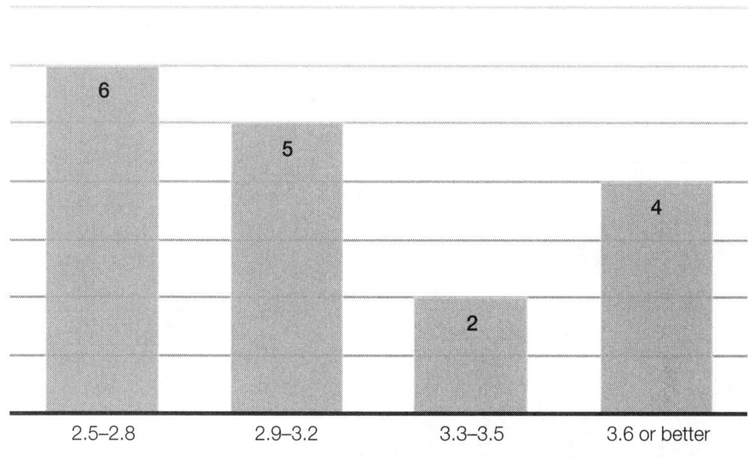

they reflected on their trek to college. At other times, the young men spoke explicitly about the education institution (Urban Prep), its teachers, its social and cultural norms, and their classmates. These narratives were made richer through descriptions of why these people, moments, interactions, and messages mattered (1) in determining each young men's individual postsecondary pathway from high school through college to completion of their degrees and (2) to their conceptions of Black manhood. Participants were asked the same set of questions, but we took the liberty of probing relevant points of significance as they came up in the interview to ensure that the interview conversation was responsive.[23] This allowed us to clarify and contextualize the participants' answers to questions posed in the research protocol. We followed up with the young men by phone or e-mail, as necessary, to clarify meanings of specific statements as we began our preliminary data analysis.

Data Analysis

Derrick and I collaborated on the UPCPS research design, participant selection, and data collection. The primary data analysis and preparation to write this book was my responsibility solely. I set out to answer the following research question in *Urban Preparation*: What factors do members of UP's

FIGURE A.3 Postsecondary institution type

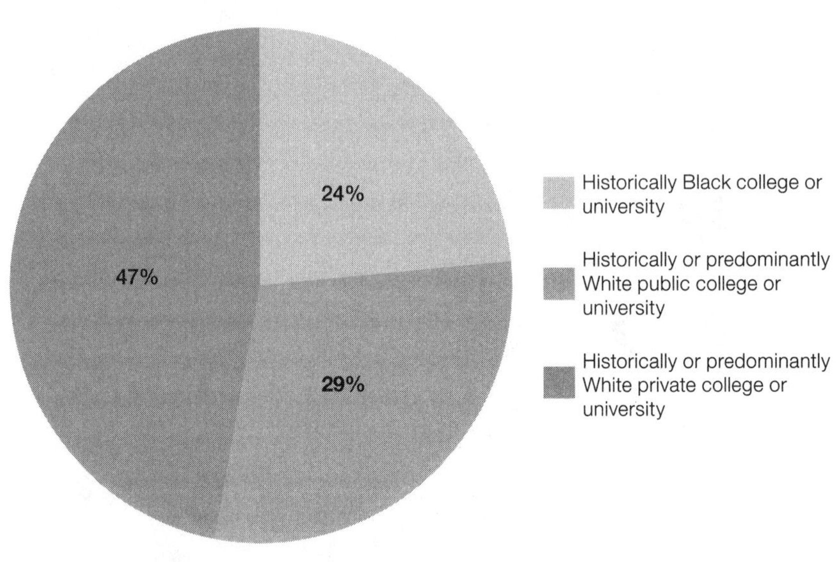

inaugural graduating class, on track to complete their undergraduate degrees within six years of initial enrollment, describe as most significant to determining their educational trajectories from Chicago's South Side to and through a four-year college or university? As is characteristic in phenomenological qualitative research, I began analyzing the data by reading and rereading the interview transcripts.[24] The first read was to get a general sense of the young men's responses to questions in the research protocol. It is at this point that I separately listed my own experiences related to the phenomenon of being a college-educated Black man who grew up on the South Side, who happened to be the founding math teacher of UP. I did this to disentangle my experiences from the young men's, such that I could focus more fully on the narratives generated from our interviews with them.

Phase 1: Textural and Structural Data Categories and Worldviews

The UPCPS participants were quite diverse with respect to the higher education institutions they chose to attend, their family structures and upbringing, personal interests, career goals, and the range of interactions with individuals

FIGURE A.4 College major

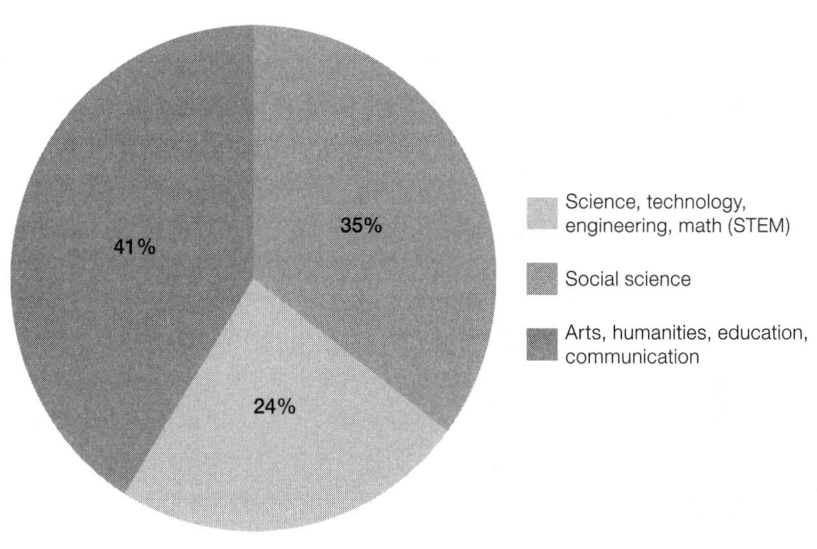

inside and outside of school (see figures A1–A6). My goal in rereading the interview transcripts was to code and catalog large chunks of data from *each* participant and place into one of two broad phenomenological categories. The first data category was textural descriptions, or the *what* of the young men's lived experiences (specific interactions, incidents, events, or moments).[25] The second was structural descriptions, or the *how* and *why* of those lived experiences. Data in the textural category were what I consider to be evidence of each young man's experiential knowledge. These were specific messages that each young man recalled during his interview (e.g., "One of my elementary school counselors recommended that I go [to Urban Prep]"). Chunks of data coded and cataloged in the structural category were each young man's description about how or why a particular moment, decision, interaction, or event mattered to him (e.g., "I think [UP] wanted Black men to do better in life and not be the typical Black man or stereotype of African American men"). Data in the structural category helped me discern the "conditions, situations, or context" important to determining each young man's educational trajectory.[26]

FIGURE A.5 Campus involvement

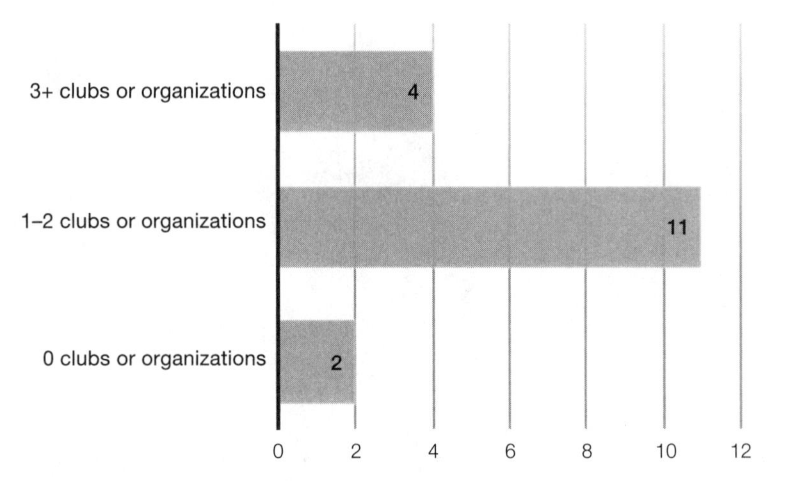

Data in the structural category are representative of the young men's thoughts and beliefs, or worldviews, about the factors determining their educational trajectories. When examining data from the textural category, gathering evidence of these young men's worldviews about the significance of certain interactions, incidents, events, or moments was essential for discerning the factors that most facilitated movement to and through college. Alford Young acknowledges that observing trends in behavior does not go far enough in comprehending the factors that determine how poor Black men from Chicago make decisions about their futures.[27] We need to know from the men what *they* think about their circumstances and the beliefs they hold about the impact of specific social and economic forces influencing the direction of their lives. Similarly, I had some sense of the various challenges these young men faced as I observed them during my year as their teacher, but there were limits to my understanding of what *they* thought or believed about the significance of those challenges for determining their educational trajectories.

Discerning the young men's worldviews was important for at least three reasons. First, they worked to triangulate specific claims made in this book about why certain factors improved or impeded their preparation to succeed

FIGURE A.6 College persistence

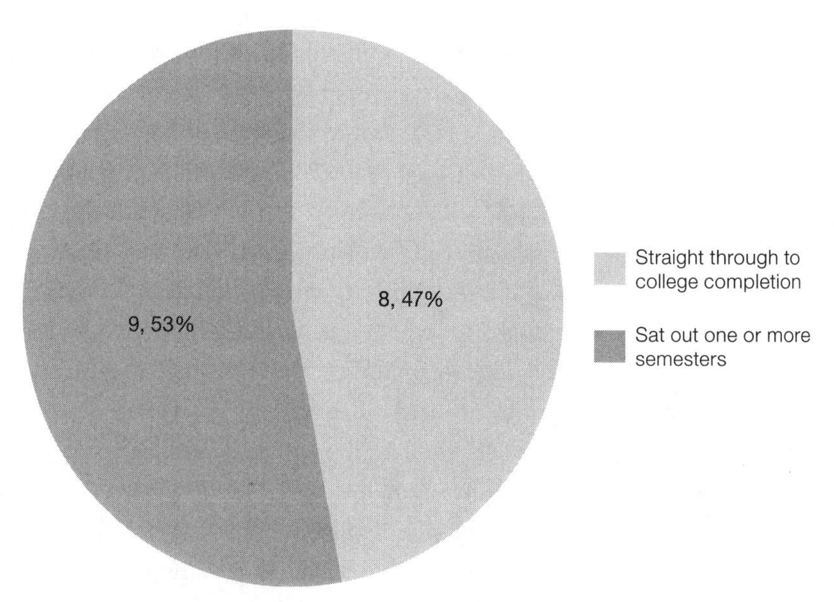

in college and life beyond college. Second, their worldviews offer a greater depth of clarity about the degree to which UP's "100% college acceptance" matters for understanding the school's overall institutional effectiveness. In other words, getting accepted to college is one thing; understanding the young men's beliefs about why getting accepted to college is significant for them considering their various social locations (e.g., race, class, gender etc.) is another issue altogether. Finally, it was insufficient to simply name the factors the young men described as most determinative of their educational trajectories. The young men's beliefs and thoughts about why these factors mattered led to a much more robust interpretation of their experiential knowledge. Hence, their worldviews allowed for substantive theorizations of race specific to its intersections with other social identities. This theorization was necessary for exposing and reflecting on common sense (White supremacist) logic influencing young Black men and boys' schooling experiences.

Phase 2: Creating Themes and Constructing a Composite Counterstory

The second phase of my data analysis centered on noting patterns within each category to derive the essence of the lived experiences being described.[28] I scrutinized data in the textural category and the structural category separately. I examined the data for the frequent reoccurrence of specific physical descriptions, ideas/concepts, and references to create themes in each category. My primary aim was to establish some intersubjective agreement about the specific factors most significant to determining these young men's educational trajectories and the reasoning from which to conclude why and how these factors were perceived to be noteworthy by the young men.[29] For example, all seventeen of the young men explicitly mentioned the UP Creed in their interview. Not only did most of them describe a specific moment when they used the Creed, they *also* articulated its importance for helping them overcome obstacles or barriers to their college completion.

It is during this phase of the data analysis that I juxtaposed individual participants' experiential knowledge (data in the textural data category) with data from the structural category to construct composite descriptions of the phenomenon.[30] All the data in these two categories were organized by their primary themes. This allowed me to then maneuver the data such that I could demonstrate how the young men's individual narratives were in conversation with one another. Next, I studied the relationships between data in the structural category with data in the textural category to begin discerning the value these young men placed on specific events, decisions, moments, incidents, and interactions. This allowed me to make inferences about the quality and contribution of *specific* lived experiences or experiential knowledge that, from the young men's narratives, were essential to either supporting or impeding their preparation to be successful in higher education. A final version of the data were then rearranged and grouped by theme.

Phase Three: Critical Race Interpretations

The third and final phase of my data analysis was a CRT interrogation of the of data gathered under each theme category. My use of CRT as an analytic framework centered on a deep examination of the relationship among race, racism, and power in the young men's narratives from a structural and institutional perspective. The resulting interpretations comprise the Zoom Out portions of chapters 2–5. I used phenomenology as the chief research methodological approach and used theorizations of race subsumed under the CRT banner, such as interest convergence, color blindness, and race neutrality, as the chief interpretive perspectives.[31] My philosophical assumptions about the significance of race and (anti-Black) racism in these young men's educational journeys are rooted in CRT propositions such as "racism is endemic to American society," "racial realism," and others described above.[32] I examined the counterstory paying explicit attention to the machinations of White supremacy for helping to make sense of these young men's descriptions of life on the South Side and the contributions of Urban Prep in their journeys to and through college.

My use of CRT as the chief interpretive toolkit for discerning why race mattered to these young men's educational trajectories also necessitated that I apply an intersectional lens to examine their composite counterstory.[33] For example, in chapter 3 I attended to the intersections of race with gender and sexuality to make sense of the ways the young men reference "brotherhood" and be(com)ing "successful Black men." An intersectional viewpoint allowed me to better discern how and why race shaded or mediated both the *what* of their journeys to college (textural) and the *how* or *why* (structural). Furthermore, attending to the intersectionality of race with gender, sexuality, and class at various points throughout *Urban Preparation* grounded my sense making around the young men's subjectivities relative to the factors they perceived most influenced their agency to attend and ultimately complete college.[34] This analysis also helped paint a picture of the ways that Black men can be both oppressed and oppressor. Intersectionality is useful for noticing how our own privilege manifests itself in various institutional contexts for which we are members. This lens also clarifies our role in ensuring that these environments are antioppressive for others who are multiply subordinated.

This last—and arguably most important—phase of the analysis was instrumental for drawing conclusions about the potential benefits and threats of specific educational ideologies, practices, and philosophies to the urban education of young Black men and boys. I constructed the counterstory by selecting what I found to be the most complete, most compelling pieces of evidence from each theme. These pieces of evidence are the dialogue quotes that drive the counterstory told in the Zoom In sections of chapters 2–5.[35] I arranged and presented the data in a way that would easily tell the story of the young men's journey from Chicago's South Side to and through college.

Positionality, Minimizing Threats to Reliability, and Establishing Trustworthiness

Taken collectively, the counterstory can be described as a *testimonio,* or a "narrative produced in the form of a printed text, told in the first person by a narrator who is also the real protagonist or witness of the events she or he recounts."[36] The young men whose narratives I feature are my former students. This provided me with an important vantage point from which to interpret and narrate the experiences and events they described during the data-gathering phase of the project. I have first-hand knowledge of Urban Prep and the population of students the school continues to serve. I submit that my witness is much more of an asset to the research design, analysis, and reporting in this book than a barrier or liability. My subjectivity as a Black man first, and researcher second, adds several benefits for data collection and analysis specific to examining these young men's own meaning making about the factors that determined their success in route to and through higher education.[37]

First, rapport and comfort with the researcher(s) is an important aspect of qualitative interviewing.[38] As such, Derrick and I were able to solicit a considerable amount of information from the young men because they knew us personally and extended to us a substantial measure of trust. To that end, it had been at least seven years since I taught any one of these young men, and at the time of data collection, I had not seen or had substantive interaction with any of the participants in at least four years. This distance minimized the degree of conviviality between us, at least initially, but there was still some familiarity. This degree of familiarity certainly increased their honesty and vulnerability during the interviews, considering the sensitive nature of some of what they divulged during our conversations.

I took several other standard measures to build trustworthiness. First, I invited the young men to check the final composite counterstory.[39] Those who were available when I reached out to them also offered me direct feedback on early drafts of the narrative portions of chapters 2–5. Michael Quinn Patton emphasizes dialogue among multiple perspectives in qualitative research.[40] This dialogue includes the conversation of the participants' experiences one with the other in the data. I examined the data for intersubjective agreement of the individual narratives collected from each participant to finalize the themes to be represented by the counterstory. No one student necessarily shared the exact same set of encounters with teachers, instruction, and the curriculum while attending UP. In the interviews, we asked participants to avoid using specific names or events and focused the protocol on very general questions so that the young men did not feel constrained to answer questions too narrowly. My research assistant and several colleagues with expertise in qualitative research and the use of CRT read the counterstory and gave me feedback on the quality and fidelity of my analyses. These conversations offered me important insight for revising final iterations of the findings presented in chapters 2–5.

Finally, I corroborated major themes from the analysis of interview data with other available documents (e.g., Illinois Report Card, articles, speeches and panel appearances by Tim King, news specials or reports, and the UP website). I wanted everything I included as evidence in this book—except for the young men's interviews, of course—to be information anybody could look up, academic or lay reader. And, again, my own personal experiences as a native Chicagoan, a former employee of Chicago Public Schools, and a founding UP teacher helped me to contextualize, define, and corroborate details included in the composite counterstory. I knew where to find information that would clarify an event, moment, incident, or decision described by the young men. Also, much of what I'd seen as a teacher at UP could not be disentangled from the young men's descriptions of their academic experiences. In psychology, this might be referred to as "memory work."[41] Being that this research was admittedly subjective, it was important to draw on my own experiences to interpret various findings from the other data in relationship to broader knowledge in the field of Black education and urban education. My own experiential knowledge and use of other forms of document data provided the context needed to extract the most honest understandings of phenomena made visible through these young men's personal narratives.

Afterword

Education opportunity for Black boys and young men continues to capture the imagination of those interested in the power and possibilities of schooling in the United States. During the past three decades, a corpus of journal articles, reports, social media commentaries, blogs, and scholarly and popular books has detailed both the promise and precarious position of Black male youth in school. While the vast majority of this work points to these students as problems, and the urban schools in which they are located as primary sources of these problems, the full story remains untold. Most of this work generally starts with a deficit-centered conceptualization and, unsurprisingly, ends with implications that are limited by the same deficit framing. By focusing on how Black boys and young men challenge urban schools, very little is really comprehended about the ways the urban schools and communities in which these youth learn and grow affect their education experiences and trajectories. This point is not meant to diminish the significant challenges Black boys face in and out of school. For sure, schooling disparities have grave consequences for economic stability, family formation, community continuity, and global competitiveness, which are acute for those in underresourced and uncaring schools. Yet, at this perilous historical moment, when the contempt for public schooling grows and investment in quality education experiences wanes, refocusing our attention on how to marvel at and ignite the magic of these students is not only timely but also necessary.

An important contribution of *Urban Preparation: Young Black Men Moving from Chicago's South Side to Success in Higher Education* is its exploration of what we know about Black boys and men in an urban school setting through their voices, their narrations of the journey to and through college. While research on Black male achievement, performance, and behavioral disparities serves as the core of most of the traditional education literature about these students, this book offers a nuanced context for understanding how urban schools limit as well as liberate the possibilities of Black boys and young men. A longer and more critical view of the historical and contemporary knowledge base about Black boys and men in schools grounds *Urban Preparation* in a way that feels both familiar and fresh in its appreciation. Considering the limitations of current deficient-oriented research of Black youth growing up poor, Chezare Warren pays needed attention to the structural realities of urban schools that produce the race, class, and gender contexts in which students develop academically and socially.

The expansion of charters, the promise of more vouchers, and the enduring implementation of whole-school reform initiatives have enlivened the current policy environment of school reform. The effects of many of these efforts, however, are unclear, and they continue to frustrate reform advocates, policy makers, educators, and parents. Whether or not reforms are missing the important day-to-day realities of urban schooling, including attention to organizational function and dysfunction, weak social infrastructure, and the inability to ensure the fidelity of implementing reform strategies, urban schools pose a particular challenge.[1] Until the lives of students inhabiting these spaces of education reform are understood beyond problem-centered narratives and numbers, efforts to increase academic and life success will be inadequate.

The importance of urban schools in advancing education opportunity is rarely questioned, yet these sites continue to be highly contested. The challenges many urban schools face are in part created by a lack of political will from stakeholders whose commitment to expanding learning opportunities, talent development, and equitable school funding is fragile. The vulnerable position of these schools is not only troubling politically, but there are also severe social and cultural consequences for the students and the communities they serve.[2] This fragility is even more pronounced when urban schools put race, gender, and class at the center of their mission. Therefore, it is not surprising that most urban schools find themselves in the crosshairs of divergent concerns about emphasizing accountability rather than innovation. To be fair, describing these two concerns as a rigid dichotomy is not completely accurate. Much evidence is available to suggest that there are real tensions between worrying about accountability and focusing on innovative social organization of schools.[3] It is also clear that pressures to raise standards and improve student achievement measured by traditional assessment approaches tame attempts to engage in imaginative reforms.[4]

This tenuous relationship between innovative efforts in structuring urban schooling and the politics of reform appears in both practice and in scholarly discourse and research on urban education. It is not difficult to understand an unease at this current moment in the political and policy landscape, when the war on public schooling rages seemingly unabated. Even in the midst of this political uncertainty, schools like Urban Prep unapologetically engage in reforms that center the identity of Black students in a larger historical narrative. The long struggle of resisting notions about the inhumanity of Black people is also tied to a politic of education, but one grounded in liberation and uplift. For sure, this pursuit of racial uplift through education has always been a dangerous enterprise.[5] Now enters the idea that schools are intentionally Black, classed, and consciously gendered—anchored in the belief that at this identity intersection lie the power and potential to change the script of how students are equipped to navigate larger contexts of domination and oppression. The education of Black boys and young men in single-sex school settings offers a unique glimpse into the black box that could help explain how to improve urban education and opportunity.

Research about the ways race, class, and gender animate urban schooling provides a compelling case study. Scholarship on urban schooling, although important in its aim to provide authentic accounts, wrestles with the uncertainty of capturing the continuing tensions between innovation and accountability. Single-sex urban schools offer a portal for understanding these tensions, especially the study of Black boys and young men in learning settings where race/class/gender is presented as implicit and explicit curriculum. For instance, how urban schools manage identity-informed missions as well as negotiate traditional achievement expectations for its students creates an angst that diminishes the production of both relevant research and practice. Researchers are dealing with this challenge on two fronts. Contemporary studies of Black boys and young men in schools tend to lessen this tension by theorizing the unique schooling experience of Black gendered bodies or by offering thoughtful critique of opportunity structures that limit education possibilities and life chances.[6] Likewise, some high school–based studies attempt to capture relevant indicators of success, such as academic performance and college admissions, in adherence to acceptable measures that hold schools accountable to public funding and private investments. Studies focusing on schools like Urban Prep, a community of practice that attempts to disrupt the legacy of anti-Black racism and restrictive gender-conforming roles, add to this body of research by expanding notions of student success.

To be clear, this is not a book about Urban Prep or schools like it. Rather, in cultivating *Urban Preparation* at the scholarly intersection of race, class, and gender, Warren intends to reveal the schisms that research on urban schooling has for too long tried to undertheorize or simply ignore. The power of this text lies in its ability to keep our eyes on pathways of possibility that implicate the daunting challenges of schooling Black and Brown children in schools, districts, and neighborhoods that too many politicians and citizens have written off or forgotten. Long-standing concerns about how Black boys and men are imagined and represented still linger. However, *Urban Preparation* highlights pathways and narratives hidden by discourses of stereotypes and deficits that kill hope by obscuring what is possible in education. And Warren reminds us that the endgame is to actualize potential and counter the perils of urban schooling for Black boys and men in our social imagination.

Creating nurturing spaces of self-discovery and community awareness where Black boys and young men are not deprived of imagining their greater selves (past, present, and future) becomes more critical given the volatile family, schooling, and community circumstances many of these students face. These concerns are not new or solely the product of the contemporary urban schooling experiences of Black boys. Urban schooling can be intentional in its objective to liberate and create learning spaces to make sense of various identity positions. In the process, identities can be created and explored with the help of caring communities, parents, teachers, and education professionals. This marks a move from recognizing potential to actualizing urban schooling as a true site for the development of social identities that build community and create education opportunity.

Schools are powerful in their potential to become counterspaces where various identities are wrestled with and experienced.[7] Just as they are supported in their academic studies and college aspirations, Black students have to be similarly supported in their negotiation of conceivable race, class, and gender identities. For too many Black male youth, their experiences of education pathways (from preschool to university) represent boundaries and constraints rather than options and opportunities. The need to conceive new meanings of education trajectories and college pathways is obvious given who students are and the contexts that inform the meaning of their lives. Identity possibilities at the intersection of race, class, and gender can constitute a reimagined hope of possible selves for Black boys and young men that is transformative and enduring.

James Earl Davis
Professor of Higher Education and
Bernard C. Watson Endowed Chair in Urban Education,
College of Education, Temple University

Notes

Foreword

1. Beverly M. Gordon, "The Necessity of African-American Epistemology for Educational Theory and Practice," *Journal of Education* 172, no. 3 (1990): 88.
2. Mwalimu J. Shujaa, *Too Much Schooling, Too Little Education: A Paradox of Black Life in White Societies* (Trenton, NJ: Africa World Press, 1994).

Introduction

1. I conceptualize *urban* as any medium to large, densely populated metropolitan region with considerable diversity (economic, racial, ethnic, religious, linguistic, etc.). I use *urban-dwelling* to represent the segregated communities of color that are disproportionately high poverty and the interlocking systems of oppression that lead to, and maintain, untenable living conditions. Throughout the text I use "young Black men and boys." I do not provide an acronym, such as YBMB, on purpose. I believe abbreviations dehumanize the population I am writing about and minimize their within-group diversity. "Young Black men and boys" is meant to be broad and encapsulating. I use it to primarily represent a school-age population (three to twenty-five). I do use *male* at different points but have attempted to limit its application because of the way this term tends to mute gender and sexuality, while at the same time privilege biological sex. I also believe that the language of "Black male" is not fully inclusive of those who choose to identify as man or boy who may not have been born with male sex organs.
2. S. D. Horsford and C. Sampson, "Promise Neighborhoods: The Promise and Politics of Community Capacity Building as Urban School Reform," *Urban Education* 49, no. 8 (2014): 955—91, doi:10.1177/0042085914557645; Peter C Murrell, *The Community Teacher: A New Framework for Effective Urban Teaching* (New York: Teachers College Press, 2001); Charles M. Payne, *So Much Reform, So Little Change: The Persistence of Failure in Urban Schools* (Cambridge, MA: Harvard Education Press, 2008); Terrance L. Green, "Leading for Urban School Reform and Community Development," *Educational Administration Quarterly* 51, no. 5 (2015): 679–711.
3. At the time this book was written, two of the seventeen young men had not completed college; one was enrolled in a community college with plans to transfer back to the university he had been attending, and the other, who dropped out due to financial hardship, was working with the university administration to reenroll.
4. Derrick R. Brooms, "'Trying to Find Self': Promoting Excellence and Building Community Among African American Males," in *Advances in Race and Ethnicity in Education African American Male Students in PreK–12 Schools,* ed. J. L. Moore and C. W. Lewis (Bingley, UK: Emerald, 2014): 61–86, doi:10.1108/s2051-231720140000002021; Edward Fergus, Pedro Noguera, and Margary Martin, *Schooling for Resilience: Improving the Life Trajectory of Black*

and Latino Boys (Cambridge, MA: Harvard Education Press, 2014); Chezare Warren, "Conflicts and Contradictions: Conceptions of Empathy and the Work of Good-Intentioned Early Career White Female Teachers," *Urban Education* 50, no. 5 (2015): 572–600; Chezare Warren, "'We Learn Through Our Struggles': Nuancing Notions of Urban Black Male Academic Preparation for Postsecondary Success," *Teachers College Record* 118, no. 6 (2016): 1–38.

5. Dolores Delgado Bernal, "Using a Chicana Feminist Epistemology in Educational Research," *Harvard Educational Review* 68, no. 4 (1998): 555–83, doi:10.17763/haer.68.4.5wv1034973g22q48; Cynthia B. Dillard, "The Substance of Things Hoped For, the Evidence of Things Not Seen: Examining an Endarkened Feminist Epistemology in Educational Research and Leadership," *International Journal of Qualitative Studies in Education* 13, no. 6 (2000): 661, doi:10.1080/09518390050211565.
6. Dillard, "The Substance of Things Hoped For."
7. Richard Delgado and Jean Stefancic, *Critical Race Theory: An Introduction* (New York: New York University Press, 2001).
8. Daniel G. Solórzano and Tara J. Yosso, "Critical Race Methodology: Counter-Storytelling as an Analytical Framework for Education Research," *Qualitative Inquiry* 8, no. 1 (2002): 29, doi:10.1177/107780040200800103.
9. Tara J. Yosso, "Whose Culture Has Capital? A Critical Race Theory Discussion of Community Cultural Wealth," *Race, Ethnicity and Education* 8, no. 1 (2005): 69–91, doi:10.1080/1361332052000341006.
10. Jessica T. Decuir and Adrienne D. Dixson, "'So When It Comes Out, They Aren't That Surprised That It Is There': Using Critical Race Theory as a Tool of Analysis of Race and Racism in Education," *Educational Researcher* 33, no. 5 (2004): 26–31, doi:10.3102/0013189x033005026; Daniel G. Solórzano and Tara J. Yosso, "Critical Race and LatCrit Theory and Method: Counter-Storytelling," *International Journal of Qualitative Studies in Education* 14, no. 4 (2001): 471–95, doi:10.1080/09518390110063365; Solórzano and Yosso, "Critical Race Methodology" Tara J. Yosso, *Critical Race Counterstories Along the Chicana/Chicano Educational Pipeline* (New York: Routledge, 2006).
11. Solórzano and Yosso, "Critical Race Methodology," 32.
12. Laurence Parker and Marvin Lynn, "What's Race Got to Do with It? Critical Race Theory's Conflicts with and Connections to Qualitative Research Methodology and Epistemology," *Qualitative Inquiry* 8, no. 1 (2002): 11.
13. Ibid., 18.
14. Solórzano and Yosso, "Critical Race Methodology," 33.
15. Ibid., 36.
16. Derrick A. Bell, *Faces at the Bottom of the Well: The Permanence of Racism* (New York: Basic Books, 1992); Daniella Ann Cook and Adrienne D. Dixson, "Writing Critical Race Theory and Method: A Composite Counterstory on the Experiences of Black Teachers in New Orleans Post-Katrina," *International Journal of Qualitative Studies in Education* 26, no. 10 (2013): 1238–58; Sharon F. Rallis, *Principals of Dynamic Schools: Taking Charge of Change* (Newbury Park, CA: Corwin Press, 1993); Sharon F. Rallis, *Dynamic Teachers: Leaders of Change* (Thousands Oaks, CA: Corwin Press, 1995); Gretchen B. Rossman and Sharon F. Rallis, *Learning in the Field: An Introduction to Qualitative Research* (Thousand Oaks, CA: Sage, 2003); Solórzano and Yosso, "Critical Race Methodology."
17. Tim King offers a testimony regarding his founding of Urban Prep and the significance of the school for "changing the narrative for Black boys." See "Tim King 10 & Change," https://www.youtube.com/watch?v=rEp5_CNhCD0.

18. Much of the information in this section is from the school's website, www.urbanprep.org, or is based on my experience as a member of the UP founding faculty.
19. Every year of its operation, the UP-Englewood campus has shared a building with a nonaffiliated, coeducational public secondary school.
20. http://www.urbanprep.org/pdf/urbanprepbrochure2014.pdf.
21. Illinois Report Card for Urban Prep-Englewood Campus, 2015–16, https://illinoisreportcard.com/School.aspx?source=profile&Schoolid=15016299025010C.
22. http://www.urbanprep.org/about/newsroom/news/news-100-percent-2016.
23. According to the Illinois Report Card, college readiness is primarily determined by the percentage of students at the school who achieve a 21 or better on the ACT assessment. While a test score is not a definitive depiction of a school's instructional effectiveness, this metric provides one important perspective about the quality of the school's academic programs. https://illinoisreportcard.com.
24. The data reported in this section is publicly available, either from UP's website (www.urbanprep.org,) or the Illinois Report Card (https://illinoisreportcard.com). I wanted to use data that can easily be found by the public. The school has annually made public announcements of its graduates' college acceptance rates. It has not published any formal announcements of its college persistence or completion rates that I have been able to find. UP has also not made annual reports available beyond 2009 on its website.
25. Urban Prep brochure, http://www.urbanprep.org/pdf/urbanprepbrochure2014.pdf.
26. Academic self-efficacy is the confidence a young person possesses in his or her ability to expertly negotiate challenging academic tasks to achieve academic success. See Martin M. Chemers, Li-tze Hu, and Ben F. Garcia, "Academic Self-Efficacy and First-Year College Student Performance and Adjustment," *Journal of Educational Psychology* 93, no. 1 (2001): 55.
27. https://www.edutopia.org/blog/swords-shields-urban-prep-tim-king.
28. Bell, *Faces at the Bottom of the Well;* Cook and Dixson, "Writing Critical Race Theory and Method"; Kimberlé Crenshaw, "Mapping the Margins: Intersectionality, Identity Politics, and Violence Against Women of Color," *Stanford Law Review* 43 (1991): 1241–99; Solórzano and Yosso, "Critical Race Methodology."
29. See Leah Clapman, "U.S. Schools Make Progress, but 'Dropout Factories' Persist," *PBS Newshour,* November 30, 2010, http://www.pbs.org/newshour/rundown/us-schools-make-progress-but-dropout-factories-persist/.
30. Michael J. Dumas, "'Waiting for Superman' to Save Black People: Racial Representation and the Official Antiracism of Neoliberal School Reform," *Discourse: Studies in the Cultural Politics of Education* 34, no. 4 (2013): 531–47; Katy Swalwell and Michael W. Apple, "Reviewing Policy: Starting the Wrong Conversations: The Public School Crisis and 'Waiting for Superman.'" *Educational Policy* 25, no. 2 (2011): 368–82.

Chapter 1

1. Gloria Ladson-Billings, "From the Achievement Gap to the Education Debt: Understanding Achievement in U.S. Schools," *Educational Researcher* 35, no. 7 (2006): 3–12, doi:10.3102/0013189x035007003.
2. Prudence L. Carter and Sean F. Reardon, "Inequality Matters," William T. Grant Foundation, http://wtgrantfoundation.org/focus-areas#reducing-inequality; J. J. Irvine, "Foreword," in *Culture, Curriculum, and Identity in Education*, ed. H. Richard Milner (New York: Palgrave Macmillan, 2010), xi–xvi; H. Richard Milner, *Start Where You Are, but Don't Stay There: Understanding Diversity, Opportunity Gaps, and Teaching in Today's Classrooms* (Cambridge, MA:

Harvard Education Press, 2010); H. Richard Milner, "Beyond a Test Score: Explaining Opportunity Gaps in Educational Practice," *Journal of Black Studies* 43, no. 6 (2012): 693–718, doi:10.1177/0021934712442539.

3. Motoko Akiba, Gerald K. LeTendre, and Jay P. Scribner, "Teacher Quality, Opportunity Gap, and National Achievement in 46 Countries," *Educational Researcher* 36, no. 7 (2007): 369–87; Prudence L. Carter and Kevin G. Welner, eds., *Closing the Opportunity Gap: What America Must Do to Give Every Child an Even Chance* (New York: Oxford University Press, 2013); Alfinio Flores, "Examining Disparities in Mathematics Education: Achievement Gap or Opportunity Gap?" *High School Journal* 91, no. 1 (2007): 29–42, doi:10.1353/hsj.2007.0022; Sally M. Reis and Joseph S. Renzulli, "Opportunity Gaps Lead to Achievement Gaps: Encouragement for Talent Development and Schoolwide Enrichment in Urban Schools," *Journal of Education* 190, no. 1 (2010): 43–49; Ross Wiener, "Opportunity Gaps: The Injustice Underneath Achievement Gaps in Our Public Schools," *North Carolina Law Review* 85 (2006): 1315-44.
4. Carter and Welner, *Closing the Opportunity Gap,* 1.
5. I use this language to specify how racist ideologies, practices, and systems specifically work to disadvantage Black people in ways completely separate from other historically marginalized racial subgroups.
6. I use *success* here to name the capacity of young Black men to get admitted to and graduate from a four-year college or university. I argue, however, that postsecondary success should not be limited solely to college matriculation and completion; there are many kinds of postsecondary success worth further consideration.
7. James D. Anderson, *The Education of Blacks in the South, 1860–1935* (Chapel Hill: University of North Carolina Press, 1988); Theresa Perry and Lisa D. Delpit, ed., *The Real Ebonics Debate: Power, Language, and the Education of African-American Children* (Boston: Beacon Press, 1998); Geneva Smitherman, *Talkin and Testifyin: The Language of Black America* (Boston: Houghton Mifflin, 1977).
8. H. Richard Milner, *Rac(e)ing to Class: Confronting Poverty and Race in Schools and Classrooms* (Cambridge, MA: Harvard Education Press, 2015).
9. Beverly Daniel Tatum, *Why Are All the Black Kids Sitting Together in the Cafeteria? And Other Conversations about Race* (New York: Basic Books, 1997).
10. Cheryl E. Matias, *Feeling White: Whiteness, Emotionality, and Education* (Rotterdam: Sense, 2016).
11. W. E. B. Du Bois, *The Philadelphia Negro: A Social Study* (Philadelphia: University of Pennsylvania Press, 1899).
12. W. E. B. Du Bois, *The Souls of Black Folk* (Chicago: A. C. McClurg, 1903).
13. Thierry Devos and Mahzarin R. Banaji, "American = White?" *Journal of Personality and Social Psychology* 88, no. 3 (2005): 447.
14. Carter Godwin Woodson, *The Mis-Education of the Negro* (Trenton, NJ: Africa World Press, 2011), 99.
15. David Wallace Adams, *Education for Extinction: American Indians and the Boarding School Experience, 1875–1928* (Lawrence: University Press of Kansas, 1995).
16. Michael J. Dumas, "Against the Dark: Antiblackness in Education Policy and Discourse," *Theory into Practice* 55, no. 1 (2015): 11–19, doi:10.1080/00405841.2016.1116852.
17. Gerren Keith Gaynor, "Hampton University Business School Bans Dreadlocks," *Black Enterprise,* August 23, 2012, http://www.blackenterprise.com/news/hampton-business-dean-bans-dreadlocks/.
18. Derrick A. Bell Jr., *Faces at the Bottom of the Well: The Permanence of Racism* (New York: Basic Books, 1992).

19. Michèle Foster, *Black Teachers on Teaching* (New York: New Press, 1997); Peter H. Irons, *Jim Crow's Children: The Broken Promise of the* Brown *Decision* (New York: Viking, 2002); Kathleen Berkeley and Vanessa Siddle Walker, "Their Highest Potential: An African American School Community in the Segregated South," *Journal of American History* 84, no. 1 (1997): 286, doi:10.2307/2952854; William H. Watkins, *The White Architects of Black Education: Ideology and Power in America, 1865–1954* (New York: Teachers College Press, 2001).
20. Derrick A. Bell Jr., "*Brown v. Board of Education* and the Interest-Convergence Dilemma," *Harvard Law Review* 93 (1979–80): 518–33.
21. William F. Tate, Gloria Ladson-Billings, and Carl A. Grant, "The Brown Decision Revisited: Mathematizing Social Problem," *Educational Policy* 7, no. 3 (1993): 255–75, doi:10.1177/089 5904893007003002.
22. Michele Foster, *Black Teachers on Teaching* (New York: The New Press, 1998); Vanessa Siddle Walker, *Their Highest Potential: An African American School Community in the Segregated South* (Chapel Hill: University of North Carolina Press, 1996).
23. Peter C. Murrell, *The Community Teacher: A New Framework for Effective Urban Teaching* (New York: Teachers College Press, 2001).
24. James D. Anderson, *The Education of Blacks in the South, 1860–1935* (Chapel Hill: University of North Carolina Press, 1988), 5.
25. Watkins, *The White Architects of Black Education;* Anderson, *The Education of Blacks in the South,* 91.
26. Bell, "*Brown v. Board of Education* and the Interest-Convergence Dilemma."
27. Rebecca Goldring, Lucinda Gray, and Amy Bitterman, *Characteristics of Public and* Private Elementary and Secondary School Teachers in the United States: Results From *the 2011–12 Schools and Staffing Survey* (Washington, DC: National Center for Education Statistics, US Department of Education, 2016); American Association of Colleges for Teacher Education Professional Education (AACTE), *The Changing Teacher Preparation Profession* (Washington, DC: AACTEPE Data System, 2013).
28. Kevin Willmot and Spike Lee, *ChiRaq,* dir. Spike Lee (40Acres and a Mule, Amazon Studios, 2015).
29. William T. Hoston, "Black-on-Black Murders: A Case Study of Chiraq, Killinois," in *Black Masculinity in the Obama Era* (New York: Palgrave Macmillan, 2014), 67–89.
30. Carter and Welner, *Closing the Opportunity Gap;* Linda Darling-Hammond, "Inequality and the Right to Learn: Access to Qualified Teachers in California's Public Schools," *Teachers College Record* 106, no. 10 (2004): 1936–66, doi:10.1111/j.1467-9620.2004.00422.x; Irvine, "Foreword"; Milner, *Start Where You Are;* Milner, "Beyond a Test Score."
31. Carter and Welner, *Closing the Opportunity Gap.*
32. Marilyn Cochran-Smith, "Color Blindness and Basket Making Are Not the Answers: Confronting the Dilemmas of Race, Culture, and Language Diversity in Teacher Education," *American Educational Research Journal* 32, no. 3 (1995): 493–522; Kenneth J. Fasching-Varner, *Working Through Whiteness: Examining White Racial Identity and Profession with Pre-Service Teachers* (Lanham, MD: Lexington Press, 2013); Daniella Ann Cook, "Shifting the Center in Teacher Education: An Introduction to the Special Issue on Critical Race Theory and Teacher Education," *Urban Review* 47, no. 2 (2014): 233–36, doi:10.1007/s11256-014-0290-9.
33. Milner, "Beyond a Test Score."
34. Wiener, "Opportunity Gaps: The Injustice Underneath Achievement Gaps in Our Public Schools."
35. Ashley Fantz, "94 out of 97 Detroit Public Schools Closed Due to Teacher 'Sickouts,'" CNN, May 2, 2016, http://www.cnn.com/2016/05/02/us/detroit-schools-teacher-sickout/.

36. Bell, "*Brown v. Board of Education* and the Interest-Convergence Dilemma."
37. Milner, "Beyond a Test Score."
38. Carter and Reardon, "Inequality Matters," 3.
39. Django Paris, "Culturally Sustaining Pedagogy: A Needed Change in Stance, Terminology, and Practice," *Educational Researcher* 41, no. 3 (2012): 93–97, doi:10.3102/0013189x12441244.
40. Linda Darling-Hammond, *The Flat World and Education: How America's Commitment to Equity Will Determine Our Future* (New York: Teachers College Press, 2010); Milner, *Start Where You Are;* Milner and Howard, *Rac(e)ing to Class.*
41. Christopher Jencks, "Whom Must We Treat Equally for Educational Opportunity to Be Equal?" *Ethics* 98, no. 3 (1988): 518–33, doi:10.1086/292969.
42. Pedro Noguera, "Urban Schools and the Black Male 'Challenge,'" In *Handbook of Urban Education,* ed. H. R. Milner and K. Lomotey (New York: Routledge, 2014), 114–28.
43. US Department of Education, Policy and Programs Study Service, "Single-Sex Versus Coeducation Schooling: A Systematic Review: Final Report," 2005, http://www2.ed.gov/rschstat/eval/other/single-sex/single-sex.pdf.
44. National Association for Single Sex Public Education, "Single-Sex Schools/Schools with Single-Sex Classrooms/What's the Difference?" http://www.singlesexschools.org/schools-schools.htm.
45. Erin Pahlke, Janet Shibley Hyde, and Carlie M. Allison, "The Effects of Single-Sex Compared with Coeducational Schooling on Students' Performance and Attitudes: A Meta-Analysis," *Psychological Bulletin* 140, no. 4 (2014): 1042–72.
46. Edward Fergus and Pedro Noguera, "Theories of Change Among Single-Sex Schools for Black and Latino Boys: An Intervention in Search of Theory" (white paper, Metropolitan Center for Urban Education, Steinhardt School of Culture, Education, and Human Development, New York University, 2010).
47. Edward Fergus, Pedro Noguera, and Margary Martin, *Schooling for Resilience: Improving the Life Trajectory of Black and Latino Boys* (Cambridge, MA: Harvard Education Press, 2014).
48. Abigail Norfleet James and Herbert C. Richards, "Escaping Stereotypes: Educational Attitudes of Male Alumni of Single-Sex and Coed Schools," *Psychology of Men & Masculinity* 4, no. 2 (2003): 136–48, doi:10.1037/1524-9220.4.2.136.
49. Fred Bonner, *Building on Resilience: Models and Frameworks of Black Male Success Across the P-20 Pipeline* (Sterling, VA: Stylus, 2014); Fergus, Noguera, and Martin, *Schooling for Resilience;* Chezare A. Warren, "'We Learn Through Our Struggles': Nuancing Notions of Urban Black Male Academic Preparation for Postsecondary Success," *Teachers College Record* 118, no. 6 (2016): 1–38.
50. Fergus, Noguera, and Martin, *Schooling for Resilience.*
51. Thomas S. Popkewitz, "History, the Problem of Knowledge, and the New Cultural History of Schooling." In *Cultural History and Education: Critical Essays on Knowledge and Schooling,* ed. Thomas S. Popkewitz, Miguel A. Pereyra, and Barry M. Franklin (New York: Routledge, 2001), 1.

Chapter 2

1. See Tama Leventhal and Jeanne Brooks-Gunn, "The Neighborhoods They Live In: The Effects of Neighborhood Residence on Child and Adolescent Outcomes," *Psychological Bulletin* 126, no. 2 (2000): 309; Annette Lareau, *Unequal Childhoods: Class, Race, and Family Life* (Berkeley: University of California Press, 2011); Frank F. Furstenberg, Thomas D. Cook, Jacquelynne Eccles, Glen H. Elder Jr., and Arnold Sameroff, *Managing to Make It: Urban Families and Adolescent Success* (Chicago: University of Chicago Press, 1999).

2. Sankofa is a pictorial representation (Adinkra) and practice that promotes African consciousness. See Christel N. Temple, "The Emergence of Sankofa Practice in the United States: A Modern History," *Journal of Black Studies* 41, no. 1 (2010): 127.
3. Chezare A. Warren, "'We Learn Through Our Struggles': Nuancing Notions of Urban Black Male Academic Preparation for Postsecondary Success," *Teachers College Record* 118, no. 6 (2016): 1–34.
4. Carla O'Connor, Jennifer Mueller, and Alaina Neal, "Student Resilience in Urban America," in *Handbook of Urban Education,* ed. H. Rich Milner and Kofi Lomotey (New York: Routledge, 2014), 75–96.
5. Fred A. Bonner, *Building on Reslience: Models and Frameworks of Black Male Success Across the P–20 Pipeline* (Sterling, VA: Stylus, 2014); O'Connor, Mueller, and Neal, "Student Resilence in Urban America," 75; Tyrone C. Howard, *Black Male(d): Peril and Promise in the Education of African American Males* (New York: Teachers College Press, 2014); Bonnie Benard, *Resiliency: What We Have Learned* (San Francisco: WestEd, 2004).
6. Derrick R. Brooms, "'We Didn't Let the Neighborhood Win': Black Male Students' Experiences in Negotiating and Navigating an Urban Neighborhood," *Journal of Negro Education* 84, no. 3 (2015): 269–81.
7. Roderick L. Carey, "'Keep That in Mind . . . You're Gonna Go to College': Family Influence on the College Going Processes of Black and Latino High School Boys," *Urban Review* 48, no. 5 (2016): 718–42, doi:10.1007/s11256-016-0375-8.
8. Fredrick Douglass, "West India Emancipation," 1857, BlackPast.Org, http://www.blackpast.org/1857-frederick-douglass-if-there-no-struggle-there-no-progress.
9. Gilberto Q. Conchas and James Diego Vigil, *Streetsmart Schoolsmart: Urban Poverty and the Education of Adolescent Boys* (New York: Teachers College Press, 2012).
10. Leventhal and Brooks-Gunn, "The Neighborhoods They Live In"; Robert J. Sampson, "Urban Black Violence: The Effect of Male Joblessness and Family Disruption," *American Journal of Sociology* 93, no. 2 (1987): 348.
11. Ralph Sampson, *Great American City: Chicago and the Enduring Neighborhood Effect* (Chicago: University of Chicago Press, 2012); William Julius Wilson, *The Truly Disadvantaged: The Inner City, the Underclass, and Public Policy* (Chicago: University of Chicago Press, 1987); Sudhir Venkatesh, *American Project: The Rise and Fall of a Modern Ghetto* (Cambridge, MA: Harvard University Press, 2000); Alford Young Jr., *The Minds of Marginalized Black Men: Making Sense of Mobility, Opportunity, and Future Life Chances* (Princeton, NJ: Princeton University Press, 2004); Kimberle Crenshaw, Neil Gotanda, Gary Peller, and Kendall Thomas, *Critical Race Theory: The Key Writings That Formed the Movement* (New York: New Press, 1996).
12. Pauline Lipman, *The New Political Economy of Urban Education: Neoliberalism, Race, and the Right to the City* (New York: Routledge, 2011).
13. "Derrion Albert," http://www.chicagotribune.com/topic/crime-law-justice/crime/derrion-albert-PECLB004341222238-topic.html.
14. Floyd D. Beachum and Carlos R. McCray, *Cultural Collision and Collusion: Reflections on Hip Hop, Culture, Values, and Schools* (New York: Peter Lang, 2011).
15. Tara J. Yosso, "Whose Culture Has Capital? A Critical Race Theory Discussion of Community Cultural Wealth," *Race, Ethnicity and Education* 8, no. 1 (2005): 69–91, doi:10.1080/1361332052000341006.
16. Ibid.
17. Ibid., 80.

18. The term *institutional assets* comes out of Terrance L. Green's work on "opportunities in geography," which maps the neighborhood institutional resources that replace inequality—the result of a lack of opportunity—with possibilities for improving the lives of urban youth growing up in low-income communities of color. Terrance L. Green, "Places of Inequality, Places of Possibility: Mapping 'Opportunity in Geography' Across Urban School-Communities," *Urban Review* 47, no. 4 (2015): 717.
19. Chezare A. Warren, "Perspective Divergence and the Mis-Education of Black Boys . . . Like Me," *Journal of African American Males in Education* 5, no. 2 (2014): 134–49; Chezare A. Warren, "Being Black, Being Male, and Choosing to Teach in the 21st Century: Understanding My Role, Embracing My Call," in *Black Male Teachers: Diversifying the United States' Teacher Workforce,* ed. C. W. Lewis and I. Toldson (Bingley, UK: Emerald, 2013).
20. Warren, "Being Black."
21. Vanessa Siddle Walker, *Their Highest Potential: An African American School Community in the Segregated South* (Chapel Hill: University of North Carolina Press, 1996); James James D. Anderson, *The Education of Blacks in the South, 1860–1935* (Chapel Hill: University of North Carolina Press, 1988); Peter C. Murrell, *The Community Teacher: A New Framework for Effective Urban Teaching* (New York: Teachers College Press, 2001).
22. The African proverb "It takes a village to raise a child" advises that a child's healthy development requires that multiple community members attend to his or her well-being and that families need other forms of support in a community to ensure every child's life success.
23. Lory Janelle Dance, *Tough Fronts: The Impact of Street Culture on Schooling* (New York: Routledge, 2002); Pedro Noguera, *The Trouble with Black Boys: And Other Reflections on Race, Equity, and the Future of Public Education* (San Francisco: Jossey-Bass, 2008).
24. Sudhir Alladi Venkatesh, *Off the Books* (Cambridge, MA: Harvard University Press, 2006); Alford A. Young, *The Minds of Marginalized Black Men: Making Sense of Mobility, Opportunity, and Future Life Chances* (Princeton, NJ: Princeton University Press, 2006).
25. See Pierre Bourdieu, *Masculine Domination,* trans. Richard Nice (Palo Alto, CA: Stanford University Press, 2001).
26. Edward Fergus, Pedro Noguera, and Margary Martin, *Schooling for Resilience: Improving the Life Trajectory of Black and Latino Boys* (Cambridge, MA: Harvard Education Press, 2014); Melissa Roderick, "What's Happening to the Boys? Early High School Experiences and School Outcomes Among African American Male Adolescents in Chicago," *Urban Education* 38, no. 5 (2003): 538–607.
27. D. J. Carter Andrews, "Black Males in Middle School: Third Class Citizens in a First Class Society," in *Advancing Black Male Student Success from Preschool Through PhD,* ed. S. R. Harper and J. L. Wood (Sterling, VA: Stylus, 2015); Melissa R. Roderick, "What's Happening to the Boys? Early High School Experiences and School Outcomes Among African-American Male Adolescents in Chicago," *Urban Education* 38, no. 5 (2003): 538–607; Terrell L. Strayhorn, "The Role of Supportive Relationships in Facilitating African American Males' Success in College," *Journal of Student Affairs Research and Practice* 45, no. 1 (2008): 26–48, doi:10.2202/1949-6605.1906; Terry K. Flennaugh, "Black Male High School Students (Un) Accepted Failure in U.S. Schools," in Harper and Wood, eds., *Advancing Black Male Student Success*; Chezare A. Warren, "Making Relationships Work: Elementary-Aged Black Boys and the Schools That Serve Them," in ibid., 21–43.
28. William H. Watkins, *The Assault on Public Education: Confronting the Politics of Corporate School Reform* (New York: Teachers College Press, 2012); Lipman, *The New Political Economy of Urban Education*; Bree Picower and Edwin Mayorga, *What's Race Got to Do with It: How Cur-*

rent School Reform Policy Maintains Racial and Economic Inequality (Bern, Switzerland: Peter Lang, 2015).

29. Stuart Greene, *Race, Community, and Urban Schools: Partnering with African American Families* (New York: Teachers College Press, 2013).
30. Terrance L. Green, "Places of Inequality, Places of Possibility: Mapping 'Opportunity in Geography' Across Urban School-Communities," *Urban Review* 47, no. 4 (2015): 717–41, doi:10.1007/s11256-015-0331-z.
31. "Chicago Board Votes to Close 50 Schools," CNN, May 22, 2013, http://www.cnn.com/2013/05/22/us/illinois-chicago-school-closures/.
32. Center for Research on Education Outcomes, "National Charter School Study" (report, Stanford University, 2013). http://credo.stanford.edu/documents/NCSS%202013%20Final%20Draft.pdf; Andrew Maul and Abby McClelland, "Review of National Charter School Study 2013," Great Lakes Center, http://greatlakescenter.org/docs/Think_Twice/TT_Maul_CREDO-2013.pdf.
33. Jaekyung Lee, "College for All: Gaps Between Desirable and Actual P–12 Math Achievement Trajectories for College Readiness," *Educational Researcher* 41, no. 2 (2012): 43–55.
34. James E. Rosenbaum and Ann E. Person, "Beyond College for All: Policies and Practices to Improve Transitions into College and Jobs," *Professional School Counseling* 6, no. 4 (2003): 252–60.
35. See Chezare A. Warren, "Conflicts and Contradictions: Conceptions of Empathy and the Work of Good-Intentioned Early Career White Female Teachers," *Urban Education* 50, no. 5 (2015): 595.
36. Christopher Emdin, *For White Folks Who Teach in the Hood . . . and the Rest of Y'all Too: Reality Pedagogy and Urban Education* (Boston: Beacon Press, 2016).

Chapter 3

1. Athena Mutua, ed., *Progressive Black Masculinities* (New York: Routledge, 2006).
2. I use the pseudonym X High School so as not to further disparage the youth and families who attend this school or the community of folks who work or serve there.
3. Barbara Rogoff, Leslie Moore, Behnosh Najafi, Amy Dexter, Maricela Correa-Chávez, and Jocelyn Solis, "Children's Development of Cultural Repertoires Through Participation in Everyday Routines and Practices" (paper, University of California, Santa Cruz, 2009), http://u.osu.edu/moore.1817/files/2009/03/Rogoff-Moore-2007-rp4muk.pdf; Frank Rudy Cooper, "Against Bipolar Black Masculinity: Intersectionality, Assimilation, Identity Performance, and Hierarchy," *UC Davis Law Review* 39 (2006): 853; Paula J. Massood, "Mapping the Hood: The Genealogy of City Space in 'Boyz N the Hood' and 'Menace II Society,'" *Cinema Journal* (1996): 85–97.
4. "I can't breathe" is what Eric Garner said repeatedly as he was being choked to death by New York City police officers. For more on this and other stories of state-sanctioned violence, see Marc Lamont Hill, *Nobody: Casualties of America's War on the Vulnerable, from Ferguson to Flint and Beyond* (New York: Simon & Schuster, 2016).
5. Mary Beth Oliver, "African American Men as 'Criminal and Dangerous': Implications of Media Portrayals of Crime on the 'Criminalization' of African American Men," *Journal of African American Studies* 7, no. 2 (2003): 3–18, doi:10.1007/s12111-003-1006-5; Michelle Alexander, *The New Jim Crow: Mass Incarceration in the Age of Colorblindness* (New York: The New Press, 2012).
6. Terri N. Watson, "'Talking Back': The Perceptions and Experiences of Black Girls Who Attend City High School," *Journal of Negro Education* 85, no. 3 (2016): 239–49.

7. Kimberlé Crenshaw, "Mapping the Margins: Intersectionality, Identity Politics, and Violence Against Women of Color," *Stanford Law Review* 43 (1991): 1241–99; Rose M. Brewer and Patricia Hill Collins, "Black Feminist Thought: Knowledge, Consciousness, and the Politics of Empowerment," *Contemporary Sociology* 21, no. 1 (1992): 132, doi:10.2307/2074808; bell hooks, *Talking Back: Thinking Feminist, Thinking Black* (Boston: South End Press, 1989); bell hooks, *Feminist Theory from Margin to Center* (Boston: South End Press, 1984); Cooper, "Against Bipolar Black Masculinity."
8. Eddie Fergus, Pedro Noguera, and Margary Martin, *Schooling for Resilience: Improving the Life Trajectory of Black and Latino Boys* (Cambridge, MA: Harvard Education Press, 2014), 37.
9. Ibid.
10. Cooper, "Against Bipolar Black Masculinity."
11. Martin Luther King Jr., "Letter from the Birmingham Jail," 1963.
12. Evelyn Brooks Higginbotham, *Righteous Discontent: The Women's Movement in the Black Baptist Church, 1880–1920* (Cambridge, MA: Harvard University Press, 1993), 187.
13. Michelle Smith, "Affect and Respectability Politics," *Theory and Event* 17, no. 3 (2014).
14. Frederick C. Harris, "The Rise of Respectability," *Dissent* 61, no. 1 (2014).
15. http://www.cnn.com/videos/us/2016/07/07/graphic-video-minnesota-police-shooting-philando-castile-ryan-young-pkg-nd.cnn; http://www.salon.com/2016/09/21/the-hard-truth-about-terence-crutcher-and-tulsa-what-kind-of-white-person-do-you-want-to-be/.
16. "Education Testing Service," *Policy Notes* 19, no. 3 (2011): 14, http://bit.ly/2hktbPZ.
17. Joseph Derrick Nelson, Garth Stahl, and Derron Wallace, "Race, Class, and Gender Identity in Boys' Education: Repositioning Intersectionality Theory," *Culture, Society and Masculinities* 7, no. 2 (2015): 171.
18. Christopher Emdin, *For White Folks Who Teach in the Hood—and the Rest of Y'all Too: Reality Pedagogy and Urban Education* (Boston: Beacon Press, 2016); Angela Valenzuela, *Subtractive Schooling: U.S.-Mexican Youth and the Politics of Caring* (Albany: State University of New York Press, 1999).
19. Eric Toshalis, *Make Me: Understanding and Engaging Student Resistance in School* (Cambridge, MA: Harvard Education Press, 2015).
20. Ibid.
21. Michael J. Dumas, "'Waiting for Superman' to Save Black People: Racial Representation and the Official Antiracism of Neoliberal School Reform," *Discourse: Studies in the Cultural Politics of Education* 34, no. 4 (2013): 531–47, doi:10.1080/01596306.2013.822621.
22. Joanne W. Golann, "The Paradox of Success at a No-Excuses School," *Sociology of Education* 88, no. 2 (2015): 103–19.
23. "Climb the mountain to college" is KIPP's school motto. See www.kipp.org. Brian Lack, "No Excuses: A Critique of the Knowledge Is Power Program (KIPP) Within Charter Schools in the USA," *Journal for Critical Education Policy Studies* 7, no. 2 (2009): 144.
24. Ibid.
25. Richard H Milner IV, "Beyond a Test Score: Explaining Opportunity Gaps in Educational Practice," *Journal of Black Studies* 43, no. 6 (2012): 693–718.
26. When I was at KIPP, the practice was that when someone did something well, the entire class would offer one clap in unison after receiving the signal from their teacher.
27. Martin Carnoy, Rebecca Jacobsen, Lawrence Mishel, and Richard Rothstein, "Worth the Price? Weighing the Evidence on Charter School Achievement," *Education* 1, no. 1 (2006): 151–61.
28. Fergus, Noguera, and Martin, *Schooling for Resilience.*

29. T. Elon Dancy, *The Brother Code: Manhood and Masculinity Among African American Men in College* (Charlotte, NC: Information Age, 2012).
30. Tony Laing, "Black Masculinities Expressed Through, and Constrained by, Brotherhood," *Journal of Men's Studies,* August 5, 2016, doi:10.1177/1060826516661186.
31. Janna Jackson, "'Dangerous Presumptions': How Single-Sex Schooling Reifies False Notions of Sex, Gender, and Sexuality," *Gender and Education* 22, no. 2 (2010): 227–38, doi:10.1080/09540250903359452; Patricia Hill Collins, *Black Sexual Politics: African Americans, Gender, and the New Racism* (New York: Routledge, 2004).
32. Lory Janelle Dance, *Tough Fronts: The Impact of Street Culture on Schooling* (New York: Routledge, 2002).
33. Joseph D. Nelson, "Relational Teaching with Black Boys: Strategies for Learning at a Single-Sex Middle School for Boys of Color," *Teachers College Record* 118, no. 6 (2016): 1.
34. Fergus, Noguera, and Martin, *Schooling for Resilience;* Chezare A. Warren, "Making Relationships Work: Elementary-Aged Black Boys and the Schools That Serve Them," in *Advancing Black Male Success: Preschool through the PhD,* ed. Shaun Harper and J. Luke Wood (Sterling, VA: Stylus, 2016), 21.
35. "El" is short for elevated train.
36. Patricia Hill Collins, "It's All in the Family: Intersections of Gender, Race, and Nation," *Hypatia* 13, no. 3 (1998): 62–82, doi:10.1111/j.1527-2001.1998.tb01370.x.
37. Nelson, Stahl, and Wallace, "Race, Class, and Gender Identity."
38. Brittney C. Cooper, Susanna M. Morris, and Robin M. Boylorn, eds., *The Crunk Feminist Collection* (New York: The Feminist Press, 2017).
39. Brittney Cooper, "The Gun Crisis We Aren't Talking About: Black Women Are Under Attack—and America Doesn't Care," *The Salon,* October 21, 2015. http://www.salon.com/2015/10/21/the_gun_crisis_we_arent_talking_about_black_women_are_under_attack_and_america_doesnt_care/.
40. Elizabeth Meyer, "Gendered Harassment in Secondary Schools: Understanding Teachers' (Non)Interventions," *Gender and Education* 20, no. 6 (2008): 555–70.
41. Steven R. Aragon, V. Paul Poteat, Dorothy L. Espelage, and Brian W. Koenig, "The Influence of Peer Victimization on Educational Outcomes for LGBTQ and Non-LGBTQ High School Students," *Journal of LGBT Youth* 11, no. 1 (2014): 1–19; Joseph G. Kosciw Neal A. Palmer, Ryan M. Kull, and Emily A. Greytak, "The Effect of Negative School Climate on Academic Outcomes for LGBT Youth and the Role of In-School Supports," *Journal of School Violence* 12, no. 1 (2013): 45–63; Meyer, "Gendered Harassment"; Elizabeth J. Meyer, *Gender, Bullying, and Harassment: Strategies to End Sexism and Homophobia in Schools* (New York: Teachers College Press, 2009).
42. Dancy, *The Brother Code.*
43. Lance T. McCready, *Making Space for Diverse Masculinities: Difference, Intersectionality, and Engagement in an Urban High School* (New York: Peter Lang, 2010).
44. Lance T. McCready, "Call and Response: How Narratives of Black Queer Youth Inform Popular Discourses of the 'Boy Crisis' in Education," *International Journal of Inclusive Education* 16, no. 4 (2012): 391–406, doi:10.1080/13603116.2011.555094.
45. Ibid., 398.
46. Ed Brockenbrough, "Emasculation Blues: Black Male Teachers' Perspectives on Gender and Power in the Teaching Profession," *Teachers College Record* 114, no. 5 (2012): 1.
47. Wayne Martino and Blye Frank, "The Tyranny of Surveillance: Male Teachers and the Policing of Masculinities in a Single Sex School," *Gender and Education* 18, no. 1 (2006): 17–33,

doi:10.1080/09540250500194914; Jackson, "Dangerous Presumptions"; Georgina Tsolidis and Ian R. Dobson, "Single-Sex Schooling: Is It Simply a 'Class Act'?" *Gender and Education* 18, no. 2 (2006): 213–28, doi:10.1080/09540250500380711; Wayne John Martino, "Male Teachers as Role Models: Addressing Issues of Masculinity, Pedagogy and the Re-Masculinization of Schooling," *Curriculum Inquiry* 38, no. 2 (2008): 189–223, doi:10.1111/j.1467-873x.2007.00405.x; G. M. Rezai-Rashti and W. J. Martino, "Black Male Teachers as Role Models: Resisting the Homogenizing Impulse of Gender and Racial Affiliation," *American Educational Research Journal* 47, no. 1 (2009): 37–64, doi:10.3102/0002831209351563; Ashley N. Woodson and Amber Pabon, "'I'm None of the Above': Exploring Themes of Heteropatriarchy in the Life Histories of Black Male Educators," *Equity & Excellence in Education* 49, no. 1 (2016): 57–71, doi:10.1080/10665684.2015.1121456.

48. Brockenbrough, "Emasculation Blues."
49. Crenshaw, "Mapping the Margins."
50. Nelson, Stahl, and Wallace, "Race, Class, and Gender Identity."

Chapter 4

1. Elyssa Cherney, "Prestigious Urban Prep Not Immune to Violence," *Chicago Tribune,* January 17, 2017, http://www.chicagotribune.com/news/local/breaking/ct-urban-prep-students-slain-met-20170116-story.html.
2. Linda Yu, "Urban Prep Graduates Turn Attention to Helping Classmates Through College," ABC 7 Chicago, February 25, 2015, http://abc7chicago.com/education/urban-prep-graduates-turn-attention-to-helping-classmates-through-college/534409/.
3. Mercedes Schneider, "Chicago's Urban Prep and 100 Percent College Acceptance: Time for the Rest of the Story," Huffington Post. June 21, 2016, http://www.huffingtonpost.com/entry/chicagos-urban-prep-and-100-percent-college-acceptance_us_5768c538e4b0092652d7ec97.
4. Karen Lewis, "Letter from CTU President Karen Lewis: 'Students Suffer in Low Performing Charter Schools," *Chicago Sun Times,* September 13, 2012, http://inthesetimes.com/working/entry/13846/letter_from_ctu_president_karen_lewis/.
5. I heard Tim King speak on a panel about the school at the 2012 Legislative Convention of the Black Caucus in Washington, DC. In his talk, he attempted to clarify misleading news reports.
6. Anthony B. Mitchell and James B. Stewart, "The Efficacy of All-Male Academies: Insights from Critical Race Theory (CRT)," *Sex Roles* 69, no. 7/8 (2013): 393.
7. Ibid.
8. Diane F. Halpern, Lise Eliot, Rebecca S. Bigler, Richard A. Fabes, Laura D. Hanish, Janet Hyde, Lynn S. Liben, and Carol Lynn Martin, "The Pseudoscience of Single-Sex Schooling," *Science* 333, no. 6050 (2011): 1706–7, http://www.feminist.org/education/pdfs/pseudoscienceofsinglesexschooling.pdf.
9. Eddie Fergus, Pedro Noguera, and Margary Martin, *Schooling for Resilience: Improving the Life Trajectory of Black and Latino Boys* (Cambridge, MA: Harvard Education Press, 2014); Erin Hyde Pahlke, Janet Shibley, and Carlie M. Allison, "Effects of Single-Sex Compared with Coeducational Schooling on Students' Performance and Attitudes: A Meta-Analysis," *Psychological Bulletin* 140, no. 4 (2014): 1042–72.
10. "Urban Prep–Englewood Campus," https://illinoisreportcard.com.
11. Now This News, May 7, 2016, https://www.facebook.com/NowThisNews/videos/1057587837664673/.

12. See www.illinoisreportcard.com; http://www.urbanprep.org/sites/default/files/documents/annual-reports/FY11%20Data%20Findings.pdf.
13. William Watkins, *The Assault on Public Education: Confronting the Politics of Corporate School Reform* (New York: Teachers College Press, 2015.)
14. Pauline Lipman,. *High Stakes Education: Inequality, Globalization, and Urban School Reform* (New York: Routledge Falmer, 2004); William J. Wilson, *When Work Disappears: The World of the New Urban Poor* (New York: Knopf, 1996).
15. Raquel Farmer-Hinton, "On Being College Prep: Examining the Implementation of a "College for All" Mission in an Urban Charter School," *Urban Review* 43, no. 5 (2011): 567–96. Through intensive interviews with high school teachers, Farmer-Hinton found that the work of building a school, a curriculum, and a culture made attending to the diverse needs of students problematic and complex.
16. This is a reference to a shrug Kanye West directed at Taylor Swift at the 2009 MTV Music Video Awards after snubbing her for winning Video of the Year. A Google Images search of "kanye shrug" will yield several pictures of the incident.
17. "Urban Prep: Englewood," Illinois Report Card, https://www.illinoisreportcard.com/School.aspx?source=trends&source2=parcc&Schoolid=150162990250100C. "Freshmen on Track" is assessed based on the number of full-year course credits (ten semester credits) and no more than one semester F in a core course. The site notes that students who finish their freshman year on track are "four times as likely to graduate from high school."
18. Tyrone C. Howard, *Black Male(d): Peril and Promise in the Education of African American Males.* (New York: Teachers College Press, 2014).
19. Derrick R. Brooms, "'I Was Just Trying to Make It': Examining Urban Black Males' Sense of Belonging, Schooling Experiences, and Academic Success," *Urban Education* (2016): 1–27, doi:10.1177/0042085916648743; Shaun R. Harper and Charles HF Davis III, "They (Don't) Care About Education: A Counternarrative on Black Male Students' Responses to Inequitable Schooling," *Journal of Educational Foundations* 26, no. 1/2 (2012): 103; Tyrone C. Howard, Ty-Ron Douglas, and Chezare A. Warren, "'What Works': Recommendations on Improving Academic Experiences and Outcomes for Black Males," *Teachers College Record* 118, no. 6 (2016): 1–6.; Brian L. McGowan, Robert T. Palmer, J. Luke Wood, and David F. Hibbler Jr., "Reframing Black Male Success in Education: Narratives of Resiliency, Inspiration, and Success," in *Black Men in the Academy: Narratives of Resiliency, Achievement, and Success,* ed. B. L. McGowan, R. T. Palmer, J. L. Wood, and D. F. Hibbler Jr. (New York: Palgrave Macmillan, 2016), 1–17; Chezare A. Warren, "'We Learn Through Our Struggles': Nuancing Notions of Urban Black Male Academic Preparation for Postsecondary Success," *Teachers College Record* 118, no. 6 (2016): 1–38.
20. Fergus, Noguera, and Martin, *Schooling for Resilience;* Shaun Harper and J. Luke Wood, *Advancing Black Male School Success from Preschool through PhD* (Sterling, VA: Stylus, 2014).
21. Anthony Graham and Kenneth A. Anderson, "'I Have to Be Three Steps Ahead': Academically Gifted African American Male Students in an Urban High School on the Tension Between Ethnic and Academic Identity," *Urban Review* 40, no. 5 (2008): 472–99; Rob Evans, "Reframing the Achievement Gap," *Phi Delta Kappan* 68 (2005): 582–89; Ronald F. Ferguson, "Teachers' Perceptions and Expectations and the Black-White Test Score Gap," *Urban Education 38,* no. 4 (2003): 460–507; Tyrone Howard, "Powerful Pedagogy for African American Students: A Case of Four Teachers," *Urban Education* 36, no. 2 (2001): 179–202.
22. Tim King, "Commentary: Swords, Shields, and the Fight for Our Children: Lessons from Urban Prep," *Journal of Negro Education* 80, no. 3 (2011): 191–92.

Chapter 5

1. Shaun R. Harper, "Black Male College Achievers and Resistant Responses to Racist Stereotypes at Predominantly White Colleges and Universities," *Harvard Educational Review* 85, no. 4 (2015): 646–74; Shaun R. Harper, "Niggers No More: A Critical Race Counternarrative on Black Male Student Achievement at Predominantly White Colleges and Universities," *International Journal of Qualitative Studies in Education* 22, no. 6 (2009): 697–712; Royel M. Johnson, "Black and Male on Campus: An Autoethnographic Account," *Journal of African American Males in Education* 4, no. 2 (2013): 103–23; Terrell L. Strayhorn, "The Invisible Man: Factors Affecting the Retention of Low-Income African American Males," *National Association of Student Affairs Professionals Journal* 11, no. 1 (2008): 66–87.
2. Shaun Harper and Christopher Newman, "Surprise, Sensemaking, and Success in the First College Year: Black Undergraduate Men's Academic Adjustment Experiences," *Teachers College Record* 118, no. 6 (2016): 1–30.
3. Ibid., 17.
4. Robert T. Palmer and Estelle M. Young, "Determined to Succeed: Salient Factors That Foster Academic Success for Academically Unprepared Black Males at a Black College," *Journal of College Student Retention: Research, Theory and Practice* 10, no. 4 (2008): 465–82; Terrell L. Strayhorn, Royel M. Johnson, and Blossom A. Barrett, "Investigating the College Adjustment and Transition Experiences of Formerly Incarcerated Black Male Collegians at Predominantly White Institutions," *Spectrum: A Journal on Black Men* 2, no. 1 (2013): 73–98.
5. Marylène Gagné and Edward L. Deci, "Self-Determination Theory and Work Motivation," *Journal of Organizational Behavior* 26, no. 4 (2005): 331–62.
6. Michael J. Dumas and Joseph Derrick Nelson, "(Re)Imagining Black Boyhood: Toward a Critical Framework for Educational Research," *Harvard Educational Review* 86, no. 1 (2016): 27–47.
7. T. Elon Dancy, "The Adultification of Black Boys: What Educational Settings Can Learn from Trayvon Martin," in *Trayvon Martin, Race, and American Justice*, ed. Kenneth Fasching Varner, Reme E. Reynolds, Katrice A. Albert, and Lori L. Martin (Rotterdam: Sense, 2014), 49–55; Michael J. Dumas, "My Brother as 'Problem' Neoliberal Governmentality and Interventions for Black Young Men and Boys," *Educational Policy* 30, no. 1 (2016): 94–113; Ann Arnett Ferguson, *Bad Boys: Public Schools in the Making of Black Masculinity* (Ann Arbor: University of Michigan Press, 2001); Gloria Ladson Billings, "Boyz to Men? Teaching to Restore Black Boys' Childhood," *Race, Ethnicity and Education* 14, no. 1 (2011): 7–15.
8. Ferguson, *Bad Boys.*
9. James Earl Davis, "Early Schooling and Academic Achievement of African American Males," *Urban Education* 38, no. 5 (2003): 533.
10. Pauline Lipman, *The New Political Economy of Urban Education: Neoliberalism, Race, and the Right to the City* (New York: Routledge, 2011).
11. Chezare A. Warren, "Perspective Divergence and the Mis-Education of Black Boys . . . Like Me," *Perspective* 5, no. 2 (2014).
12. Mauriell H. Amechi, Jonathan Berhanu, Jonathan M. Cox, Keon M. McGuire, Demetri L. Morgan, Collin D. Williams Jr, and Michael Steven Williams, "Advancing Black Male Success: Understanding the Contributions of Urban Black Colleges and Universities," *Urban Education* 12 (2015); Terrell L. Strayhorn, "The Invisible Man: Factors Affecting the Retention of Low-Income African American Males," *National Association of Student Affairs Professionals Journal* 11, no. 1 (2008): 66–87; Luke J. Wood, "Examining Academic Variables Affecting the

Persistence and Attainment of Black Male Collegians: A Focus on Academic Performance and Integration in the Two-Year College," *Race, Ethnicity and Education* 17, no. 5 (2012): 601–22.

13. Derrick R. Brooms, Joe Goodman, and Jelisa Clark, "'We Need More of This': Engaging Black Men on College Campuses," *College Student Affairs Journal* 33, no. 1 (2015): 105–23; S. R. Harper, "Am I My Brother's Teacher? Black Undergraduates, Racial Socialization, and Peer Pedagogies in Predominantly White Postsecondary Contexts," *Review of Research in Education* 37, no. 1 (2013): 183–211; Bryan K. Hotchkins and T. Elon Dancy, "Black Male Student Leaders in Predominantly White Universities: Stories of Power, Preservation, and Persistence," *Western Journal of Black Studies* 39, no. 1 (2015): 30.
14. Laura W. Perna, "The Key to College Access: Rigorous Academic Preparation," in *Preparing for College: Nine Elements of Effective Outreach,* ed. William. G. Tierney, Zoe. B. Corwin, and Julia. E. Colyar (Albany: State University of New York Press, 2005), 113; Terrell L. Strayhorn, "Bridging the Pipeline: Increasing Underrepresented Students' Preparation for College Through a Summer Bridge Program," *American Behavioral Scientist* 55, no. 2 (2010): 142–59; George L. Wimberly and Richard J. Noeth, "College Readiness Begins in Middle School" (ACT Policy Report, American College Testing ACT, Inc., 2005), https://eric.ed.gov/?id=ED483849ERIC.
15. Sara Goldrick-Rab, Robert Kelchen, Douglas N. Harris, and James Benson, "Reducing Income Inequality in Educational Attainment: Experimental Evidence on the Impact of Financial Aid on College Completion 1," *American Journal of Sociology* 121, no. 6 (2016): 1762–1817; Bridget Terry Long and Erin Riley, "Financial Aid: A Broken Bridge to College Access?" *Harvard Educational Review* 77, no. 1 (2007): 39–63; Michael B. Paulsen and Edward P. St. John, "Social Class and College Costs: Examining the Financial Nexus Between College Choice and Persistence," *Journal of Higher Education* 73, no. 2 (2002): 189–236; Kara Dukakis, Nina Duong, Jorge Ruiz de Velasco, and Jamila Henderson, "College Access and Completion Among Boys and Young Men of Color: Literature Review of Promising Practices" (white paper, John W. Gardner Center for Youth and Their Communities, Graduate School of Education, Stanford University, 2014), https://gardnercenter.stanford.edu/publications/college-access-and-completion-among-boys-and-young-men-color-literature-review; Robert Palmer and Marybeth Gasman, "'It Takes a Village to Raise a Child': The Role of Social Capital in Promoting Academic Success for African American Men at a Black College," *Journal of College Student Development* 49, no. 1 (2008): 52–70; Terrell L. Strayhorn, "The Role of Supportive Relationships in Facilitating African American Males' Success in College," *Journal of Student Affairs Research and Practice* 45, no. 1 (2008); Robert T. Palmer, Ryan J. Davis, and Dina C. Maramba, "The Impact of Family Support on the Success of Black Men at an Historically Black University: Affirming the Revision of Tinto's Theory," *Journal of College Student Development* 52, no. 5 (2011): 577–97.
16. Terrell L. Strayhorn, Royel M. Johnson, and Blossom A. Barrett, "Investigating the College Adjustment and Transition Experiences of Formerly Incarcerated Black Male Collegians at Predominantly White Institutions," *Spectrum: A Journal on Black Men* 2, no. 1 (2013): 73–98.
17. James D. Anderson, *The Education of Blacks in the South: 1860–1935* (Chapel Hill: University of North Carolina Press, 1988); Derrick P. Alridge, "African American Educators and the Black Intellectual Tradition," in *The Sage Handbook of African American Education,* ed. Linda C. Tillman (Thousand Oaks, CA: Sage, 2009), 23; Michèle Foster, *Black Teachers on Teaching* (New York: The New Press, 1997).
18. Verve is a preference of young people to enjoy doing multiple activities at the same time and of teachers to use multiple and different activities to teach content. See Kenneth M. Tyler, A. Wade Boykin, and Tia R. Walton, "Cultural Considerations in Teachers' Perceptions of

Student Classroom Behavior and Achievement," *Teaching and Teacher Education* 22, no. 8 (2006): 998–1005.

19. Foster, *Black Teachers on Teaching;* Vanessa Siddle Walker, *Their Highest Potential: An African American School Community in the Segregated South* (Chapel Hill: University of North Carolina Press, 1996).
20. Booker T. Washington, *Up from Slavery* (New York: Penguin Books, 1986).
21. Warren, "Perspective Divergence."
22. Carter G. Woodson, *The Miseducation of the Negro* (New York: Tribeca Books, 1933).

Chapter 6

1. James D. Anderson, *The Education of Blacks in the South, 1860–1935* (Chapel Hill: University of North Carolina Press, 1988); Joel Spring, *American Education,* 17th ed. (New York: Routledge, 2015); Steven Tozer, Paul C. Violas, and Guy B. Senese, *School and Society: Historical and Contemporary Perspectives,* 7th ed. (New York: McGraw-Hill, 2012).
2. Michael Dumas and kihana miraya ross, "Be Real Black for Me: Imagining BlackCrit in Education," *Urban Education* 51, no. 4 (2016): 415–42; Michael J. Dumas, "'Losing an Arm': Schooling as a Site of Black Suffering," *Race, Ethnicity and Education* 17, no. 1 (2013): 1–29; Michael J. Dumas, "Against the Dark: Antiblackness in Education Policy and Discourse," *Theory into Practice* 55, no. 1 (2015): 11–19.
3. Dumas, "Against the Dark."
4. A couple of websites to see Black inventions include http://www.huffingtonpost.com/entry/black-inventors_us_56d0d33ee4b0bf0dab3236d5 and http://www.avengingtheancestors.com/releases/wedidit.htm.
5. A 2016 Netflix documentary titled *13th* helps explain how the Thirteenth Amendment of the US Constitution works to end slavery except in the case that a person can be seen as criminal. Thus, to be criminalized gives the nation-state the right to reclaim Black people as state property. Spencer Averick and Ava Duvernay, *13th,* dir. Ava Duvernay (Netflix, 2016).
6. Pew Research Center, "On Views of Race and Inequality, Blacks and Whites Are Worlds Apart" (report, Pew Research Center, 2016), http://www.pewsocialtrends.org/files/2016/06/ST_2016.06.27_Race-Inequality-Final.pdf.
7. See Frank Rudy Cooper, "Against Bipolar Black Masculinity: Intersectionality, Assimilation, Identity Performance, and Hierarchy," *UC Davis Law Review* 39 (2006): 853.
8. See Linda C. Tillman, *The Sage Handbook of African American Education* (Thousand Oaks, CA: Sage, 2009).
9. A. Garza, "A Herstory of the #BlackLivesMatter Movement," *Feminist Wire* [blog], 2014, http://thefeministwire.com/2014/10/blacklivesmatter-2/ ; Marc Lamont Hill, *Nobody: Casualties of America's War on the Vulnerable, from Ferguson to Flint and Beyond* (New York: Simon & Schuster, 2016).
10. Movies like *Dangerous Minds, The Principal, Lean on Me,* and *Freedom Writers* are examples of the ways urban schools are constructed in the mainstream media. The documentary *Waiting for Superman* also adds to the deficit depiction of urban schools. Also, so much of the local news about urban schools suggest they are dangerous places and should be abandoned.
11. Http://www.urbanprep.org/sites/default/files/documents/annual-reports/FY11%20Data%20Findings.pdf.
12. These are traditional neighborhood high schools on the South Side, a few of which the young men would have attended had they not been admitted to Urban Prep.
13. Carter G. Woodson, *The Miseducation of the Negro* (New York: Tribeca Books, 1933).

14. Dumas and ross, "Be Real Black for Me"; Dorothy E. Roberts, "BlackCrit Theory and the Problem of Essentialism," *University of Miami Law Review* 53 (1998): 855.
15. Dumas, "Losing an Arm"; Dumas and ross, "Be Real Black for Me."
16. Dorinda J. Carter Andrews, "The Construction of Black High-Achiever Identities in a Predominantly White High School," *Anthropology and Education Quarterly* 40, no. 3 (2009): 297–317; Dorinda J. Carter Andrews, "Black Achievers' Experiences with Racial Spotlighting and Ignoring in a Predominantly White High School," *Teachers College Record* 114, no. 10 (2012): n10; Carla O'Connor, "Dispositions Toward (Collective) Struggle and Educational Resilience in the Inner City: A Case Analysis of Six African-American High School Students," *American Educational Research Journal* 34, no. 4 (1997): 593–629.
17. For instance, Carla Shedd examines the ways Black students in Chicago navigate their neighborhoods, life opportunities, and encounters with urban policing and argues that we laud young people as the future, yet "more often than not, their voices remain unheard or ignored" (p. 5). Carla Shedd, *Unequal City: Race, Schools, and Perceptions of Injustice* (New York: Russell Sage Foundation, 2015).
18. Eddie Fergus, Pedro Noguera, and Margary Martin. *Schooling for Resilience: Improving the Life Trajectory of Black and Latino Boys* (Cambridge, MA: Harvard Education Press, 2014).
19. See Pedro A. Noguera, "The Trouble with Black Boys: The Role and Influence of Environmental and Cultural Factors on the Academic Performance of African American Males," *Urban Education* 38, no. 4 (2003): 431–59; Robert T. Palmer, James L. Moore III, Ryan J. Davis, and Adriel A. Hilton, "A Nation at Risk: Increasing College Participation and Persistence among African American Males to Stimulate U.S. Global Competitiveness," *Journal of African American Males in Education* 1, no. 2 (2010): 105–24.
20. Noguera, "The Trouble with Black Boys," 436.
21. Ebony O. McGee, "Threatened and Placed at Risk: High Achieving African American Males in Urban High Schools," *Urban Review* 45, no. 4 (2013): 448.
22. Ricardo D. Stanton-Salazar, "A Social Capital Framework for the Study of Institutional Agents and their Role in the Empowerment of Low-Status Students and Youth," *Youth & Society* 43, no. 3 (2011): 1067.
23. For instance, see Carla R. Monroe, "Why are 'Bad Boys' Always Black? Causes of Disproportionality in School Discipline and Recommendations for Change," *The Clearing House* 79, no. 1 (2005): 45–50; H. Richard Milner IV, "Why Are Students of Color (Still) Punished More Severely and Frequently Than White Students?" *Urban Education* 48, no. 4 (2013): 483–89.
24. Travis J. Bristol, "Teaching Boys: Towards a Theory of Gender-Relevant Pedagogy," *Gender and Education* 27, no. 1 (2015): 53–68; Iesha Jackson, Yolanda Sealey-Ruiz, and Wanda Watson, "Reciprocal Love Mentoring Black and Latino Males Through an Ethos of Care," *Urban Education* 49, no. 4 (2014): 394–417; Julia C. Ransom, "Caring for Black Males in Schools: An Ethnographic Exploration of Educational Experiences of Black Males in a GED Program," *Urban Education Research and Policy Annuals* 4, no. 1 (2016).
25. Joseph B. Richardson, "Men Do Matter: Ethnographic Insights on the Socially Supportive Role of the African American Uncle in the Lives of Inner-City African American Male Youth," *Journal of Family Issues* 30, no. 8 (2009): 1041–69; Stanton-Salazar, "A Social Capital Framework"; Chinwe J. Uwah, H. George McMahon, and Carolyn F. Furlow, "School Belonging, Educational Aspirations, and Academic Self-Efficacy Among African American Male High School Students: Implications for School Counselors," *Professional School Counseling* 11, no. 5 (2008): 296–305; Derrick R. Brooms, "'I Was Just Trying to Make It': Urban Black Males' Sense of Belonging, Schooling Experiences, and Academic Success," *Urban Education* (2016):

1–27, doi:10.1177/0042085916648743; H. Richard Milner IV, "African American Males in Urban Schools: No Excuses—Teach and Empower," *Theory and Practice* 46, no. 3 (2007): 239–46; Ivory A. Toldson, *Breaking Barriers: Plotting the Path to Academic Success for School-Age African-American Males* (Washington, DC: Congressional Black Caucus Foundation, 2008).

26. Chezare A. Warren, "Making Relationships Work: Elementary-Aged Black Boys and the Schools That Serve Them," in *Advancing Black Male Success: Preschool Through PhD*, ed. Shaun Harper and J. Luke Wood (Sterling, VA: Stylus, 2016), 21.
27. Ty-Ron M. O. Douglas, *Border Crossing Brothas: Black Males Navigating Race, Place, and Complex Space* (New York: Peter Lang, 2016).
28. Anthony L. Brown, "'Brothers Gonna Work It Out': Understanding the Pedagogic Performance of African American Male Teachers Working with African American Male Students," *Urban Review* 41, no. 5 (2009): 416–35; Marvin Lynn, "Education for the Community: Exploring the Culturally Relevant Practices of Black Male Teachers," *Teachers College Record* 108, no. 12 (2006): 2497–522; Chance W. Lewis, "African American Male Teachers in Public Schools: An Examination of Three Urban School Districts," *Teachers College Record* 108, no. 2 (2006): 224–45; Chezare A. Warren, "Being Black, Being Male, and Choosing to Teach in the 21st Century: Understanding My Role, Embracing My Call," in *Black Male Teachers: Diversifying the United States' Teacher Workforce,* ed. C. W. Lewis and I. A. Toldson (Bradford, UK: Emerald, 2013), 167–82.
29. Douglas A. Guiffrida, "Othermothering as a Framework for Understanding African American Students' Definitions of Student-Centered Faculty," *Journal of Higher Education* 76, no. 6 (2005): 701–23; Lynette Mawhinney, "Othermothering: A Personal Narrative Exploring Relationships Between Black Female Faculty and Students," *Negro Educational Review* 62/63, nos. 1–4 (2011–12), 213–32; Marvin Lynn, "Education for the Community: Exploring the Culturally Relevant Practices of Black Male Teachers." *Teachers College Record* 108, no. 12 (2006): 2497.
30. Ebony Elizabeth Thomas and Chezare A. Warren, "Making It Relevant: How a Black Male Teacher Sustained Professional Relationships Through Culturally Responsive Discourse," *Race, Ethnicity and Education* 20, no. 1 (2017): 87–100.

Chapter 7

1. Charles M. Payne, *So Much Reform, So Little Change: The Persistence of Failure in Urban Schools* (Cambridge, MA: Harvard Education Press, 2008).
2. Anthony S. Bryk, Penny Bender Sebring, Elaine Allensworth, Stuart Luppescu, and John Q. Easton, *Organizing Schools for Improvement: Lessons from Chicago* (Chicago: University of Chicago Press, 2010), 9.
3. Fred A. Bonner, ed., *Building on Resilience: Models and Frameworks of Black Male Success Across the P—20 Pipeline* (Sterling, VA: Stylus, 2014); Shaun Harper and J. Luke Wood, eds., *Advancing Black Male Student Success From Preschool Through PhD* (Sterling, VA: Stylus, 2016); Tyrone C. Howard, *Black Male(d): Peril and Promise in the Education of African American Males* (New York: Teachers College Press, 2014); Chezare A. Warren, Ty-Ron M. O. Douglas, and Tyrone C. Howard, "In Their Own Words: Erasing the Deficits: My Brother's Keeper and Contemporary Perspectives on Black Male School Achievement," *Teachers College Record* 118, no. 6 (2016): 1–6.
4. Pedro A. Noguera, "How Listening to Students Can Help Schools to Improve," *Theory into Practice* 46, no. 3 (2007): 205–11.

5. Ibid.
6. For similar findings about other single-sex schools for boys of color, see Eddie Fergus, Pedro Noguera, and Margary Martin, *Schooling for Resilience: Improving the Life Trajectory of Black and Latino Boys* (Cambridge, MA: Harvard Education Press, 2014).
7. Tyrone C. Howard, Ty-Ron M. O. Douglas, and Chezare A. Warren, "'What Works': Recommendations on Improving Academic Experiences and Outcomes for Black Males," *Teachers College Record* 118, no. 6 (2016): 1.
8. Patrisse Cullors, TED Talk, November 2016, https://www.ted.com/speakers/patrisse_cullors.

Appendix

1. John W. Cresswell, *Qualitative Inquiry and Research Design: Choosing Among Five Approaches* (Thousand Oaks, CA: Sage, 2013); Clark Moustakas, *Phenomenological Research Methods* (Thousand Oaks, CA: Sage, 1994); Gretchen B. Rossman and Sharon F. Rallis, *Learning in the Field: An Introduction to Qualitative Research,* 2nd ed. (Thousand Oaks, CA: Sage, 2003).
2. William F. Tate, "Critical Race Theory and Education: History, Theory, and Implications," *Review of Research in Education* 22 (1997): 195, doi:10.2307/1167376.
3. Gloria Ladson-Billings and William F. Tate IV, "Toward a Critical Race Theory of Education," *Teachers College Record* 97, no. 1 (1995): 47–68.
4. M. J. Dumas and K. M. Ross, "'Be Real Black for Me': Imagining BlackCrit in Education," *Urban Education* 51, no. 4 (2016): 415–42, doi:10.1177/0042085916628611.
5. Adrienne D. Dixson and Celia K. Rousseau, "And We Are Still Not Saved: Critical Race Theory in Education Ten Years Later," *Race Ethnicity and Education* 8, no. 1 (2005): 7–27, doi :10.1080/1361332052000340971; Gloria Ladson-Billings, "Just What Is Critical Race Theory and What's It Doing in a Nice Field Like Education?" in *Foundations of Critical Race Theory in Education,* ed. E. Taylor, D. Gillborn, and G. Ladson-Billings (New York: Routledge, 2009), 17–36; Gerardo R. López and Chezare Warren, "Critical Race Theory," *Oxford Bibliographies Online Datasets,* doi:10.1093/obo/9780199756810-0124; Marvin Lynn and Adrienne D. Dixson, *Handbook of Critical Race Theory in Education* (New York: Routledge, 2014); Marvin Lynn and Laurence Parker, "Critical Race Studies in Education: Examining a Decade of Research on U.S. Schools," *Urban Review* 38, no. 4 (2006): 257–90, doi:10.1007/s11256-006-0035-5.
6. Derrick Bell, *Faces at the Bottom of the Well: The Permanence of Racism* (New York: Basic Books, 1992); Kimberle Crenshaw, "Mapping the Margins: Intersectionality, Identity Politics, and Violence against Women of Color," *Stanford Law Review* 43, no. 6 (1991): 1241, doi:10.2307/1229039; Richard Delgado and Jean Stefancic, *Critical Race Theory: An Introduction* (New York: New York University Press, 2001).
7. Derrick A. Bell Jr., "A Hurdle Too High: Class-Based Roadblocks to Racial Remediation," *Buffalo Law Review* 33 (1984): 1–34; Cheryl I. Harris, "Whiteness as Property," *Harvard Law Review* 106, no. 8 (1993): 1707–91; Mari J. Matsuda et al., eds., *Words That Wound: Critical Race Theory, Assaultive Speech, and the First Amendment* (Boulder, CO: Westview Press, 1993).
8. Derrick A. Bell, "*Brown v. Board of Education* and the Interest-Convergence Dilemma," *Harvard Law Review* 93 (1979–80): 518–33.
9. Bell, "A Hurdle Too High"; Kevin Edward Kennedy and Derrick A. Bell, "And We Are Not Saved: The Elusive Quest for Racial Justice," *Michigan Law Review* 86, no. 6 (1987): 1130, doi:10.2307/1289158; Mari J. Matsuda, "Public Response to Racist Speech: Considering the Victim's Story," *Michigan Law Review* 87, no. 8 (1989): 2320–81, doi:10.2307/128930; Laurence Parker and David O. Stovall, "Actions Following Words: Critical Race Theory

Connects to Critical Pedagogy," *Educational Philosophy and Theory* 36, no. 2 (2004): 167–82, doi:10.1111/j.1469-5812.2004.00059.x; Laurence Parker and David O. Stovall, "Actions Following Words: Critical Race Theory Connects to Critical Pedagogy," *Educational Philosophy and Theory* 36, no. 2 (2004): 167–82, doi:10.1111/j.1469-5812.2004.00059; David Stovall, "Forging Community in Race and Class: Critical Race Theory and the Quest for Social Justice in Education," *Race, Ethnicity and Education* 9, no. 3 (2006): 243–59, doi:10.1080/13613320600807550; David Stovall, "When the Rubber Meets the Road: CRT Goes to High School," in *Critical Race Theory in Education: All God's Children Got a Song,* ed. A. D. Dixson and C. K. Rousseau (New York: Routledge, 2006), 231–40.

10. Kennedy and Bell, "And We Are Still Not Saved"; Richard Delgado, "Critical Legal Studies and the Realities of Race—Does the Fundamental Contradiction Have a Corollary?" *Harvard Civil Rights–Civil Liberties Law Review* 23 (1988): 407–13; Richard Delgado, "Storytelling for Oppositionists and Others: A Plea for Narrative," *Michigan Law Review* 87, no. 8 (1989): 2411–41, doi:10.2307/1289308; Crenshaw, "Mapping the Margins."
11. Kimberle Crenshaw et al., eds., *Critical Race Theory: The Key Writings That Formed the Movement* (New York: New Press, 1995); Delgado and Stefancic, *Critical Race Theory;* Matsuda et al., eds., *Words That Wound.*
12. Laurence Parker and Marvin Lynn, "What's Race Got to Do with It? Critical Race Theory's Conflicts with and Connections to Qualitative Research Methodology and Epistemology," *Qualitative Inquiry* 8, no. 1 (2002): 7–22, doi:10.1177/107780040200800102.
13. Eduardo Bonilla-Silva, *Racism Without Racists: Color-Blind Racism and the Persistence of Racial Inequality in the United States,* 3rd ed. (Lanham, MD: Rowman & Littlefield, 2010); Ashley W. Doane and Eduardo Bonilla-Silva, *White Out: The Continuing Significance of Racism* (New York: Routledge, 2003); Amanda E. Lewis, *Race in the Schoolyard: Negotiating the Color Line in Classrooms and Communities* (New Brunswick, NJ: Rutgers University Press, 2003); Mica Pollock, *Colormute: Race Talk Dilemmas in an American School* (Princeton, NJ: Princeton University Press, 2004); Howard C Stevenson. *Promoting Racial Literacy in Schools: Differences That Make a Difference* (New York: Teachers College Press, 2014).
14. Christopher Dunbar, "Critical Race Theory and Indigenous Methodologies," *Handbook on Critical and Indigenous Methodologies,* ed. N. K. Denzin and Y. K. Lincoln (Thousand Oaks, CA: Sage, 2008), 85–99, doi:10.4135/9781483385686.n5.
15. Dolores Delgado-Bernal, "Critical Race Theory, Latino Critical Theory, and Critical Raced-Gendered Epistemologies: Recognizing Students of Color as Holders and Creators of Knowledge," *Qualitative Inquiry* 8, no. 1 (2002): 105–26, doi:10.1177/107780040200800107.
16. Ibid., 120.
17. Shaun R. Harper et al., "Succeeding in the City: A Report from the New York City Black and Latino Male High School Achievement Study" (report,Center for the Study of Race and Equity in Education, University of Pennsylvania, Philadelphia, 2014); Tyrone C. Howard et al., "The Counternarrative: Reframing Success of High Achieving Black and Latino Males in Los Angeles County" (report, UCLA Black Male Institute, Los Angeles, 2016); "Recommendations for Policymakers: Advancing the Success of Boys and Men of Color in Education" (policy report, Project Males, University of Texas, Austin, 2015).
18. John W. Creswell, *Qualitative Inquiry and Research Design: Choosing Among Five Traditions* (Thousand Oaks, CA: Sage, 2012), 156; Charles Teddlie and Fen Yu, "Mixed Methods Sampling: A Typology with Examples," *Journal of Mixed Methods Research* 1, no. 1 (2007): 77–100.
19. See Student Right-to-Know Act, https://nces.ed.gov.
20. Michael Quinn Patton, *Qualitative Research* (New York: John Wiley & Sons, 2005).

21. Irving Seidman, *Interviewing as Qualitative Research: A Guide for Researchers in Education and the Social Sciences* (New York: Teachers College Press, 2013), 16.
22. Max Van Manen, *Researching Lived Experience: Human Science for an Action Sensitive Pedagogy,* 2nd ed. (New York: Routledge, 2016).
23. Herbert J. Rubin and Irene S. Rubin, *Qualitative Interviewing: The Art of Hearing Data,* 3rd ed. (Thousand Oaks, CA: Sage, 2012).
24. Van Manen, *Researching Lived Experience.*
25. Creswell, *Qualitative Inquiry and Research Design.*
26. Ibid., 80.
27. Alford A. Young, *The Minds of Marginalized Black Men: Making Sense of Mobility, Opportunity, and Future Life Chances* (Princeton, NJ: Princeton University Press, 2004).
28. Ibid., 194.
29. Ibid.
30. Ibid., 194.
31. See Delgado and Stefancic, *Critical Race Theory.*
32. Bell, *Faces at the Bottom of the Well.*
33. Crenshaw, "Mapping the Margins"; Leslie McCall, "The Complexity of Intersectionality," *Signs: Journal of Women in Culture and Society* 30, no. 3 (2005): 1771–800.
34. Tyrone C. Howard and Rema Reynolds, "Examining Black Male Identity Through a Raced, Classed, and Gendered Lens," in *Handbook of Critical Race Theory in Education,* ed. Marvin Lynn and Adrienne Dixson (New York: Routledge, 2014).
35. Daniel G. Solórzano and Tara J. Yosso, "Critical Race Methodology: Counter-Storytelling as an Analytical Framework for Education Research," *Qualitative Inquiry* 8, no. 1 (2002): 23–44.
36. John Beverley, "Testimonio, Subalternity, and Narrative Authority," in *Handbook of Qualitative Research,* ed. Norman K. Denzin and Yvonna S. Lincoln (Thousand Oaks, CA: Sage, 2000), 555.
37. Susan L. Morrow, "Quality and Trustworthiness in Qualitative Research in Counseling Psychology," *Journal of Counseling Psychology* 52, no. 2 (2005): 250.
38. Creswell, *Qualitative Inquiry and Research Design;* Rossman and Rallis, *Learning in the Field.*
39. John W. Creswell and Dana L. Miller, "Determining Validity in Qualitative Inquiry," *Theory into Practice* 39, no. 3 (2000): 124–30.; Yvonna S. Lincoln and Egon G. Guba, *Naturalistic Inquiry,* vol. 75 (Thousand Oak, CA: Sage, 1985).
40. Patton, *Qualitative Research.*
41. Carla Willig, *Introducing Qualitative Research in Psychology: Adventures in Theory and Method* (Philadelphia: Open Press, 2001), chap. 8.

Afterword

1. Charles M. Payne, *So Much Reform, So Little Change: The Persistence of Failure in Urban Schools* (Cambridge, MA: Harvard Education Press, 2008); Geoffrey D. Borman, Gina M. Hewes, Laura T. Overman, and Shelly Brown, "Comprehensive School Reform and Achievement: A Meta-Analysis," *Review of Educational Research* 73, no. 2 (2003): 125–230.
2. David Stovall, "Against the Politics of Desperation: Educational Justice, Critical Race Theory, and Chicago School Reform," *Critical Studies in Education* 54, no. 1 (2013): 33–43.
3. Hava Rachel Gordon, "'We Can't Let Them Fail for One More Day': School Reform Urgency and the Politics of Reformers-Community Alliances," *Race, Ethnicity and Education* 19, no. 1 (2014): 1–22; A. Wade Boykin and Pedro Noguera, *Creating the Opportunity to Learning: Moving from Research to Practice to Close the Achievement Gap* (Washington, DC: Association for Supervision and Curriculum Development, 2011).

4. Jeffrey R. Henig, Richard C. Hula, Marion Orr, and Desiree S. Pedscleaux, *The Color of School Reform: Race, Politics and the Challenge of Urban Education* (Princeton, NJ: Princeton University Press, 2008).
5. James D. Anderson, *The Education of Blacks in the South, 1860–1935* (Chapel Hill: University of North Carolina Press, 1988).
6. Michael J. Dumas and Joseph Derrick Nelson, "Re(Imagining) Black Boyhood: Toward a Critical Framework for Education Research," *Harvard Educational Review* 86, no. 1 (2016): 27–47; T. Elon Dancy, "(Un)Doing Hegemony in Education: Disrupting School-to-Prison Pipelines for Black Males," *Equity & Excellence in Education* 47, no. 4 (2014): 476–93.
7. Pedro Noguera, Edward Fergus, and Margary Martin, *Schooling for Resilience: Improving Life Trajectories for Black and Latino Boys* (Cambridge, MA: Harvard Education Press, 2014).

Acknowledgments

This book is a manifestation of things "exceedingly abundantly above all that [I could] ask or think." Thank you, Father, for trusting me with this ministry.

I have an extraordinary village of love and support that I do not take for granted. To my parents, Lumsden Cox and Sheila Warren; my "Magra," Carmeta Moncrieffe, the Jamaican immigrant who is *the* picture of love and sacrifice; my beautiful sister, Bueana Cox, and my nephew, Mr. Piercen—thank you for your patience with me and for being my biggest fans. I love you. To the rest of my family, near and far—every cousin, aunt, and uncle on both sides—thank you for your unwavering love, kind words, and encouragement.

Thank you, Brian, Maurice, Sam, Kobie, and Antonio, for listening as I whined about the difficulty of writing this book and for reminding me of my gifts and cheering me on along the way. And to the many others in my village who intimately know my journey, who have, in one way or another, contributed to my growth and development—my Abundant Grace Assembly family, UIC graduate school peeps, Penn GSE friends and colleagues, Ali Michael, my FaithFul Praise family (I will always love and miss you, Janiele), Tyson and Terrence and your partners, Jasmine, the brothers of Megisté Areté and sisters of Elogeme Adolphi, the Rho Chapter of Alpha Phi Alpha Fraternity, my line brothers, the Lansing E-Board, my EOW peeps, CRSEA leadership, CPS colleagues, and former students—I thank you all for your persistent love and support.

To the seventeen young men whose stories are featured in this book, I am honored that you've allowed me to share with the world the important lessons I began learning from you as your ninth-grade math teacher. Thank you for trusting me to think *with* you and learn *from* you. I hope that I've made you proud. I look forward to the great things you will accomplish and the lives you will impact. And to the "young men of Urban Prep" from the school's founding class, as well as other UP students past and present, thank you for allowing the rest of the world to watch you shine.

To Dr. Derrick R. Brooms, my collaborator, friend, and colleague. I am incredibly grateful for your brotherhood, and I appreciate your contributions to this research. Thank you for helping to make a book like this possible. And my other brother and sister scholar "friendleagues," your camaraderie makes the academy more humane. Thank you for reminding me of why I do this work and challenging me to continue doing it with excellence. Drs. Nathan Alexander, Bianca Baldridge, Erica Bullock, Travis Bristol, Brian Burt, Roderick Carey, Ty-Ron Douglas, Maisie Gholson, Terrance Green, Kevin Lawrence Henry, Bryan Hotchkins, LaTeefah Id-Deen, Greg Larnell, Ebony McGee, Keon McGuire, Gholdy Muhammad, Joseph Nelson, Camika Royal, Rema Reynolds, Ebony Elizabeth Thomas, Derron Wallace, and Ashley Woodson—I could go on and on. (If I missed you, it's the heart count, not the head count that matters.) Y'all are some of the most brilliant people on the planet, and I'm just glad to know you. And to all my scholar cousins rewriting the academic script so that we leave academia better than we found it—LET'S DO THIS!

To my Michigan State University intellectual community I say with all seriousness, I don't think I could ask for a better cadre of students and colleagues to work with and learn alongside each day. Thank you to my chair and dean and to the staff, faculty colleagues, and graduate students in the Department of Teacher Education for inspiring me to always put my best foot forward. And to Django, Rae, Glenn, Terah, Terry, Sonya, Dorinda, Alyssa, Tam, Delia, Maribel, Yomaira, Tacuma, Vaughn, Joanne, Sara, Dustin, Vanessa, Mari, Christa, Ginny, and Xhercis—thank you for all you do to sustain *this* community. Your commitment to justice—not just equity, diversity, and inclusion—challenges and motivates me in ways I can't describe. Let's continue doing work that matters! #StayMadAbby.

And I thank the intellectual giants whose scholarship continues to shape my thinking and whose example ensures that Black boys from the South Side of Chicago, like me, will never have to apologize for studying issues of race and racism in education. And though there are far too many of you to name here, thanks to all my senior colleagues who have taken risks and carved out new areas of study making it possible for a book like *Urban Preparation* to be written. I have so much respect and admiration for you. If you think I'm talking about you, I am! Your contributions are deeply felt and appreciated.

To Dave Stovall, Marisha Humphries, Ivory Toldson, Chance Lewis, James Moore, Howard Stevenson, Shaun Harper, Marvin Lynn, and Steven Tozer—thank you for your tremendous investment of time and mentorship, for every reference letter and e-mail or text exchange in my time of need. Each of you has taught me remarkable lessons about the ethics of conducting justice-centered research and doing scholarship that matters to real people. Most importantly, your words of encouragement at some point in my journey sparked the confidence I needed to pursue ideas and projects that I'm passionate about, including those documented in this text. Thank you.

H. Rich Milner, ever since I first read your work as a first-year doctoral student, I've wanted to be just like you. You and Pedro Noguera are my academic heroes. Authoring the first book in a series that you are editing is a dream come true. I am humbled to be connected to you in this way and will continue to learn from your example. Onward and upward, good brother. And James Earl Davis, I hope to one day become a fraction of the scholar/brother/mentor/role model that you have been to me. Thank you for your sage advice and for thinking highly enough of me to contribute to this volume. Most of all, thank you for being you. You set the standard for the type of human being we (should) all want to be—kind, patient, warm, and just easy to be around. And thanks for reminding me to "just say 'the founders.'"

I extend my thanks to everyone who read drafts and/or discussed with me the ideas in this book: Dave Stovall, Justin Cole, Dani Parker-Moore, Marcus Campbell, Terrence Pruitt, Terrance Green, Nina Johnson, Michael Dumas, Ashley Woodson, Lloyd Matthew Talley, Lance McCready, Royel Johnson, Derrick Brooms, Joanne Marciano, Joseph Nelson, Derron Wallace, Antonio Pee, Marvin Lynn, Cody Harrell, Coach Joy, and my Faculty Success Bootcamp small group. *Thank you* seems insignificant. Nonetheless, please know that I am super grateful for the time and attention each of you gave to helping transform my musings into something that will have a lasting impact on education research and practice.

And finally, to my editor, Douglas Clayton; my copy editor, Joanna Craig; and the editorial team, marketing department, and advisory board at the Harvard Education Press—thank you. Working with HEP has been an exceptionally pleasant experience. I am overwhelmed with gratefulness for your belief in this project and for all the work each person invested to ensure a stellar final product.

About the Author

Chezare A. Warren is an assistant professor in the Department of Teacher Education at Michigan State University. He is the 2014 recipient of the Outstanding Dissertation Award from the American Association of Colleges for Teacher Education, and he completed a postdoctoral research fellowship in the Graduate School of Education at the University of Pennsylvania. A Chicago native, Warren has over a decade of professional experience as a public school educator. His research interests include urban teacher preparation, culturally responsive teaching, and critical race theory in education, and his scholarship has been published in several peer-reviewed journals, including *Urban Education, Urban Review, Journal of Negro Education, Race, Ethnicity and Education*, and *Teachers College Record.* Warren is past president of the Critical Race Studies in Education Association. He holds a BS in elementary education from the University of Illinois at Urbana-Champaign, a MA in school leadership from Concordia University–Chicago, and a PhD from the Policy Studies in Urban Education program at the University of Illinois at Chicago.

Index